AMERICAN PROTESTANT THEOLOGY

American Protestant Theology

A Historical Sketch

LUIGI GIUSSANI

Translated by Damian Bacich

Introduction by Archibald J. Spencer

McGill-Queen's University Press
Montreal & Kingston • London • Ithaca

ISBN 978-0-7735-4197-9 (cloth)
ISBN 978-0-7735-4300-3 (paper)
ISBN 978-0-7735-8951-3 (ePDF)
ISBN 978-0-7735-8952-0 (ePUB)

Legal deposit third quarter 2013
Bibliothèque nationale du Québec

First paperback edition 2014

Originally published in *Hildephonsiana*, a series of theological and religious studies, from the publications of the Episcopal Seminary of Milan, Italy. Publisher: "La scuola cattolica," Venegono Inferiore (Varese), Italy, 1969.

Imprimatur. In Curia Arch. Mediolani die 6–5–1969.
J. Schiavini, Vicar General

Printed in Canada on acid-free paper that is 100% ancient forest free (100% post-consumer recycled), processed chlorine free

McGill-Queen's University Press acknowledges the support of the Canada Council for the Arts for our publishing program. We also acknowledge the financial support of the Government of Canada through the Canada Book Fund for our publishing activities.

Library and Archives Canada Cataloguing in Publication

Giussani, Luigi, author
[Teologia protestante americana. English]
American Protestant theology: a historical sketch / Luigi Giussani; translated by Damien Bacich; foreword by Archibald J. Spencer

Translation of: Teologia protestante americana.
Includes bibliographical references and index.
Issued in print and electronic formats.
ISBN 978-0-7735-4197-9 (bound). – ISBN 978-0-7735-4300-3 (pbk.).
ISBN 978-0-7735-8951-3 (ePDF). – ISBN 978-0-7735-8952-0 (ePUB)

1. Theology, Doctrinal – United States – History. 2. Protestant churches – United States – Doctrines – History. I. Bacich, Cosmos Damian, translator II. Title. III. Title: Teologia protestante americana. English.

BX4811.G5713 2013   280'.40973   C2013-902420-4
C2013-902421-2

This book was typeset by Interscript in 10.5/13 Sabon.

Contents

Introduction

The task of introducing a previously published book to readers in a new language is fraught with ambiguity. Where does one start? What parameters should guide such an operation? What information about the author should be included? Such questions cannot be answered by seeking out a few examples of where it has been done elsewhere. The exercise reveals no "standard introduction." In fact, it only reveals a wide-open field in which the book being introduced can sometimes be overtaken by the introduction itself. One great example of this is J.B. Baillie's introduction to the English edition of G.W.F. Hegel's *Phenomenology of Spirit*, one best left until after you read the book itself;[1] it is a categorical mistake to read this introduction beforehand.

As far as one can tell, based on some of the better efforts this author has read, an introduction to a good book should offer the reader a basic orientation to the author, the situation in which the book came about, and an essential guide to accessing the work in terms of its genre, organization, strengths, weaknesses, and/or lacunae. This will be our aim here with respect to Luigi Giussani's *American Protestant Theology: A Historical Sketch*.[2] However, because Giussani is relatively new to North Americans, a little more background information is needed to explain how a Protestant theologian, now in the Baptist tradition, came to be writing an introduction to a book originally written in Italian, presumably (originally) for a Catholic scholarly audience.

That the subject is American Protestant theology makes this situation that much more unique. What possible motivation existed for the production of this book by a Catholic Italian theologian who spent the majority of his life in his native land? To answer that question, some biographical background seems to be called for.

MONSIGNOR LUIGI GIUSSANI: A BRIEF BIOGRAPHY

Monsignor Luigi Giussani, who was born in Italy in October 1922 and died there in February 2005, was a Roman Catholic priest, scholar, theologian, high school teacher, and professor who founded the lay Catholic movement Communion and Liberation.[3] He lived most of his life in and around Milan. Upon his entrance to the priesthood his plan was to follow the life of a scholar and seminary teacher, but because of his concern for youth, he decided early on to radically alter his teaching career. In 1954, he asked his superiors if he could move to the education of high-school youth.

From 1965 to 1969, Giussani carried out research in American Protestant theology, spending the second half of 1965 in the United States. His earlier work in this field, in the seminary, had resulted in his doctoral dissertation, "Il senso cristiano dell'uomo secondo Reinhold Niebuhr." His new research culminated in the writing of the work under consideration here, with the full Italian title, *Grande linee della teologia Protestante Americana: Profilo storico dalle origini agli anni 50* (*Outline of American Protestant Theology: An Historical Profile from Its Origins to the 1950s*). This was later shortened to *Teologia Protestante Americana: Profilo storico*.[4]

After his sojourn in America, Guissani returned to his native land and became professor of theology at the Università Cattolica del Sacro Cuore in Milan, but more importantly, he returned to his leadership of the youth movement that he had started before he left. The movement officially became Communion and Liberation in 1968.[5]

It is significant, as we shall see below, that *Teologia Protestante Americana*, or *American Protestant Theology*, is to be understood in distinction from European or British Protestant theology. Giussani sees the American religious spirit as a unique expression of its Protestant heritage.

Later in his life, Giussani became closely acquainted with Pope John Paul II, who conferred on him the title of Monsignor in 1983. Furthermore, he was well acquainted with Pope Benedict XVI, who presided at his funeral as Cardinal Joseph Ratzinger. From 1983 until his death, Father Giussani (or "Don Giuss," as he was affectionately known to the members of CL) would come to have an enormous impact on Italian and European religious life and culture. Today, his influence extends to more than eighty countries, including Canada and the United States, all of which have become hosts to groups of Catholic brothers and sisters drawn together by Giussani's writings, personality, and, most importantly, his witness to the event of the Incarnation. Interestingly, there are many people of other Christian faiths who count themselves – and are counted – as members of Communion and Liberation.

Giussani's influence had many sources, not the least of which was his winsome personality. His *charism*, combined with his keen sense of awareness of the spiritual situation of his day, his critical acumen in almost all matters of culture, and a sharp theological mind made him one of the most formative theologians of young Italian minds from 1954 until his death. (Only John Paul II can compare with such influence among Italian youth in Catholic circles.) This influence increased exponentially with the establishment of a religio-cultural fair in 1980 called simply the "Meeting for Friendship among Peoples," or just Il (or the) Meeting. This event has become a major conduit for exposing the world to Guissani's thought. The Meeting is an annual late summer festival of scholarship, the arts, commerce, politics, and religious dialogue that sees almost one million visitors descend on Rimini, Italy, every year, for a week. I have been invited to attend these meetings several times in the recent past as a speaker. The only conclusion that can be drawn about Giussani is that his influence there is pervasive. With only fourteen staff and over three thousand young volunteers, the annual Meeting at Rimini is a grand testimony to Giussani's ongoing influence today.

Although Giussani's exploits are little known in North America, there is no question that his influence will eventually extend to our continent as well, especially with more of his works being translated into English. Giussani was a prolific writer and in his lifetime contributed works on education, theology, philosophy of religion, history, and spirituality. His trilogy, which includes *The Religious Sense*, *At the Origin of the Christian Claim*, and *Why the Church?* represents his best synthesis of all these efforts.[6] These works are a monumental contribution to religious life, thought, and practice in the wake of modernity's failed agenda. Although Giussani never uses the word "postmodern" in any technical sense, the term may well be applied to this trilogy, given its eclecticism, especially in *The Religious Sense*.

Where Giussani's influence will go from here, no one can tell, but it is a fact that his death has only led to an expansion of the lay movement that he founded and an ongoing interest in the *charism* that was his life. This present essay, it is hoped, will go a considerable way towards introducing Guissani's ideas beyond the usual boundaries of the Catholic faith, to which at the present time his thought and life are largely confined in North America.

Indeed, the work of Luigi Giussani has broad implications not only for Protestant-Catholic dialogue but also for dialogue about and with other religions and the religious nature of humanity in general.[7] The reason for this resides in Giussani's unique approach to the problem of religion, an approach that is at once firmly ensconced in his Catholic faith, as expressed in Vatican II, and at the same time open to the world, in Giussani's perpetual search for what is truly human and truly Divine. To understand *American Protestant Theology* in terms of what it means for Giussani's calling, it would be worthwhile to summarize briefly the principles of the religious, historical, and communal roots of the true humanity that Guissani espouses, especially as it is contained in his trilogy.

But, first a comment on Protestant engagement with Guissani and my connection with Guissani's work.

PROTESTANT ENGAGEMENT WITH GIUSSANI

Allow me here to indicate my connection with Giussani, the man and his work. In my theological training and religious experience, nothing had ever led me to any great interest in ecumenism or dialogue with the other "catholic" faiths, up to and even beyond my engagement with Giussani. Indeed, even in the writing of my initial review of *The Religious Sense*, I never thought of it as an ecumenical piece. I did, however, note in that review how intrigued I was by this apparently unknown person who had managed to write a work on religion that was on the order of Kant, Schleiermacher, or Edwards, all Protestants who had written influential tracts defining the nature of "true religion." But, members of the movement Communion and Liberation thought otherwise with respect to my apparent ecumenical bent in the review, especially the translator and editor of *The Religious Sense*, Professor John Zucchi of McGill University in Montreal. After the publication of my review, I was contacted "out of the blue" by Professor Zucchi with a request to further engage with Giussani's work.[8] For almost two years, I heard nothing further from Zucchi. In the meantime, I was asked to review the second volume of Giussani's trilogy, *At the Origin of the Christian Claim*, and was about to review the third volume when the invitation finally came from Zucchi to come to McGill University and offer a response to *Why the Church?* in the form of a formal lecture. Subsequent to this lecture, which was offered jointly with Professor Janine Langan of the University of St Michael's College, Toronto, and Bishop Terrence Prendergast of Halifax (now Archbishop of Ottawa), I was invited to Italy to engage with Giussani, quite literally on his own turf. Thus, in 2003, I delivered a lecture at the Meeting. Not only was my ecumenical interest deepened and broadened at that time, but my continuing interest in Giussani's writings was guaranteed by my personal encounter with the man himself.

I was deeply impressed by this man's faith, and also by his humility, candour, and graciousness, which were everywhere in evidence. At no time was I made to feel inferior because of my Protestant faith. Quite the opposite! Guissani was as much interested in my spiritual journey as I was in his. This was due in no small part to his appreciation of and respect for the history of Protestant thought in North America, especially that of Jonathan Edwards.[9] Since that time, I have published other articles and written lectures for presentation to audiences as far away as Dublin, Seattle, and on many other occasions, Italy itself.

Since my initial engagement with Giussani, he has come to the attention of many other Protestant theologians including such influential voices as John Milbank and Stanley Hauerwas. Giussani's eclecticism and the broad range of his engagement with classical Western thought makes him the ideal Catholic postmodern, with whom more engagement will assuredly be forthcoming. It is hoped that the translation and publication of *American Protestant Theology* will further that engagement in a positive direction.

GIUSSANI'S TRILOGY

To understand Giussani's thought, we would do well to rehearse briefly the conception of the essential religious nature of humanity that Giussani sees as the basic core of human life, which he calls "the religious sense." Everything in the trilogy proceeds from that basis. A brief overview will bear this out.

The Nature of the Religious Sense According to Giussani

I have suggested in my review of *The Religious Sense* that "it is nothing short of a full affirmation of the co-inherence and coexistence of reason and religion in somewhat neo-Thomist terms."[10] By "religious sense," Giussani means that which lies at the very essence and root of human rationality and consciousness. It is that aspect of the human individual that affords Christianity a *reasonable basis*, as an instance of the revelation of God as mystery.

To properly understand and establish the validity of this religious sense, three premises need to be put forward and assumed. The first is that of *realism*, that is, the urgent necessity not to give a more important role to a scheme already in our minds, but rather to cultivate an "intuitive, passionate, insistent ability to observe the real event, the fact."[11] This will require a method that is imposed by the "fact" of the object itself. The experience of the object presents us with its own "method for knowing it" as a religious experience. The criteria of this method must emerge from "the inherent structure of the human being, the structure at the origin of the person."[12] This is possible because religious experience is fundamentally the same for everyone since we all have the same human *needs*. This criterion is an objective one "with which nature thrusts man into a universal comparison, endowing him with that nucleus of original needs, with that elementary experience which mothers in the same way provide to their children."[13]

This first premise points naturally to a second, that of *reasonableness*, that is, "the mode of action that expresses and realizes reason, the capacity to become aware of reality."[14] Reasonableness is part of the universal human experience and points us, by and large, back to realism. Reality, arrived at through reason, has to come about in a reasonable way. Indeed, the term "reasonable" is, in some sense, more important and useful than "reason," because the latter has a tendency to be used in an "unreasonable" manner. Reason is "reasonable" when it is open to reality through the employment of adequate motives, that is, as a capacity to know life in all its complexity and multiplicity. Such a view of reason yields "moral certainties," which in turn, lead to what Giussani calls, in somewhat Schleiermacherean terms, a "universal intuition." Life together (*convivenza*) leads us to universal intuitions about an "other" beyond our capacity to reason it: "In this sense, the question of moral certainty is the main problem of life as existence, but, through it, also of life as civilization and culture."[15] To understand these first two principles, and to make sense of them, requires a method, which amounts to "a locus of adequate motives." It is a method yielded up to us by the object itself in terms of what Giussani calls the "reasonableness of life."

This means that a third proposition must be assumed. If reality is known through a method of reasonableness imposed on the knowing subject by its relationship to the object, then morality will necessarily have an impact on the dynamic of knowing. This, says Giussani, is the *epistemological* problem. Reason is inseparable from the unity of the "I" and, as such, cannot be seen as some mechanism separated off from the knowing "I."[16]

Reason is necessarily bound to feeling and is, indeed, "conditioned" by it: "In order for reason to know an object, it must also take into account feeling, the 'state' of the soul by which it is filtered and with which it is, in any case, involved."[17]

This epistemological nexus is unavoidable as a part of human experience, even in the sciences. True knowledge can only be arrived at when all human factors, especially feelings, are highlighted and given their proper value. Indeed, knowledge of an object can only increase with the increase of intensity of feeling towards the object: "The impact of feeling does not diminish, but increases where the object becomes more filled with meaning." Such a "feeling" is really the heart of the epistemological problem and necessarily involves the question of morality in the process of knowing. Again, motivation is central in this "dynamic of knowing an object." If certitude is to be attained in religious knowledge, then one must "love the truth of an object" more than one's opinions that may have already been formed about it, either from tradition or misinterpretation. This is not to suggest that our knowledge of the object is free of presuppositions but, rather, that we desire to know the object "in a true way" beyond any of our attachments that we bring to it. The reality of life, in all its reasonableness, necessarily imposes certain preconceptions of that reality. The point is to recognize this and strive for "an attitude with which we reflect upon our freedom and use its energy in a way that is true to its purpose."[18] Of course, Giussani does not go on to describe what he thinks this "purpose" to be, nor how one can arrive at the knowledge of it, except to say that it is life lived from a reasonable perspective.

Reality, reasonableness, and morality lead us to the inexorable conclusion that humanity is, in fact, "moved solely by love and affection. It is primarily the *love of ourselves as destiny*, the affection for our own destiny, that convinces us to undertake this work ... to become habitually detached from our own opinions and our own imaginations ... so that all of our cognitive energy will be focused upon a search for the truth of the object, no matter what it should be."[19] It is the supreme emotion (feeling) that drives us towards truth. The very presence of things, and of the cosmos, invites us to analogy, to the substitution of the sign for the "thing-in-itself." For to do otherwise, or to deny it, is irrational, or put better, unreasonable. This is what gives us openness and freedom to be the self. It constitutes this very self. *The self is openness to the mysterious you which I am.*

The world is the parable that interprets this openness. It is the playing field where this freedom is exercised. It both veils and unveils in that it points to this other but in terms that make the other evident yet unknowable. It is this pointing towards the other that gives the human a religious sense. Reason is the energy that calls us to recognize the reality of the world as a sign: "Reason, in order to be faithful to its nature and to the nature of such a calling, is forced to admit the existence of something else underpinning, explaining everything." Quoting St Thomas Aquinas, Guissani calls for a necessary revelation in order to "render this salvation more universal and more certain."[20]

Our nature as creatures of need, combined with reason, intuits an answer to our fundamental questions in terms of a mysterious other. This is reason's pinnacle and vertiginous position. We are dependent upon this unreachable, unknowable mystery. This is our *religious sense*. Against this, we are pushed back, in fear and terror, into reflection on an expanse. Subsequently, we tend to identify one or other aspect(s) of this experience with the absolute as a means and way of redemption. Appeals are made to a word from the divine other that comes out of this experience.

Thus, we have the hypothesis of Revelation. It is the entry of the Divine into history through mundane human experience, as in the case of Christianity. As God acts, he makes human action (or reaction), possible and significant.

The Nature of Revelation: At the Origin of the Christian Claim

The second volume of Giussani's trilogy, *At the Origin of the Christian Claim*, amounts to an investigation into how the ultimate questions of the earliest disciples about this revelation were decisively answered by the totalizing message of "Jesus Christ the risen Lord." This was a conclusion at which they arrived simply because life "spurs reason to search for a solution. Indeed reason's very nature implies that a solution exists."[21] That is, human reason must be "confirmed by revelation." Reason cries out for it and launches itself towards this hypothesis, "which is so rational and so much part of our nature that, to some degree, it always emerges."[22] This impulse towards revelation is inherent in our drive for knowledge, our need for mediators of knowledge, our experience of proximity to God, our common appeal to revelation, and our Western appeal to the faith of Israel. If there were an accusation that could be levelled at this universal religious impulse, as conceived by culture today, it would be that of the claim to "exclusive truth." Yet, Christianity does just this. For Giussani, this is a claim that can only be justified or not, when we return to the "origins of the Christian claim."

Considered on its own merits as a human construct, Christianity would certainly be wrong to make such a claim in the face of other religions. If, however, we understand the Christian claim to be an expression of the "enigma" as a fact within the history of this human religious trajectory, then this fact must be regarded or examined on its own merits. Were we to suppose that the enigma (mystery, God) became flesh, then this "supposition would correspond to the need for revelation."[23] To deny this would be irrational and contrary to the *human religious sense*. Were this to be the case, then could not Christianity prove to be "a more human synthesis, a more complete way of valuing the factors at play"?[24] Announced as a fact of history, the Christian claim must be taken seriously as a problem to be solved, and not as a "despotic irrational claim." That is, it concerns a question of fact – Incarnation – not opinion.

For Giussani, the origin of the problem as a fact of history lies not so much in the event itself as in the "perceptive experience of the earliest disciples" and their careful formulation of the primitive "Christology" or Messianism. Although the event is a mystery, almost imperceptible, the conviction (of the disciples) is the fulfilment of humanity's deepest longings, needs, and questions. It was, as such, a totalizing event.

Giussani, however, is not satisfied to lay all the weight of the exclusive claims of Christianity on the basis of the experience of the earliest disciples. He takes great pains to point out that Christ himself, through a "slow pedagogy," taught his disciples to think of him as "God." Jesus' claim is simply a fact that lays bare "the basic position of the human heart – whether closed or open – to the mystery of being."[25] As such, the Christian problem is resolved in the same terms in which it presents itself: "either we are dealing with madness or this man, who says he is God, really is God."[26] Our free decision to penetrate this mystery "is a decision with hidden roots bound to our attitude to reality as a whole." It is that "supreme something" which sees Jesus as the ultimate good and worth our free commitment.

To understand this Christian claim, we must be educated into "Christ's conception of life," which is an education in "morality for understanding," as per the third principle of method indicated in *The Religious Sense*. What is at stake is the "correspondence of human existence as a whole to the form of Christ."[27] Jesus' own outlook on the value of humanity, dependence upon the Divine, self-existence, sin, and human freedom answers the ultimate questions about these core human realities in a definitive way: "Following Christ (faith) thus generates a characteristic existential attitude by which man walks upright and untiring towards a destination not yet reached although sure (hope)."[28] Thus, the event of the Incarnation, as mystery, is an "ethical urgency" and an "education to the ideal." It was "an extraordinary historical reality" in which Jesus moved his disciples from "awe to conviction" because the answers he gave to the questions of ultimate concern convinced them that he was the "God-man." The greatest task of Christianity is to announce, with the same conviction that was present "at the origins of the Christian claim," that Jesus of Nazareth is God.

The Church: The Contemporaneous Christ Is an Education in the Fact of History

The third offering in Giussani's trilogy provides the most fundamental context in which humanity must begin to realize the Incarnation as a fact of history. Space does not permit a full investigation of how *Why the Church?* suggests that the Church embodies this divine revelation of the Incarnation as the continuing contemporaneousness of Christ. Allow me, therefore, to point out three crucial aspects of the book before drawing the lines of connection with the previous volumes; in chapter 9 of *Why the Church?* Guissani focuses on experience as the verifying principle of the fact of the Incarnation and its ongoing reality in the life of the Church.

First, the fundamental presupposition of the religious sense is carried forward in the volume's opening pages as a continuation of the claim uncovered in the analysis of the origins of Christianity. As such, "the Church is a religious life" that appeals, either negatively or positively, to the religious sense: "This theme of the religious sense is important for an understanding of the originality of Christianity, which is nothing more than the answer, through Christ and the Church, to our religious sense."[29] Thus, the Church is the means whereby Christ continues to be present, educating believers and unbelievers as to his reality and as to how he is the answer to all their concerns.

Second, the continuity of this appeal to the religious sense by Christ, in the ongoing history of the Church, is attested to by the Church's own self-awareness.[30] Both structurally and dogmatically, it can be demonstrated that in its bond with Jesus Christ, the Church "represents Him, in the full and ancient meaning of the term … really makes Him present."[31] The Church does this as a sociologically identifiable community invested with the power of the Holy Spirit that issues in a "new type of life." Despite its frailty on the human side, "there was (and is) the certainty of a new humanity, the humanity of Christ capable of transforming any kind of miserable humanity … according to its own possibilities, but supported by grace."[32] This unified witness to the continuing presence of Christ in the life of the Church is supremely exemplified for Giussani in the conversion and life work of Cardinal John Henry Newman. The unity of the witness, discovered by Newman in his *Development of Doctrine*, to this ongoing presence of Christ should "inspire self-questioning, pushing us on to a personal comparison from which our lives will surely emerge richer and fuller, that is to say truer and more human."[33]

Third, and on the basis of the forgoing points, Giussani understands the Church to be "the effective sign" of the Divine in history: "In summary the Church stands before the world as a social reality filled with the Divine."[34] The Church challenges history just as Christ did, and as he continues to do. As the divine sign (Sacrament), the Church is "the saving power of Christ in the world … coincides with the Christian community, the Church, as the subject and sacrament of his power": "Thus the Sacrament is the Divine which makes an appeal to our senses through the sign, becoming a presence which reaches out beyond the limits of the sign itself. It is a presence at work in us in an ineffable way. It confers upon us our new stature as new men (through our free participation). And it is a unifying power because the Sacrament is only given in the context of the unity of all Christians."[35]

But, how do we come to know that the Church is the authentic "prolongation of Christ in time and space"?[36] Giussani tries to answer that question in chapter 9 of *Why the Church?* and in so doing brings the full ramifications of his appeal to the religious sense into clear view. In continuing to address humanity as the presence of Christ, the Church will, as did Christ, appeal to "the man who compares everything to his elementary experience."[37] Following the religious epistemology of the German philosopher Bernhard Welte, Giussani writes, "as we already said in the first volume of this trilogy, this is why the complete man, equipped with a critical sense and capable of global judgment, will be the man who has trained himself to compare everything with the bundle of profound needs which constitute the core of his true 'I,' a core uncensored by outside intervention."[38] That is, "it serves the immediacy we call experience."

Such experience provides us with a critical faculty to decide, as long as it is "immediate experience" – and not the collection of confusing emotions and experiences that are put in our way as blocks to this immediate experience. The Church, as the sum total of the self-revelation of the Divine in history, subjects itself to the gamble of human "reasonableness." It promises to those who believe an experience of the Divine that transcends normal human experiences. This experience imparts new life: "The problem of verifying such a far-reaching claim must have as its starting point an 'encounter,' a physical presence."[39] That is, it must have a community that can verify this claim: "And the Church is this physical presence: it cannot cheat in making its proposal. It cannot just hand over a book and a series of formulas to exegete for its life, and it must offer life, and it must enfold the experience of men deep within the embrace of its claim."[40] But, humanity must not cheat either: "Man's prospect is true journeying, but his heart must be willing." The minimum requirement is merely a "poverty of Spirit" that comes with an open hand to receive. This is the beginning of the fulfilment of our religious sense.[41]

Some Reflections on Giussani's Trilogy vis-à-vis Protestant Theology

Of course many Protestants will want to take issue with Giussani at several points. But let me begin by suggesting what I consider to be some of his positive contributions to our understanding of faith, religion, and Christianity, from a Protestant perspective.

To say the least, Giussani's appeal to the religious sense constitutes a tour-de-force justification of the basic religious essence of the human individual, and it will demand the attention of detractors from his position. Guissani has succeeded in offering a cohesive argument that is not only intellectually challenging but also well illustrated. It is innovative in its descriptions of reason, reasonableness, intuition, and feeling, providing new ways of understanding concepts that have fuelled philosophical and theological debate for centuries. In this regard, Giussani can neither be described as a modernist nor a postmodernist, although he draws from both impulses. He is more of an ultramodernist, in that his appeal is to the collective witness of the Church in the totality of its historical and contemporary existence. Certainly, he may not necessarily provide definitive, ultimate, or even provisional solutions to these problems, but he does offer a fresh approach that is not entirely trapped within the modernist-postmodernist philosophical debate about religion.

Giussani is to be commended for the way in which he combines epistemology with a moral ontology that does not fall into the same traps that Kant's moral imperative does, with its contradictory understanding of the self-legislating will. Giussani seems to move in this direction at first, but avoids it through a thorough grounding of the human in God's prior act of grace. Yet, this moral responsiveness, based as it is in the intuiting individual, is capable of a religious knowledge that moves us in the direction of divine encounter, as mystery. Here, again, Giussani is neither modern nor postmodern. His moral ontology seems to trade on the best from the Christian and the German Idealist traditions.

Giussani seems to avoid the pluralist and exclusivist trap with his appeal to the Christian claim as a *fact* of history. He simply puts the Christian claim out as one that must pass the test of history in the life of the Church. All are free to decide, but this does not change the fact of the Incarnation. It merely allows for a level playing field on which the claims of Christianity must be given the same consideration as those of any other religion, with their claims to exclusive truth.

Finally, on the positive side of the equation, I would commend the clear Christological grounding of the religious sense, the experience and pedagogy of the earliest community of faith, and the sacramental presence of Christ throughout the history of the Church. Giussani's

Catholic ecclesiology reaps the benefits of this Christological orientation and issues, in a clear pedagogy into the way of Christ as a core task of the Church. His section on the sacramental presence of Christ is the best Catholic sacramental theology since Schillebeeckx's *Christ the Sacrament*.[42]

GIUSSANI'S INTEREST IN AMERICAN PROTESTANT THEOLOGY

It is this author's studied opinion that Giussani's interest in American Protestant theology is not purely academic. As noted above, in the delineation of his key ideas, it is clear that Guissani absorbed certain Protestant impulses in his description of the religious sense. If there is a key motivation for his interest before his formal study of the question, it remains locked up between the lines of his earlier work, especially on the formation of youth. The implications are that Guissani promoted a more personal understanding of faith than his Catholic communal faith perhaps allowed for or taught.

The sense is that he wanted the youth under his care to both be able to express their faith and to have more of a personal stake in it. Did Giussani detect in his Catholic faith either a lack or hidden-ness of the spiritual resources needed to attain this personalization of faith that he saw, somehow, emulated in Protestant theology in America, however "wrong headed"? Again, no literary testimony before *American Protestant Theology* exists to verify this as a motivating factor his interest in this topic. But, it is everywhere attested to in his subsequent writings, as will become clear as we approach the content of the book itself. At any rate, it is the only internal witness we have, other than a purely academic motivation, regarding any deeper motivations for his interest; if there were more, Giussani appeared to be very judicious about saying so.

As mentioned above, Giussani was keenly interested in a Protestant-Catholic rapproachment, a fact of which I have direct, first-hand evidence, from our conversation together that warm summer day in August 2003. As is clear from the book itself, this is not a clinical, objectivist exposition of American Protestant theology. The very choices he makes in the organizations, movements, personalities, and key ideas that he covers already indicate an interest in getting at the heart of the personal nature of religion in Protestant America. Giussani's interest is not so much in the movement of the Holy Spirit within it, as it is in the movement of the human religious heart, which I think he suspects is, nevertheless, a movement of the Holy Spirit. There is a decidedly religious phenomenological bent to his inquiry, however. For instance, when in *American Protestant Theology* he writes of the beginnings of the Great Awakening that "the intense stress placed on conversion as the event that seizes the entire person, and on the fervour of a devotion that is confirmed and nourished by expression, while springing from the urgency of renewing a declining religiosity, strives, however, to be motivated in a theological vision and to create its own continuity through an intellectual education" (20), Guissani is clearly offering a phenomenological description of the event.

But, within this sentence itself, there is a clear tension he feels between this event as a humanly derived religious experience and a witness to its theological (read, Divine) orientation. This tension regarding the personal appropriation of religion is one that Guissani shares with one of his key figures of interest, Jonathan Edwards. One can almost read Giussani's own "bursting forth" as he summarizes this tension in Edwards. He writes, "This tension burst forth in a clamorous [notice, he did not say calamitous] way in Edwards' life, even though the force of his thought doubtless exceeds mere reduction to pragmatic categories, just as his doctrine did not exhaustively originate in the revival of the fact, although it was congenial to it" (20).

Further on, it is clear that Giussani does not want to write Edwards off as a "Protestant sectarian" but to show the religious roots from which his rational, and yet, clearly theological, approach to Christian faith comes. That is, while he refused to reduce religion and its doctrines to mere "religious phenomena" or "rational means," Edwards, nevertheless, committed himself to a "dense cogent logic" in its exposition (20). As we have seen above, Giussani's own approach to the religious sense is not so far from the internal tension that he ascribes to Edwards.

The religious sense is by no means a purely "religious phenomenology" nor is it pure doctrinal faith. It is, rather, the self-expression of the internal tension of what it is to be a religious human being. Did Giussani see this in Edwards better than he did in his own Roman Catholic contemporaries, or at least equally so? We are just asking at this point, but the question is at least plausible. Space does not permit a full explication here of how his engagement with American Protestant theology triggered this tension within Giussani, both in his description of American Protestantism and in his own religious self-consciousness. I am alerting the reader to it here in respect to Edwards, but such tension can also be seen in how Giussani deals with Boston Personalism, Reinhold Neibuhr, and Paul Tillich. Thus, it was not without reason that Guissani wrote *American Protestant Theology*.

In his contact with the human expression of faith in American Protestant thought, Luigi Guissani came, in some way, face to face with his own humanity, and – dare I say? – in some respects he liked what he saw. He liked it insofar as it testified to something about himself and about those whom he loved in his homeland. It is entirely possible that Giussani received from his contact with American Protestantism a witness to the religious impulse that he felt to be basic in all humans and, furthermore, to be a key instinct to reawakening his own Catholic brothers and sisters. If there is a reason this book should be published in English, this is it.

To be sure, treatments of American Protestant theology, especially in its Liberal expressions, abound. In terms of content, coverage, and depth of research Gary Dorrien's *The Making of American Liberal Theology* is, in many respects, far beyond what Giussani offers.[43] And yet, there are some lessons Dorrien could learn from Giussani, not the least of which is the internal tension alluded to above. Dorrien is much more the phenomenologist of religion than Giussani, a position no doubt attributable to the fact that Dorrien is a late-modern Protestant who seems to have long ago lost contact with his internal religious sense.[44] There is a position that Catholicism offers more safeguards against this loss of the religious sense, due to its grounding in a more ecclesial and communal sense of its reality.

Another reason why *American Protestant Theology* should be published now is simply because it is a witness to a new form of ecumenical dialogue between Catholics and Protestants that Giussani exemplifies; in this respect, he was ahead of his time.

Guissani demonstrates a clear understanding of his subject. Nowhere is he polemical, denigrating, or condescending. He deals objectively, charitably, and fairly with each Protestant expression, movement, and personality. Yet, he is not interested in a reductionism of religion. He sees American Protestant faith for what it is and does, without asking it to become something else in the interest of some greater good. As we have said, what Giussani seeks is a phenomenology of religion that, nevertheless, testifies to something beyond its being merely human.

Indeed, he wants the truly human, the divine intentionality in all religion, to come to the surface. It is only at that level that he makes judgments, but they apply across the board.

Finally, *American Protestant Theology* should be published in English if only to demonstrate how scholarly and careful Giussani was in his academic pursuits. One of the hindrances to the reception of Giussani in the English-speaking world is his seeming eclecticism and somewhat disorderly interdisciplinarity (my coinage).

Giussani is no confused religionist. He knows his subject matter intimately. He is more than capable as a scholar and deftly moves in and out of topics, personalities, and movements with ease. Indeed, a brief comparison between the book by Dorrien, mentioned above, and this one demonstrates that Giussani had a precise sense of how Protestant theology in America unfolded. Although some of the names and movements in Dorrien's book are not accounted for in Giussani, who was only sketching an outline, nevertheless, the broad strokes are clearly visible. This would be remarkable enough for any American-born theologian or historian. It is all the more remarkable when you consider that Giussani's knowledge of English extended to reading and nothing more. In fact, Giussani's scholarly legacy is only now being fully disclosed.

As more of Guissani's work becomes available in English, the full scope of his power as a theologian, philosopher of religion, and pastor/priest will become all the more evident. We have now only to point the reader to some basic features of Giussani's *American Protestant Theology* before we conclude and move to the work itself.

THE BASIC FEATURES OF *AMERICAN PROTESTANT THEOLOGY: A HISTORICAL SKETCH*

In *American Protestant Theology*, Giussani's approach is historical but neither strictly chronological nor thematic. His choice and arrangement of the material can be explained as follows.

The very first point to understand clearly about this book is its claim to be a sketch, one that only gives a *selective* account of American Protestant theology up to the time the author concluded its writing. Unless this is kept in mind, the average Protestant reader is likely to be disappointed that his or her "hero of the faith" was overlooked or given short shrift. Giussani is aiming at the core of a religious phenomenology that he sees emerging in American

Protestant theology, not merely a history. His selection of the materials is guided by no other intention.

One might wonder why, for instance, he did not focus directly on the various "schools" of Liberal Protestantism at Harvard, Yale, or Chicago, the true leading centres of Protestant Liberal thought in the 1950s and 1960s. However, one could argue that Giussani encounters the best spirit of those schools in his focus on Reinhold Niebuhr and Paul Tillich, the latter being the leading light at Harvard and Chicago during the time of his writing.

One might also quibble that some of America's most influential female theologians, like Georgia Harkness, were also missed. But his comments on H.E. Fosdick and E. Mays seem to make this point moot, other than the "need" to include women. This was a need not as keenly felt by scholars in the 1950s and 1960s as it is today, however regrettable this fact is.

When comparing Giussani's approach to that of Gary Dorrien's massive three-volume *Making of American Liberal Theology*, the outline of development, including similar themes, is remarkable. The lineage in Dorrien's first volume of his trilogy is almost identical to Giussani's description, as is the characterization of the period from 1805 to 1900 as a striving after "progressive religion," which both Dorrien and Giussani agree was rooted in the emergence of Arminian theology at the turn of the nineteenth century. Dorrien suggests that by the end of the nineteenth century Arminianism "belonged to a groundswell of religious practice and denominations in the New England states."[45] Meanwhile, in *American Protestant Theology* (17ff), Giussani suggests, as does Dorrien, that this marked a passage from the predominant Puritan Calvinism of the eighteenth century to the intervention of Enlightenment rationalism, which would wind up supplanting the former in guiding American culture. As both Guissani and Dorrien suggest, this led to a complementarity between revelation and reason "but eventually suggested that religion was about inspiring and obliging human beings to fulfill their divinely inspired capacity for goodness and progress."[46] Thus, Giussani is on stable ground if we are to judge his and the more recent approach of Dorrien as reliable guides to the development of American Protestant theology in its Liberal vein. We will leave for now the glaring absence, in both of their works, of the debate between Liberalism and Protestant Conservativism, which on the Conservative side, continues to influence American theology to this day.

Comparing the tables of contents of the two books is a good indication of how well attuned Giussani was to his task in his own time. This is especially true with Giussani's placement of the theologians Reinhold Niebuhr and Paul Tillich, whom he calls "Neo-liberals." Guissani sees these two theologians as attempting to move beyond the impasse created by Enlightenment Liberal-Protestant progressivism. Neo-liberals exchange the language of process, progress, morality, and evolutionary idealism for the language of angst, crisis, existence, encounter, and paradox. That is, in place of the philosophically inspired language of moral and technological progress, they substitute the more orthodox theological language of sin, redemption, tragedy, and transcendence (see 106ff herein).[47]

Giussani was very aware that one could not simply make a hard and fast dichotomy between American Liberal Protestantism and its sister movement commonly known as neo-liberal, dialectical, or existential theology. Giussani writes, "We have provided an emphasis and more space has been dedicated to the literature of the New Theology and the Social Gospel, which bridges the nineteenth and twentieth centuries, out of the conviction that this literature will show the roots of much of the theme and underlying methodology that guided the approach, as inspiration and as program, of certain very new currents that, at the present time, are agitating the American theological climate. Our broad attention to Niebuhr's discourses and to Tillich's work is motivated by the decisive influence that the former's ethical development and the latter's Weltanschauung have had on the whole scene of American religious thought" (xxiv). Of course, Giussani could have described this religious tradition, as some do, in strictly European Protestant terms in its origins, but he is far too sensitive to the Edwardsian spirit of religion in America to make that mistake.

Guissani's goal is to expose what he considers to be the uniquely "American spiritual milieu" in his concentration upon these more programmatic theologies. The degree to which he succeeds will have to await the judgment of the readers of this volume; nevertheless, Gary Dorrien's work treats this theological lineage as summative of the most influential aspects of the religious milieu of America, and certainly Giussani has anticipated this spirit very well for a man who was neither born nor bred in that milieu.[48] This is a clear indication of Giussani's great capacity for religious-theological interpretation on a fundamentally anthropological level. His phenomenological intuition constitutes one of his greatest contributions to the religious thought of the twentieth century and is the undercurrent that the reader must be alert to in reading *American Protestant Theology*.

In many respects Giussani here is "priming the pump" for some of his more influential later works on religion and theology, especially *The Religious Sense*. This can be observed in the way he deals with this in three of the main characters of Protestant thought in America, Jonathan Edwards, Reinhold Niebuhr, and Paul Tillich. What indications of this phenomenology of religion should readers be alert to in this respect?

The Phenomenology of Religion in Jonathan Edwards

Jonathan Edwards helped engender the "Great Awakening," and Giussani sees the essence of American religious history expressed in its experiential-emotional aspect, which he thinks Edwards both represents and masterfully tapped into. In an excellent analysis of Edwards, in *American Protestant Theology*, Giussani describes this basic religious phenomenology as follows: "The new orientation of theological discourse will normally assume the experiential fact of conversion as the catalyst of its entire disposition and as the centre of its systematic solution, by exalting the paradigmatic criterion of direct experience in the pietistic view, or practical results in the more moralistic conception" (20). This was the basic phenomenology that motivated Edwards' preaching, writing, and overall theology. It was a phenomenology born of Edwards' contact with philosophy, especially the empiricism of John Locke, as much as it was of his own religious experiential observation. This was a "natural theology" for Edwards, and it deeply informed the whole of the religious nature of humanity in his opinion. It is in this modality that we must speak of "a primary of direct experience" (10), and it had no small impact on Giussani himself. This whole world of Newtonian-Lockean cause-effect experience must, for Edwards and Giussani, be grounded in the sovereignty of a final cause as the only possible explanation of this experience: "Faithful to his psychological and phenomenological position, Edwards holds that the virtuous fact bespeaks a radical reference to 'something beautiful, or rather some kind of beauty or excellency'" (27).

Giussani sees in this phenomenology, however Protestant in its orientation, a reflection of his own tradition of the beatific vision of virtue. In the works of Edwards, Guissani does not see merely individual religious experience but an experience that exhibits "the passion for the objectivity of order and the rational zest for the system integrated into the individual event and into a context that was established and consecrated" (29). Of course, this reflects Giussani's own Roman Catholic milieu, but now with the more prominent emphasis on individual encounter that will eventually mark both his own religious experience and his description of it in *The Religious Sense*. (It can be argued that in the total corpus of Giussani's works the key words to look for are expressed in the phrase "the existential encounter with Jesus Christ," albeit qualified in terms of "within the Church.")

The Phenomena of Religion in Reinhold Niebuhr

It is this fundamentally American understanding of religious phenomenology that Giussani finds at work in his second most important Protestant protagonist, Reinhold Niebuhr.

Giussani's familiarity with Niebuhr goes back to his graduate theological studies and his 1954 doctoral dissertation, "Il senso cristiano dell'uomo secondo Reinhold Niebuhr."[49] There and in *American Protestant Theology*, the full implications of Giussani's earlier interest in Niebuhr become clear. He is substantially concerned with the anthropologically driven phenomenology that Niebuhr's social-ethical theology exhibits.

Reinhold Niebuhr was an American-born Protestant theologian whose career was established mostly at Union Theological Seminary in New York. He spent a great deal of his theological career writing about the nature and ethical scope of humanity.[50] In Niebuhr's work, Dialectical Theology and Liberal Protestant Theology were to come under criticism regarding their respective theologies of human subjectivity. However, like the dialectical theologians, especially Barth and Brunner, Niebuhr reaches the conclusion that modern culture, the Liberal Protestant "god of idealist philosophy," in particular, tends to identify God with some level of human consciousness or order of nature. Humanity has thereby created a "God" who is but an exaggerated reflection of that same humanity. In the assertion of human autonomy and freedom, humanity fails to recognize its true stature before God, considering its own cultural and rational achievements as the essence of self-transcending activity.[51]

Such conceptions of the self are, for Niebuhr, empty. No matter how easy and good the conscience of modern humanity feels, it is hopelessly lost in contradictory human understandings of this "self." Indeed, "the most surprising aspect of modern man's good conscience is that he asserts and justifies it in terms of the most varied and even contradictory metaphysical theories and social philosophies." Niebuhr concludes, "without the presuppositions of the Christian faith the individual is either nothing or becomes everything."[52] However, "in the Christian faith man's insignificance as a creature, involved in the process of nature and time, is lifted into significance by the mercy and power of God in which his life is sustained. But his significance as a free spirit is understood as subordinate to the freedom of God. His inclination to abuse his freedom, to overestimate his power and significance and to become everything is understood as the primal sin. It is because man is involved in this primal sin that he is bound to meet God first as judge, who humbles his pride and brings his vain imagination to naught."[53]

Despite Niebuhr's agreement with Dialectical Theology on this point, he feels that their respective anthropologies in general and ethics in particular "threaten to destroy all relative moral judgments by their exclusive emphasis upon the ultimate religious fact of the sinfulness of all men."[54] Not only that, they also imperil the "relative moral achievements of history." For Niebuhr, it is Barth who is the real culprit here. In agreement with Brunner's side of the debate, Niebuhr affirms that "Protestant theology is right in setting grace in contradiction to nature in the sense that the vicious cycle of false truth, apprehended from the standpoint of self, must be broken and the self cannot break it." In that sense, the apprehension of the truth in Christ must be viewed as a miracle: "But Protestant theology, more particularly radical Protestant theology (Barth), is wrong in denying the 'point of contact' (*Anknüpfungspunkt*) which always exists in man by virtue of the residual element of *justitia originalis* in his being."[55]

In his treatment of Niebuhr herein, Giussani begins with precisely this anthropological stance that he finds in Niebuhr. In *American Protestant Theology*, Guissani characterizes Niebuhr's religious phenomenology as follows. While it is true that Niebuhr's theology participates broadly in the redempto-centric nature and specificity of the American religious experience, "Niebuhr's work … is already marked and shaken by the subterranean fact of the experience he lived in Detroit in a world dominated by Ford [Motor Company] and the men excited by his programs, the experience therefore, of the contrast between proclaimed ideas and social reality" (152). This principle of experience, Giussani thinks, is summed up for Niebuhr in a "philosophy of history" that yields a principle similar to that of Jacques Maritain, that is, that history is a redemptive process that is often misunderstood by both individual and collective humanity. It is, rather, a theology of history that fundamentally orients the human to its proper religious experience, not a philosophy of history. This theology of history includes both an "orientation of the self towards a 'unity of experience' and towards its 'creaturely nature'" (151ff). This is the axiomatic centre from which the human experiences ultimate necessity, or "religious dependence" (151–2 and 171–2).

The second aspect of this religious phenomenology is our "capacity for freedom," which according to Niebuhr makes us "responsible creatures in nature," with a rational capacity. As with Edwards, this is our capacity to reflect, empirically and experientially, on our own experience (20). In a concise summary of Niebuhr's thought Giussani writes, "Historical knowledge and awareness of what exists are ultimately the same event. Precisely because the essential and absolute originality of freedom represents the substance of the object for both of them; and it is by memory that those cognitive moments are constituted" (155). Revelation trades upon this fundamental religious ontology in that it is "substantially subjective" because it is "eminently psychological." It takes the symbols, language, and rites of communal life to awaken this consciousness, and thus, human community is essential as the "common fabric of all temporal events" (158).

This quintessential ontology finds expression for Giussani as an "intuition innate to humanity." From a methodological standpoint, the intuitions of faith function as a working hypothesis which, when compared with the data of experience and of history, are found to be "in accord with that experience" (159). The parallels to Giussani's later expression of this phenomenology in *The Religious Sense* (especially chapter 3) are unmistakable.

This religious intuition is the "precondition" that gives orientation to faith and existence. It is the singular contribution of the Protestant faith that it has made this basic intuition more radically individual, but this is also, and at once its greatest weakness for Giussani. Without the Church – its dogmas, rites, and symbols – there can be no other verification of this religious sense. Thus, "it may be said that a natural connotation of faith is the need for convergence, for communion."[56]

For Giussani, the only possible unity for such a human religious phenomenology can be a point outside of it, vested in a divine action, namely, Jesus Christ and his sacrifice. Only in that act is our participation in the Kingdom possible. The "aporia" of Niebuhr's thought is its incapacity to see the Divine apart from its ontological expression in human religious experience. If we are not to confuse this with ourselves, or nature, or some other aspect of existence, it needs an orientation beyond its confirmation in individual experience, in community.

The Phenomena of Religion in Paul Tillich

In Giussani's account of American Protestant theology, there can be no greater confirmation of the radical subjectivity suggested in the Edwardsian-Niebuhrian religious phenomenology than Paul Tillich's theological enterprise. This is despite the fact that Tillich is more European than American.

Tillich went to the United States partly at the behest of the brothers Reinhold and Richard Niebuhr. But, Tillich was also considerably motivated by a deteriorating social-political situation in Germany, his native land. He was very much a child of the late modern "crisis of the European mind" that was the final stage of German Romanticism, Idealism, and the monistic philosophies of nature represented in Spinoza, Schelling, and especially Hegel. Giussani is well aware of Tillich's European heritage and does not seek to downplay it. He writes, "The figure of Tillich thus emerges outside the natural lines of the American Protestant theological tradition and, despite the fact that most of his production belongs to his émigré period, it ultimately is that of a European thinker" (124). But this does not disqualify Tillich as a fully participating member of the American Protestant scene. Rather, there is a good degree of correspondence between the two: "No other Spiritual position or intellectual discourse could better enter into a suitably intense dialogue with Liberal American theology in its Realist or Neo-orthodox conversions than that of Paul Tillich" (124).

But, American Protestant thinkers were not content merely to emulate this "Neo-orthodoxy." Rather, they sought to appropriate its most biblical aspects into their "empirical temperament," which had been the heritage of American religion since the New England theology, especially that of Edwards. The term that Tillich uses to typify this temperament is "correlation." It is pragmatic and psychological in tendency and, therefore, less dogmatic and/or systematic. Unlike true dialectical thought, this American version does not draw an absolute line between nature and grace, but sees both as inimical to revelation, as a dialectical unity rather than an absolute paradox: "Tillich's position is in agreement with this type of dialectical unity, and it is that demand for pragmatic verification that his 'experiential method' would value" (125). This makes Tillich more than just a dialogue partner with European tendencies. Rather, "Tillich is a master within the world of American Protestant thought and is accepted as tremendously suited to the urgencies and accents proper to that world" (125). This constitutes a considerably precise insight on Giussani's part, because it is a point that often escapes many of the Protestant admirers of Tillich's thought in the United States at that time.

As he moves on in his exposition of this emphasis in Tillich, Guissani is able to adduce much evidence that he himself is no mere third-party commentator on Protestant theology in America. This is particularly the case with Tillich's method of correlation, a method that is most natural to the American Protestant spirit because it "makes an analysis of the human situation out of which the existential questions arise" (127).[57] This amounts to the same "empirical" religious intuition that has been an enduring aspect of American Protestant theology, expressed well in Tillich's dictum that "religion is the substance of culture and culture is the form of religion" (132).[58] In this respect, Giussani sees Tillich as the quintessential American Protestant, despite his European upbringing, education, and indeed, final orientation.

SUMMARY

The language of American Protestant theology, in its more dialectical-existentialist mode, appears everywhere in the pages of Luigi Giussani's later works. Terms such as "ultimate concern," "need," "reasonableness," and "encounter" are transformed by Giussani to suit their emphasis in a more Roman Catholic context. The degree to which there is an influence from this tradition of American Protestant theology on Giussani's thought can hardly be said to have been well established in this introduction. However, there can be no doubt that Giussani wanted to adapt a more personal expression of faith to his own Catholic context, clearly correcting what he sees to be its excesses, but at the same time, availing himself of its ability to call people of faith to a more substantial awareness of our religious reality. Surely, Guissani's desire to reinvigorate the faith of his own tradition, especially among youth, was a motivating factor in his decision to investigate the religious phenomenology of American Protestant theology. Much more could be said on behalf of this intuition were we to fully exposit the other aspects, personalities, and movements that Giussani includes, but that would be obviating the book itself. Thus, enough has been said to introduce the reader to Giussani and his thinking on this. Now on to *American Protestant Theology: A Historical Sketch*.

Archibald J. Spencer, ThD
Associated Canadian Theological Schools
Northwest Baptist Theological Seminary at Trinity Western
University, Langley, British Columbia

Preface to the First Edition

American Protestant theology has not received much attention among Italian scholars. Only very recently do Niebuhr and Tillich appear to represent that appeal guaranteed by a profound and constructive originality, a contribution that addresses the anxiety about perceived problems: we currently see, for example, the favour that the themes of the "death of God" and "secularization" and their principal literary expressions enjoy.

The lack of attention to this theology shows up particularly at the level of a general overview. But, if an overview that is the fruit of a broad development of research is offered, it will, in turn, become the springboard for greater interest and the spur for new research.

After several years of involuntary delay, a desire awakened by research into the overall spiritual and cultural context in which to situate Niebuhr's theological discourse – research determined by the first edition of his *Faith and History* (1949) – developed into a study program aimed at situating *the most serious and culturally significant theological expression* of the adventurous spiritual life of American Protestantism within a historical outline. The usual meaning of "theological" here – especially for the nineteenth and twentieth centuries – must, necessarily, be broadened based on its etymological meaning, and must integrate the whole wide reflection centred on the contents offered by Christian tradition and on the words, formulae, and religious values signified by that tradition. Seminaries, schools, and theological faculties represent the characteristic sphere of this work in the nineteenth and twentieth centuries.

It is impossible to draw a sharp line between theological discourse and religious philosophy; therefore, some authors, who could be more strictly considered philosophers, are included in the development of the description, because they are expressions of a religiously imbued sphere that directly influenced the life of a church and the consciousness of the clergy. This is the case, for example, with certain exponents of the Transcendentalism and the Personalism of Boston.

We have provided an analytical emphasis, and more space has been dedicated to the literature of the New Theology and of the Social Gospel, which bridge the nineteenth and twentieth centuries, out of the conviction that this literature will show the roots of much of the theme and underlying methodology that guide the approach, as inspiration and as program, of certain very new currents which, at present, are agitating the American theological climate. Our broad attention to Niebuhr's discourse and to Tillich's work is motivated by the decisive influence that the former's ethical development and the latter's Weltanschauung have had on the whole scene of American religious thought.

Awareness of the limits of this initial approximation is mitigated by the expressly informational character of this work, even if elements of a judgment and discursive factors cannot avoid presupposing this description, and discretely defining it.

These limitations notwithstanding, I hope that this attempt of mine to offer something of initial usefulness to those interested in the American spiritual milieu will not be in vain.

Luigi Giussani
Milan, 30 May 1968

AMERICAN PROTESTANT THEOLOGY

1

Puritan Origins

1 RELIGIOUS INSPIRATION

The important role the religious factor played in the formation and character of the colonies that would later make up the United States of America is well known. The first societies to colonize the new land took care to make it known that the spread of religion was one of their goals, indeed, their "maine and cheefe purpose,"[1] asserted a leaflet published in 1615 by the council of the first English colonial enterprise in America, the Virginia Company.

The strongest reason for the influence exerted by the religious factor in the Protestant colonies of seventeenth-century America is found in the fact that many of them declared themselves to be havens for those persecuted for their faith. Naturally, these emigrants carried with them the beliefs of the European religious groups to which they belonged. Thus, already in the seventeenth century, we find Anglicans, Calvinists, Lutherans, and "sectarians" of various orientations, especially Baptists. Anglicanism had been bound, as the "Established Church," to that Crown whose religious despotism many had fled, or whose political dominion the new colonies would later have to struggle against in the War of Independence. It was, therefore, a minority denomination, even though it was officially established in the two "royal" colonies of Virginia and Maryland. Lutheranism was also a minority, and its influence was nullified by the isolationism of the religious and civil life of the German and Swedish immigrants, an isolationism also fomented by their strict attachment to their native languages.

The type of Protestantism that, among all the rest, would determine American culture was Calvinism. It is emblematic that in the first representative assembly of the English colonies in America, held in Jamestown, Virginia, on 30 July 1620, of the thirty-four laws passed, twelve had to do with religious life, and they were of a markedly Puritan inspiration. From Calvinist Puritanism derives "the moralism or the legalism of American piety at its origins, the rigorous regulation of life by means of ordinances which gave it more an Old Testament than a Christian character."[2]

Federal Theology

The emigrants to New England (Plymouth, Massachusetts; New Haven, Connecticut) brought with them – one may recall the famous Pilgrim Fathers who came ashore at Cape Cod from the *Mayflower* in 1620 – a particular conception of church and a particular concrete experience, radically nonconformist, if not necessarily separatist from the Church of England:[3] namely, Congregationalist or Independent.

This ecclesiology was originally seen in the writings of Henry Jacob (1563–1624), an Anglican minister from Kent, especially in his *The Divine Beginning and Institution of Christ's True Visible or Ministerial Church* (1610). Jacob held that the Church is formally present wherever there is a group of "devout and holy Christians *consociated together* to serve God ... in conformity with his word."[4] It is directly to such a union, created by free "convention" or "covenant," that God grants his power and Christ his guidance. No ecclesiastical organization can claim hierarchical rights over it.

A similar conception – which had its first live experiment in Southwark in 1616 – is connected to a theology followed by the Puritans of east central England, whence came the emigrants to Massachusetts, and which represented a mitigated form of Calvinism ("the Puritan Middle-Way") known as "Federal (or Covenant) Theology." The conception of God who, in an absolute way outside of time, predestines some to glory and others to damnation, with no consideration for human action, was substituted by the idea of a dual "covenant." In the former, man was seen as having been able to reach eternal life through works of obedience; once Adam broke this covenant, God was seen as having granted a second kind of covenant, in which he would save man with his pure grace, by means of faith.

The most widely read authors of New England in the seventeenth century belonged to this theological current, authors such as William Perkins (1558–1602) and John Preston (1587–1628). One of the most widespread texts of systematic theology was the *Medulla Theologiae* of the Scotsman William Ames (1576–1633), who published it in 1623 in Holland, where he had taken refuge, and where, from 1626 to 1632, he was rector of the University of Franeker. In 1643, ten years after his death, the work was translated into English with the title *The Marrow of Sacred Divinity*.

It was the idea of the "covenant" that clearly had decisive influence on Congregationalist ecclesiology.

In disfavour or persecuted because of their non-alignment with the official religious doctrines of the state, many of the Independents migrated to America before or around the middle of the seventeenth century, thus, transplanting their conception of church onto American soil. In New England, "a church was constituted by a group of Christians uniting into a voluntary agreement, known as a convenant [sic] … The early covenants were simply promises to worship together, following the divine commandments and promising faithfulness to each other, and were largely free of doctrinal statements. The absence of doctrinal matter in the covenants was largely due to the creedal uniformity prevailing, rather than to any lack of concern in the matter of doctrine."[5]

2 THE INTELLECTUAL LIFE AND THE BEST-KNOWN LITERATURE

A fervid intellectual life characterized these groups; many emigrants were academics and men of learning: "They did not travel to the New World in the hope of improving their situation or enhancing their wealth. They tore themselves away from the pleasures of home in obedience to a purely intellectual need. They braved the inevitable miseries of exile because they wished to ensure the victory of *an idea*."[6] From the flourishing Puritan colonies of New England, there flowed a truly active contribution of thought, and the course of American theology had begun.

This intellectual activity is documented in the many works written in the young colonies by strong and capable personalities. Among these works are those of Thomas Shepard (1605–1649): *The Sincere Convert* (1640) and *A Defence of the Answer* (1648); of Peter Bulkeley (1641–1688): *The Gospel-Covenant* (1646); of Thomas Cobbet: *A Just Vindication of the Covenant* (1648); of Thomas Hooker (1586–1647):[7] *The Soule's Preparation for Christ* (1632), *The Unbelievers Preparing for Christ* (1638), *The Faithful Covenanter* (1644), and

The Application of Redemption (1657), "his most lasting prose,"[8] a posthumous publication of his last sermons; and of John Norton (1606–1663): *The Orthodox Evangelist* (1657).

The theologian who dominated the first Puritan period in New England, however, was John Cotton (1584–1652). After a complete academic curriculum at Cambridge University, he had been a very well known preacher in the Church of Saint Rodolph in Boston, Lincolnshire, until his flight to America in 1633, in order to avoid the heavy hand of Bishop Laud, a persecutor of nonconformists. In the "second Boston," he would become the key personality of religious and cultural life, the perfect interpreter of Calvinist Puritanism. One historian sums up the image of his presence in that new world in this way: "He wielded with strong and brilliant mastership the fierce theocracy of New England. Laymen and clergymen alike recognized his supremacy and rejoiced in it. He was the unmitred pope of a pope-hating commonwealth."[9]

Larzer Ziff's critical biography lists thirty titles of his works and leaflets, some of which were published posthumously as editions of his courses of preaching or teaching. Among these works, the most significant from the theological point of view are the following: *A Treatise I. of Faith, II. Twelve Fundamental Articles of Christian Religion, III. A Doctrinal Conclusion, IV. Questions and Answers upon Church-government* (1713 edition of his teachings dated between 1634 and 1635); *The Keyes of the Kingdom of Heaven and the Power Thereof, according to the Word of God, Tending to Reconcile some Present Differences about Discipline* (1644);[10] *A Treatise of the Covenant of Grace as it is Dispensed to the Elect Seed, effectually unto Salvation, being the Substance of Divers Sermons Preached upon Acts 7.8* (a 1659 edition of two other preceding redactions of sermons dating back to 1636); *The Covenant of God's Free Grace* (1645); and above all, *The Way of the Congregational Churches Cleared* (1648).

The content of all this speculation had been suggested by the profound awareness of a particular vocation within the situation in which the authors and their companions found themselves: God had directly inspired their migration so that the new land could be the land of the people of God, the land of the covenant between people and God, as had happened to the "Israel of old." All events drew their meaning from this hypothesis, and for the individual or for the community, they were rigidly taken as signs of approval or of condemnation, of verification of divine election and of human fidelity.[11]

This leads to an understanding of the two characteristics that qualify Puritan theology at its origins: the stature of the ecclesiological problem in relation to social life as a whole and the pragmatic attitude.

3 CONGREGATIONALIST ECCLESIOLOGY

Congregationalist ecclesiology was robustly present in New England in all its consequences.

The ecclesiological conception of the first generation found its most mature expression in a document that would govern the life of the of Massachusetts congregations for a century and a half. A synod of ministers and laymen representing the churches entrusted to John Cotton of Boston, Richard Mather of Dorchester, and Ralph Partridge of Duxbury the preparation of a "model of government for the church." In the 1648 session at Cambridge, on the basis of a proposal of Richard Mather, and taking as a doctrinal position the federal theology of the 1646 Westminster Confession of Faith, what would be called the "Cambridge Platform" was compiled in seventeen chapters.

The "church" is a community of "elected," that is, of members in whom the Spirit has manifested himself by means of the capacity for "prophesying," a particular gift for testifying. These elect form themselves into a group – or "congregation" – by means of a free convention. About the "form" of the Church, the Platform asserts that it consists in a "visible covenant, agreement; or consent, whereby [the elect] give themselves unto the Lord, to the observing of the ordinances of Christ together in the same society, which is usually called the 'church covenant,' for we see not otherwise how members can have church power over one another mutually."[12]

The power of Christ the head belongs "to all together the body of each church, and not to one member apart or to several members separated from the whole or to another congregation which acts for them."[13] In a complete sense, each congregation, thus, realizes the idea of church in a totally self-sufficient way: "Although churches be distinct, and therefore may not be confounded one with another, and equal, and therefore have not dominion one over another; yet all the churches ought to preserve church communion one with another, because they are all united unto Christ, not only as a mystical, but as a political head." Thus, the synods between the churches, "though not absolutely necessary to the being, yet many times, through the iniquity of men and perverseness of times, [are recognized as] necessary to the well-being of churches."[14]

The members of the community "are a church before they have officers, and without them," because a "church being a company of people combined together by covenant for the worship of God, it appears thereby that there may be the essence and being of a church without any officers."[15] The members elect the presbyters (elders) and the other officials of the congregation: but once they have received it, the "elders" have a power which, having come from God by means of that method, is no longer simply at the mercy of the electors. In his *The Keyes of the Kingdom of Heaven* (1644), John Cotton defines the makeup of a congregation and affirms this sort of hierarchy to be the realization of the symbol of the two keys given to Peter: one, the key of faith, is common to all believers; the other, that of power for the ordering and guidance of the community, is given to the elders alone. Cotton recalls a popular comparison: "A Queene ... may call her servants, her mariners, to pilot and conduct her over the sea to such an Haven: yet they being called by her to such an office, shee must not rule them in steering their course, but must submit herselfe to be ruled by them, till they have brought her to her desired Haven. So is the case between the Church and her Elders."[16]

Samuel Stone (1602–1663) of Hartford, a disciple and colleague of Thomas Hooker, vividly defined the manner of common life within the Congregationalist group or community as "a speaking *Aristocracy* in the face of a silent *Democracy*."[17]

The Theocratic Ideal

Joined to this ecclesiology was a strictly theocratic ideal of the *res publica*, in which only the members of the church were citizens in full right, "freemen" and therefore, electors, "voters":[18] thus, in society there could be freedom only for the just, and the sinner had to be subject to the saint, with "the ministers serving as a court of last resort to interpret the divine law to the subject-citizens of Jehovah."[19] Cotton, however, insisted on the fact that exclusion from the church did not necessarily imply being ostracized from public life, from "civill Commerce," because men "may discover such hypocrisie as may make them unfit for the Church, but yet they may not altogether be unfit for the Common-wealth."[20]

The magistrates had been put at the head of the people of God by means of the votes of the electors, and they were, thus, removable only for grave moral reasons. Cotton wrote, in 1636, "I do not conceyve, that ever God did ordeyne democracy as a fitt government eyther for church or commonwealth. If the people be governors, who shall be governed?"[21]

Church and state were conceived of as two organizations of the same genus, having the same author, God, with man the common subject and the glory of God the common purpose, but of different species, one regarding the inner life of man and the other the outer. Church and state are, thus, two separate and concomitant institutions: "As it is unlawful for church officers to meddle with the sword of the magistrate, so it is unlawful for the magistrate to meddle with the work proper to church officers."[22]

In those things that had to do with "the civill peace," however, the church was required to be subject to the "power of the sword." Now, regarding this civil peace, in Cotton's view, one must keep in mind that to the civil authority belongs the "establishment of pure Religion, in doctrine, worship, and government, according to the word of God, as also the reformation of all corruptions in any of these."[23] The Cambridge Platform stated as a principle in this sense that "it is the duty of the magistrate to take care of matters of religion, and to improve his civil authority for the observing of the duties commanded in the first, as well as for observing of the duties commanded in the second table." In particular, it specified, "If any church, one or more, shall grow schismatical, rending itself from the communion of other churches, or shall walk incorrigibly and obstinately in any corrupt way of their own, contrary to the rule of the Word; in such a case, the magistrate is to put forth his coercive power, as the matter shall require."[24] The derivation from God of such public power made it clear that any eventual exercise of this power over the church would have to be accepted with "patient suffering … without hostile or rebellious resistance."[25]

Congregationalism and the Establishment of American Democracy

Directly out of Congregationalist ecclesiology another kind of discourse developed, one that would have an extreme importance in American history. Indeed, the democracy inherent to the original structure of Congregationalism was defended in the books of John Wise (1652–1725): *The Churches Quarrel Espoused* (1710) and *A Vindication of the Governement of New England Churches* (1717). It was to be these books, republished fifty years later, that would give

Americans the ideological motivation for their struggle for independence: the people as the original holder of the power of God, God-given freedom as the primordial right of every man, and the communitarian structure foreseen by Christ solely in democratic terms and, therefore, the nature of government as essentially popular.

John Wise had systematized ideas that were deeply precious to the Congregationalist world. Every Congregationalist minister, once appointed, gave his "election sermon." For a century and a half, these sermons addressed nothing but arguments on the sovereignty of God by means of the laws of nature, on the freedom and equality native to men, and on the divine value of civil power; thus, a mentality was prepared and supported that would find its vindication in the War of Independence (1775–83).

4 PRAGMATIC ATTITUDE

To stress the pragmatic attitude of the New England theologians means identifying a methodology that will remain a permanent characteristic of American religious thought. Committed to confronting the concrete tasks of colonization, all of those makers of a new history sought their inspiration and ideological framework in the Puritan theological literature that preceded them, and they became its passionate interpreters in the new setting. And, in that setting, full of concrete needs, they found harmonious guidelines and mentality in that literature: "Ames's *Medulla* candidly affirmed theology as a practical discipline, not speculative ... John Preston maintained that the aim of theology is action, and in his sermons he apologized if he held too long 'on the doctrinal side.' Thomas Hooker did not intend to hold forth on metaphysical speculation: 'While we are speaking and disputing about what we ought to do,' he said, 'we neglect too long to do what we ought, and we become incapable of doing what we intend.'"[26]

The "primacy of direct experience," as Mauro Calamandrei calls it,[27] is demonstrated in a double connotation.

It is seen first, especially in Cotton, in the intense affirmation of the Spirit as the inspirational origin and the criterion of reference for the true believer. For the "born again," all questions find a ready response in inner movement. The witness that this movement gives has more value than concepts from texts and formulae. The behaviour of the believer, more than by the words of Scripture or by church rules, is determined by the dictates of the Spirit, by inner revelation: "Let not men be afraid, and say, That we have no *revelation* but the *word*: for I do believe, and dare confidently affirme, that if there were no revelation but the word, there would be no spiritual grace revealed to the soul; for it is more then the Letter of the Word that is required to it: not that I look for any other matter besides the *word*. But there is need of greater light, than the *word* of itself is able to give."[28]

The second connotation of the prevalence of experience over speculation and theory is found in the value given to practical efficiency as a criterion, that is, by the need for validation based on experiential results. If a man is chosen by God and justified, his life cannot be in contradiction to this; he will inevitably do good. Thus, good works are the "sign" of his election and of his rebirth, produced by God. Thomas Hooker wrote, "Each one must, and, if he is touched by grace, can give that appropriate and special evidence, those unfailing and inevitable fruits of his working which will undoubtedly reveal to others, and assure his own conscience, that the blow [of grace] has surely struck [upon him]."[29] A first "sign" is given by the experience of a new frame of mind: "Thus the saints have a lived awareness of the work of grace: in virtue of it, they recognize this [work] with the same certainty as from touching a flame they recognize that fire burns, or from tasting honey they recognize that it is sweet"; "as a woman carrying a child in her womb feels such nausea or disturbances that from this she knows that she is with child."[30]

The conception of "signs" of election played a decisive role – as already mentioned – for the very formation of the church community, in that a particular inspired testimony or "confession," which made rebirth "visible," was required for becoming a member of the church. In fact, adherence to formulae was not sufficient: "The difference will ever hold between the word read, and preached."[31]

Challenges to apologetic positions were settled by "signs." In defence of the institutions and of the methods practised in New England, John Davenport (1597–1670), responding to nine questions submitted by a minister of Somersetshire, and Richard Mather (1596–1669), responding to a questionnaire of thirty-two propositions,[32] did not turn to scriptural citations to develop their explanation, but rather to an indication of effects, of verifiable demonstrations of goodness.

5 ALTERNATIVES TO RELIGIOUS PURITANISM

Rigid Puritanism, even at its beginnings, was not without alternative aspects.

John Cotton was the unwavering advocate of the absoluteness of God's initiative over the elect: "Not Obedience first, nor Faith first, nor any thing else first, but [the Spirit] himselfe is *Donum primum & primarium*, and in him, all his goodnesse."[33] The intransigent position of Cotton on the absolute initiative of grace in justification, to the complete exclusion of any intervention of human works, was especially defined in a debate at the end of 1636, and was shared by only one other minister, John Wheelwright (1594–1679), while his other colleagues were, as formulated in the thirteenth question of the debate, for "evidencing Iustification by Sanctification." Cotton maintained, "Justifying faith cannot safely build or rest upon any ground, save onely upon Christ and Righteousnesse."[34] Cotton's radical stance in affirming the independence of God's initiative from man's work – therefore, the defence of a pure "covenant of faith" in which divine gratuitousness acts without any conditions in its choices and elections – thus, came into conflict with implications that led to the conception of a "covenant of works," in which divine gratuitousness was bound to a human response or human behaviour. Such a bond was conceived of as the conditional link between divine action and man's attitude: if man offers his faith and his works to God, God will then offer the signs of his election and regeneration to man. The English puritan Richard Sibbes (1577–1635) stated, "Though God's grace do all, yet we must give our consent."[35] In addition, Peter Bulkeley specified authoritatively, "God hath so linked together the blessing of the Covenant (which is his to give) with the duty and way of it (which is ours to walk in) that we cannot with comfort expect the one; but it will work in us a carefull endeavour of the other."[36]

Thus, the ideal of an orderly theocratic "respublica" was established, in one sense, by Antinomism – the movement founded in 1638 by Anne Hutchinson (1590–1643), promoter of the "inner light," as the sole vehicle of the divine will, totally free from any rule whatsoever – and, in another sense, by Roger Williams (1603–1683), exponent of freedom of religion, and, together with his followers who had fled Massachusetts, founder in 1635 of a new colony, Rhode Island, based upon that principle.[37]

6 THE SECOND PURITAN GENERATION: EVOLUTION OF AN ORIGINAL CONCEPTION

Cotton Mather observed, with melancholy, that the "prosperous and prevailing condition might be res unius aetatis."[38]

The period following the intense beginnings soon saw a relaxation of ecclesiological intransigence. The synod held in Boston in 1662 voted in favour of the validity of infant baptism administered by any baptized person and not only, as was previously held, that of those who had given testimony of a particular experience of grace or "regeneration" and who were, therefore, full-fledged members of the congregation. This position was called the "Half-Way Covenant" and, despite the struggle in the press that later ensued, it prevailed.

Harvard College

From a cultural standpoint, the second generation could not have the same pedigree as the first, educated at Oxford and Cambridge (it is estimated that 130 university professors emigrated to New England by 1645). Instead, the latter were formed in the school of the colonies.

The Founding Fathers, indeed, immediately set about to secure a method for cultural education. Wertenbaker cites the following report: "After God had carried us safe to New England, and we had builded our houses, provided necessaries for our livelihood, reared convenient places for God's worship and settled the civil government; one of the next things we longed for and looked after was to advance learning, and perpetuate it to posterity, dreading to leave an illiterate ministry to the Churches when our present ministers shall lie in the dust."[39] And the theologian prince among the Fathers of New England wrote, "*Zeale must be according to knowledge*, knowledge is no knowledge without zeale, and zeale is but a wilde-fire without knowledge."[40]

In 1636, the "General Court of the Massachusetts Bay Colony" – the colony of the Pilgrim Fathers – voted for the foundation of a "College," which opened its doors in 1640 and was baptized with the name of John Harvard (1607–1638). Harvard, a graduate of Cambridge, died of tuberculosis at a young age after one short year as minister at Charleston, whence he had emigrated, and had bequeathed half of his estate along with his library to the proposed school.

The seriousness of intention and planning did not forestall periods of hardship, so much so that the "Reforming Synod" of 1679 noted, "When *New-England* was poor, and we were but few in Number comparatively, there was a Spirit to encourage Learning, and the College was full of Students ... but it is deeply to be lamented, that now, when we are become many, and more able than at our beginnings, that Society and other inferior Schools are in such a low and languishing State."[41]

Be that as it may, at the end of the seventeenth century, most of the ministers of Massachusetts and Connecticut were graduates of Harvard College.

The Most Influential Authors

At the Boston Synod, there emerged the brilliant oratory of one minister, Jonathan Mitchell (1624–1668), who died not long afterwards, and who is remembered in the pamphlets *A Defense of the Answer and Arguments of the Synod* (1664) and *Nehemiah on the Wall in Troublesome Times* (1667).

The most widely known characters of the new period are two figures who, while sharing the Half-Way Covenant, for the most part, played a conservative role: they are Increase Mather (1639–1723) and Cotton Mather (1663–1728), father and son, respectively. With the latter, "although belonging to the third generation, his labors fell almost entirely within the life-span of the second-generation leaders."[42] Among the works of Increase Mather, the following bear mentioning: *The Doctrine of Divine Providence* (1684), *An Essay for the Recording of Illustrious Providences* (1684), and *The Order of the Gospel* (1700). Cotton Mather's abundant production included, along with the "imposing" *Magnalia Christi Americana* (1702), which "defends the virtuousness of New England and condemns New England's depravity ... a summation and synthesis of the New England apocalypse,"[43] three works that, according to Perry Miller, justify "his place in American literature":[44] *Bonifacius: An Essay upon the Good that is to be Devised* (1710), *The Christian Philosopher* (1721), and *Manuductio ad ministerium* (1726).

A vast systematizing of the dominant theological currents of the previous era was published by two Harvard doctors in 1726. It was compiled based on the lectures of the vice president of the college, Samuel Willard (1640–1707), and given the title *A Complete Body of Divinity*.

The liberalizing movement, in lively contrast to the Mathers, centred around the pastor of the Church of Northampton, Solomon Stoddard (1643–1729). An energetic writer, in his work *The Doctrine of Instituted Churches Explained, and Proved from the Word of God* (1700), Stoddard defended a more open ecclesiology, according to which, after the issue of baptism, that of the Lord's Supper needed to be reviewed, in the sense that all should have access to this supreme act of the Christian community, without distinction between those who "make a serious profession of the true Religion, together with those that do descend from them, till rejected of God."[45] This was the definition that Stoddard gave of "visible saints," that is, of "non-scandalous" Christians: thus, all "visible saints" could have access to the Lord's Supper. The original tradition held that the Holy Meal was reserved, as culmination of the Christian life, to "full Covenanters," that is, those who had been numbered among the full-fledged members of the church by means of the determined witness of the Spirit. Instead, according to Stoddard, even young children should be allowed access to Communion, as soon as they were able to "discern the Lord's Body." It was absurd, he insisted, that persons with the seed of grace at birth should reach the age of forty or fifty "and yet not [be] capable of coming to the Lord's Supper, for want of the Exercise of Faith [that is, of the required testimony of particular experience]; they are not to be denied because of the weakness of Grace, they that have the least Grace need to have it Nourished and Cherished."[46]

Stoddard was also a powerful preacher, and his pastoral and evangelizing activities are referenced in his other writings, primarily *The Safety of Appearing at the Day of Judgment in the Righteousness of Christ* (1687), a basic text for the clergy for more than a half century, and later, *Guide to Christ* (1714) and *A Treatise Concerning Conversion* (1719).

The Saybrook Platform

Within this ecclesiological conception, the basis for a radical challenge to the free Congregationalist mindset of the ecclesiastical government was introduced by the synod originally called by the directors of Yale College and which met in 1708 at Saybrook, with the aim of injecting new life into the state of religion.

The Saybrook Platform, adopted by the Puritan churches of Connecticut in its first edition of 1710 at New London, is the first book to be printed in Connecticut. It contains three documents: the first adopts the Calvinist "Savoy Confession of Faith," formulated by the English Congregationalists in 1658; the second recovers the Congregationalist-tending "Heads of Agreement" of 1691, voted on in London; the third, instead, expresses the fifteen innovative "Articles." It [the Saybrook Platform] states that "the Churches, which are Neighbouring each to other, shall Consociate," with ultimate power of judgment and of discipline, exercised with the criterion of the majority of participants present: the pastor and church that do not accept the definitions "after due patience used ... shall be reputed guilty of Scandalous Contempt & dealt with as the Rule of God's Word in such case doth provide, and the Sentence of Non-Communion shall be declared against such Pastor and Church."[47]

With the autonomy of the individual church, the idea of the community of the "Covenanters" as the authentic place of the Spirit and sole and ultimate sphere of his suggestion was, thus, compromised.

2

New England Theology

I A NEW PROBLEMATIC

At the end of the seventeenth century and the beginning of the eighteenth, grave concerns burdened the genuine Puritans. Reduced religious fervour and interest caused a decline in the frequency of the "tests" that proved the "conversion" conferring the right to full membership in the community of the faithful. Thus, the idea was increasingly asserted that the Holy Spirit could become present and act not only in a direct way, but also through certain *means* available to human initiative, such as Scripture reading, prayer formulae, attendance at divine services, and the exact observance of the law.

1 Arminianism

Nevertheless, on the level of doctrine, Calvinist purity was attacked, above all, through the spread of Arminian ideas. This type of theological thought, which derives its name from Jacobus Arminius (1560–1609), professor at the University of Leiden in Holland, arose in reaction to Calvinist rigidity regarding the relationship of grace to freedom. Salvation cannot be set by God through a choice that redeems some and condemns others without taking into account human freedom: "[God] cannot will to do … that which He cannot do of right. For His will is restricted by justice," Arminius wrote. In an analogous way, divine grace is not irresistible even to the elect, but conditioned on human willingness and initiative: only those who "are ready for the conflict, and desire His (Christ's) help,"[1] are to be saved by merciful divine operation.

The Arminian doctrine was adopted by the Anglicans in the eighteenth century as more correspondent than pure Calvinism to the "sweet reasonableness" that their great theologian Richard Hooker (1554–1600) had recommended.

In the America of the first half of the eighteenth century, the Arminian position found vigorous support in the eminent Anglican pastor, philosopher, and friend of Berkeley, Samuel Johnson (1696–1772), who in 1746 edited *A New System of Morality*,[2] in which the capacity of human freedom in the face of its destiny is energetically recognized. Samuel Johnson constitutes the initial sign, as it were, of the passage from the dominance of Puritan thought to the intervention of Enlightenment Rationalism, which would wind up supplanting the former in guiding American culture.

2 *Man's Works in the Covenant of God*

But, liberation from the harsh Calvinistic concept of freedom's relation to divine action and salvation soon found fertile ground beyond Anglicans in America: "In 1726 Cotton Mather boasted that there was not a single Arminian in New England; by 1734 the Matherian party were to endorse a jeremiad of John White's that called Arminianism the great sin of the land."[3]

In reality, as previously noted, this danger crept in through the same conditionality of the Covenant between God and man that the "federal" theologians of New England understood as a truly binding contract between two parties, as Sibbes defines the "Covenant of Grace": "It has pleased the great God to enter into a treaty and covenant of agreement with us his poor creatures, the articles of which agreement are here comprised. God, for his part, undertakes to convey all that concerns our happiness, upon our receiving of them by believing in him."[4] Or, even more clearly: "In a Covenant, first there must be conditions and Articles of agreement betweene the parties offered and consented unto: and secondly, a binding one another to the performance thereof by Bond ... It is just so here: ... [the Lord] propounds the Law, and saith, That if we keepe the law, he will blesse us abundantly in all things ... Then the people they agree, and say, Content Lord, whatever thou saist, we will doe."[5]

Thus, the religious Revival technique preached by Cotton Mather clearly contains accents of that doctrine that, as a good conservative, he doggedly opposed in theory: "My Brethren, This is the Way. And now, what remains to be endeavoured, is, To use a Sacred Violence upon you."[6]

Unconscious incoherence was completely camouflaged by a terminology packed with subtle distinctions, and the distinctions seemed to assure a position of balance in the face of error, in which, on the one hand, man's freedom in the contractual bond and the absolute nature of divine action, on the other hand, were saved by means of a conception of "works" as "rule of virtue" – as testimony to and not a precondition for faith, which, therefore, remained a gratuitous gift.

Indeed, in praxis and doctrine, the turn of the century saw the rigid Calvinist concept of God's absolute dominion and his unconditional initiative threatened.

II JONATHAN EDWARDS

1 The "Great Awakening" and the Activity of Jonathan Edwards

Jonathan Edwards (1703–1758), perhaps the greatest thinker America ever produced, stands as the defender of the absolute nature of divine sovereignty against all the liberalizing trends that diminished religious engagement favoured.

His figure emerges along with the socio-religious phenomenon known as the "Great Awakening," an extremely emotional revival of religious life that developed its greatest impetus from the preaching of Edwards, but as a movement anticipated and went beyond the sphere of action of his person, and in an almost periodic revival characterizes American religious history.

The beginnings of the Great Awakening are connected to the pietistic impetus of Reformed Europeans through the activities of the Dutch pastor Theodore Jacobus Frelinghuysen (1691–1748), who arrived in New Jersey in 1720. Nevertheless, a noteworthy contribution to its development was made by early Methodism, along with the evangelical zeal of George Whitefield (1714–1770), companion to the Wesley brothers in the foundation of the new English spiritual movement and who arrived in America in 1740 with the first of his seven voyages to the New World. The intense emphasis placed on conversion as the event that seizes the entire person, and on the fervour of a devotion that is confirmed and nourished by expression, while springing from the urgency of renewing a declining religiosity, strives, however, to be motivated in a theological vision and to create its own continuity through an intellectual education. As if to follow the example of the famous and fleeting Log College of Pastor Gilbert Tennent (1703–1764) at the origins of the Great Awakening, many scholastic institutes date their beginnings to the Revivalist era, such as New Jersey's Presbyterian College, Dartmouth College (which sprang from an Indian mission), the Baptist College of Rhode Island (now Brown University), and Queen's College (now Rutgers University) of the Dutch Reformed Church. The historian McLoughlin observes that among the factors common to American Revivalist movements two should be highlighted: "a grave theological reorientation" and "an ecclesiastical conflict associated with this reorientation."[7]

The new orientation of theological discourse will normally assume the experiential fact of conversion as the catalyst of its entire disputation, and as the centre of its systematic solution, by exalting the paradigmatic criterion of direct experience in the pietistic view, or practical results in the more moralistic conceptions, or social efficiency in the more secularized systems, as we shall see in the second half of the nineteenth century. These would all enter into sharp tension with the resistance of the supporters of the established ecclesiastical and theological forms, on the one hand, and with the reaction of the most rationalistic trends, on the other.

This tension burst forth in a clamorous way in Edwards' life, even though the force of his thought doubtless exceeds mere reduction to pragmatic categories, just as his doctrine did not exhaustively originate in the Revival fact, although it was congenial to it. The very makeup of his preaching is quite different from that of the Revival propagandists: he would close himself off for as many as thirteen hours at home studying, the result of which were sermons dense with a cogent logic that he read from "semi-legible manuscripts." Be that as it may, his doctrine, which was both rigid and opposed to the compromises that most had come to accept, particularly in his dogged aversion to the theory and practice of "means" (in which there was a tendency to reduce the religious phenomenon to rational human norms, delivering it from the sovereign and mysterious initiative of God) caused him to renounce his ecclesiastical office in 1750. Since 1727, he had been a Congregationalist minister in Northampton, Massachusetts, where, after two years of collaboration, he succeeded his famous grandfather, Solomon Stoddard. He then retired to an

Indian mission at Stockbridge, and there remained until February 1758, when he was elected president of New Jersey College (Princeton). One month later he died of smallpox.

2 *Literary Production*

The eight years spent among the Indians not only did not diminish but, indeed, increased the quantity of his writing, which had begun at a very young age. From this early period, two insightful compositions stand out from the others: *Of Insects* and *Of Being*, both pervaded by surprising advances; for example, his insistence "on sight, on vision, was to be a way of speculation for a lifetime. It granted him a personal sensitivity to the vividness of immediate experience; and it provided him with a habit of 'seeing' even the most abstruse theological ideas as if they were as clearly apprehended as the sun on its horizon or the leaf turning in the breeze."[8]

His thirty-six works can be divided between those determined by the Great Awakening and those better understood as a systematic rethinking of the great themes of American Calvinism.

"REVIVALISTIC" WORKS Among the former are four works meant to interpret and defend the Revival event as a work of the Spirit of God. The first is an attentive report on the extraordinary religious experience witnessed by the author: *A Faithful Narrative of the Surprising Work of God*, originally a letter sent to a Boston pastor, published in 1737. *The Distinguishing Mark of a Work of the Spirit of God*, published in 1741 and made up of sermons given in New Haven, takes a critical stance in order to evaluate the distinction between authentic and false piety. The third, *Some Thoughts Concerning the Present Revival*, written in 1742, delves deeper into critical observation by distinguishing between "occasional causes" or secondary effects – like "enthusiasm, superstition, or intemperate zeal" – from the "proper" or final cause of spiritual experiences.

The last among these writings, *A Treatise Concerning Religious Affections* (1746), has been defined as "the most profound exploration of the religious psychology in all American literature."[9]

A powerful organic development,[10] it revives the fundamental critical concern: "Therefore, it greatly concerns us to use our utmost endeavors clearly to discern, and have it well settled and established, wherein true religion does consist. Till this be done, it may be expected that great revivings of religion will be but of short continuance: till this be done, there is but little good to be expected, of all our warm debates, in conversation and from the press, not knowing clearly and distinctly, what we ought to contend for."[11] Calvinists distinguished between "common" operations – what we might call "natural" – and "salvific" or "gracious" operations of the Spirit of God, which generated the true religion that the Scriptures speak of. In contrast to his prior writings, in *Religious Affections*, Edwards restricts his analysis to this latter category and identifies the fruits of the Spirit and, therefore, true religion, with the "affections," that is, feelings or emotions that he describes: "True religion, in great part, consists in holy affections."[12] In his analysis of the phenomena that took place in the Revival, he finds fundamental and crucial features that correspond to the "sentiments" of renewed life described by St Paul: joy, contrition of heart, gratitude, compassion, zeal, love for Christ. He premises the first part with the words of 1 Peter 1:8 that speak of the love of Christ that is yet not seen and of joy "unspeakable and full of glory." The proof of true religion is in the emotion that characterizes such feelings. Among the twelve "distinguishing signs of truly gracious and holy affections" – which is the theme of the third part – the first and foremost is that of "a new inward perception or sensation of their minds, entirely different in its nature and kind, from anything that ever their minds were subjects of before they were sanctified."[13] An experience that really overflows with intensity and made up of natural experience is provoked: "the exercises of a principle of new nature, or the sensations of a new spiritual sense."[14]

Edwards' entire activity is based upon the empiricism of Locke, whose essay, *Concerning Human Understanding*, which Edwards read in his second year at Yale (1717), made such a decisive impression on him that he wrote a youthful work titled *The Mind* (or *Notes on the Mind*). This work is also pervaded by the intuitions that will form the outline of his future thought, for example, the profound unity between body and mind in every act, idea, or moral decision – "To live in bodily excitement and vividness is to live in what Edwards called 'essential good,'"[15] the denial of the difference between natural knowledge and "supernatural" knowledge, that is, the denial that there is a solution of continuity between nature and grace.

Edwards had already expressed these ideas fundamental to his conception of Christian life in the sermon published the year prior to the first explosion of the Great Awakening, *A Divine and*

Supernatural Light (1734), where he stated that for man revelation lies in "a true sense of the divine excellency of the things revealed in the word of God, and a conviction of the truth and reality of them thence arising."[16] Edwards specifies that the "new spiritual light"[17] is not a new faculty of knowledge but a new foundation placed in the nature of the soul in order to generate a new exercise of the very same faculty of knowing. That foundation is given by the nature of the divine things in themselves, which takes the place of natural or sensual things in activating the human mind, thereby causing it to express unusual effects such as a new "light" and "taste" in which direct apprehension of the Divine takes place.

The primacy of direct experience reaches its culmination in Edwards. In sense experience, the essential unity of the person as intellect and "heart" is marked out. In it, as the physical location of manifestations, the transcendent and mysterious level of Being in itself is revealed. Insofar as it is provoked by the Spirit, it coincides with the space of conversion or sanctification, and therefore, there is a new representation of things (a new "idea" in the Lockean sense), seen and loved as they are in themselves, therefore, in relationship with God.

THE TREATISE ON LIBERTY Among Edwards' works not directly inspired by the Great Awakening, but which constitute a systematic recovery of important Calvinist themes, the most justifiably famous is *A Careful and Strict Enquiry into the Modern Prevailing Notions of that Freedom of Will, Wich is Supposed to be Essential to Moral Agency, Vertue and Vice, Reward and Punishment, Praise and Blame* – more commonly known as *Freedom of the Will*, or, as Edwards himself used to refer to it, *Enquiry*. Published in Boston in 1754, the work is located among the great classics of Protestantism. The organization and the powerful coherency of its argument are all the more striking the more one thinks of the precarious and fretful conditions and the discontinuity in which Edwards drafted it as a missionary among the Indians: "many a chapter must have been temporarily laid aside while the great theologian paused to catechize the Indian boys or to set them a spelling lesson."[18] It has been calculated that this heavy volume was brought to completion in four and a half months, stating, "So far as I am aware, no similar example, of power and rapidity united, is to be found on the annals of Mental effort."[19]

What matters most to Edwards is reaffirming the absolute sovereignty of God. Moreover, in a reality entirely based on the Newtonian conception of a scientifically registered mechanical order, freedom understood as self-determination would constitute a fact whose origin would not be God and, therefore, an event lacking a cause: "That whatsoever begins to be, which before was not, must have a cause why it then begins to exist, seems to be the first dictate of the common and natural sense which God hath implanted in the minds of all mankind, and the main foundation of all our reasonings about the existence of things, past, present, or to come ... So that it is indeed repugnant to reason, to suppose that an act of the will should come into existence without a cause, as to suppose the human soul, or an angel, or the globe of the earth, or the whole universe, should come into existence without a cause."[20]

The human act of will coincides with the fascination for the good that seems greatest – says Edwards in this rewriting of St Augustine's *delectatio victrix* – "because an appearing most agreeable or pleasing to the mind, and the mind's preferring and choosing, seem hardly to be properly and perfectly distinct."[21] Willing consists in the strongest inclination or motive, and therefore, ultimately coincides with the judgment with which the intellect definitively formulates that motive. Thus was created the ironclad causal structure that, in the final analysis, has God as its sole determining factor wherein the idea of human self-determination threatened to create the absurd void of an exception: "For if the determination of the will, evermore, in this manner, follows the light, conviction and view of the understanding, concerning the greatest good and evil, and this be that alone which moves the will, and it be a contradiction to suppose otherwise; then it is *necessarily* so, the will necessarily follows this light or view of the understanding, not only in some of its acts, but in every act of choosing and refusing. So that the will doesn't determine itself in any one of its own acts; but all its acts, every act of choice and refusal, depends on, and is necessarily connected with some antecedent cause; which cause is not the will itself, nor any act of its own, nor anything pertaining to that faculty, but something belonging to another faculty, whose acts go before the will, in all its acts, and govern and determine them every one."[22] In this context, freedom, as Edwards will recall in a letter to the Reverend John Erskine, is "the power, opportunity, or advantage that anyone has to do as he pleases ... conducting, *in any respect*, according to his pleasure."[23]

Not the capacity to choose, but the obvious practicability of what has been chosen: this is freedom. And the determinism of such a conception, in order to save the morality of human agency, defined the state of necessity of the will as a "moral necessity" distinct from a "natural necessity" not because in the former the concept of determination is confirmed to a lesser degree, but because it is confirmed according to a different modality of factors, thus, recalling the Lutheran distinction between necessities of "compulsion" and of "immutability": "Moral necessity may be absolute, as natural necessity ... But ... they must be distinguished by some names or other; for there is a distinction or difference between them, that is very important in its consequences: which difference does not lie so much in the nature of the connection, as in the two terms connected. The cause with which the effect is connected, is of a particular kind; viz. that which is of a moral nature; either some previous habitual disposition, or some motive exhibited to the understanding. And the effect is also of a particular kind; being likewise of a moral nature; consisting in some inclination or volition of the soul, or voluntary action."[24]

The moral judgment, either of praise or reproach, on such an action springs from the fact that the I with its feeling and value is implicated: it does not develop "properly because [actions] are *from* us, as because we are *in them* ... not so much because they are from some *property* of ours, as because they are our *properties*."[25]

THE "UNCOMPLETED SUMMA" Against his Arminian and Deist adversaries, Edwards had invented a complete rational defence of Christian doctrine from the orthodox Calvinist standpoint: *A Rational Account of the Main Doctrines of the Christian Religion Attempted*, in which he wished to show "how all arts and sciences, the more they are perfected, the more they issue in divinity."[26] Out of that intention, three important treatises remain, making up an "Uncompleted Summa,"[27] as it were.

The first in order of publication is *The Great Christian Doctrine of Original Sin defended; Evidences of its Truth produced, and Arguments to the Contrary answered*, published in 1758, shortly before the author's death, and written the preceding year. It marks the strongest critique of the thesis held by the English "dissenter" John Taylor (1694–1761), in his *The Scripture Doctrine of Original Sin* (1740), which entered America in the midst of the Revival; its thesis was that the doctrine of the imputation of the sin of Adam could be considered neither biblical nor rational. In that treatise, Edwards testifies that *Freedom of the Will* was meant to be the essential preparation for the magnum opus, the undermining of an otherwise "unassailable" fortress, upon which depended all of the theological controversies "concerning Original Sin, the sovereignty of grace, election, redemption, conversion, the efficacious operation of the Holy Spirit, the nature of saving faith, perseverance of the saints, and other principles of like kind."[28]

The second work written in the intense years of Stockbridge – *A Dissertation Concerning the End for Which God Created the World*, probably from 1754–55, and published posthumously in 1765 – contains as the dialectical pole of *Freedom of the Will*, in as much as the argument poses God's absolute self-determination: "there is something in that disposition in God to communicate goodness, which shews him to be independent and self-moved in it, in a manner that is peculiar, and above what is in the beneficence of creatures. Creatures ... are excited by some object that they find ... but God, being all and alone, is absolutely self-moved. The exercises of his communicative disposition are absolutely from within himself, not finding any thing, or any object to excite them or draw them forth; but all that is good and worthy in the object, and the very being of the object, proceeding from the overflowing of his fullness."[29] The same absolute immanence exhausts the idea of the "end" of God's actions: "a disposition in God, as an original property of his nature, to an emanation of his own finite fullness, was when excited him to create the world; and so that the emanation itself was aimed at by him as a last end of creation."[30] This immanence defines God's virtue: "God, being, as it were, an all comprehending Being, all his moral perfections, as his holiness, justice, grace and benevolence are some way or other to be resolved into a supreme and infinite regard to himself; and if so it will be easy to suppose that it becomes him to make himself his supreme and last end in his works."[31] And Edwards' central passion is unleashed in almost liturgical terms: "The beams of glory come from God, and are something of God, and are refunded back again to their original. So that the whole is *of* God, and *in* God, and *to* God, and God is the beginning, middle and end."[32]

The third fragment of the uncompleted *Rational Account* is a systematic treatise on ethics, "the least polemical and most sweetly reasoned of all his writings,"[33] composed in 1755 and published posthumously in 1765 together with the aforementioned work: *The Nature of True Virtue*. Less bulky than the two larger works, it is no less important or significant for Edwards' thought or in terms of potential intrinsic value: "Although not widely read, it has been said to have few peers in the field of ethics."[34]

Faithful to his psychological and phenomenological position, Edwards holds that the virtuous fact bespeaks a radical reference to "something beautiful, or rather some kind of beauty or excellency."[35] Beauty means being in as much as it is "immediately pleasurable": "when a form or quality appears lovely, pleasing and delightful in itself, then it is called beautiful; and this agreeableness or gratefulness of the idea is *beauty*."[36] It is evident that not every meaning of beauty implies a virtuous fact, but the moral event lies where there is a consensus and agreement of merit and praise, therefore, where the "intelligent being" is involved. Clearly, therefore, virtue is "founded in sentiment" and not reason, because "the way we come by the idea of beauty is by immediate sensation of the gratefulness of the idea called beautiful; and not by find out by argumentation any consequences, or other things with which it stands connected."[37] Virtue is thus said to belong the category of "heart" and not of speculation.

The essential question is, therefore: "what that is, which renders any habit, disposition, or exercise of the heart truly beautiful?" or more specifically, "what is the nature of the true virtue?" Edwards premises his answer by distinguishing two inflections of beauty. There is a "particular" beauty, "by which a thing appears beautiful when considered only with regard to its connection with, and tendency to, some particular things within a limited, and as it were, a private sphere." Out of this type of beauty springs the vision of egocentric interest that measures conveniences and establishes proportions, all in search of "means" for the organization of its own ends. Then there is a "general" beauty, "by which a thing appears beautiful when viewed most perfectly, comprehensively and universally, with regard to all its tendencies, and its connections with every thing to which it stands related."[38] The notes of a tune, exemplifies Edwards, can make up a harmony among themselves and, yet, be out of tune with the overall musical discourse: "True virtue most essentially consists in *benevolence to being in general*. Or perhaps, to speak more accurately, it is that consent, propensity and union of heart to being in general, which is immediately exercised in a general good will."[39] Although he uses Platonic terms that were circulating in England during the seventeenth century and borrows categories in vogue from the aesthetic optimism of Shaftesbury and Hutcheson, Edwards nevertheless, pursues a discourse that is irreducibly his. His beauty is not an abstract idea but, rather, an imposing and concrete intuition in the perception of the real. But, above all, the "general" context necessary for considering true virtue none other than the ends of God, "God himself is in effect being in general,"[40] and thus, "it may be asserted in general, that nothing is of the nature of true virtue, in which God is not the first and the last; or which ... have not their first foundation and source in the apprehensions of God's supreme dignity and glory, and in answerable esteem and love of him, and have not respect to God as the supreme end."[41]

Disinterested benevolence, which defines the very virtue of God, "this absolute benevolence," enters the history of American Protestant theology as an ethical accent that strips human action of any possible presumption: that is how it would clearly and systematically resound two centuries later in Niebuhr's ethics. Yet, as Perry Miller notes, "True Virtue is all the greater a study because its composer knew that, but the absolute standard therein declared, he himself was as culpable as any."[42]

REFERENCE TO A THEOLOGY OF HISTORY In a letter, dated 19 October 1757, to the trustees of the College of New Jersey (Princeton) who had invited him to take over the presidency of the college, Edwards wrote, "I have on my mind and heart (which I long ago began, not with any view to publication), a great work, which I will call a *History of the Work of Redemption*, a body of divinity in an entire new method, being thrown into the form of history."[43] The reference to the undertaking regards some sermons of 1739, which were published in Scotland in 1774, with some pages re-edited and lengthened towards the end of Edwards' life. The preoccupation with a theology of history – which in a barely sketched-out tangle testifies to the freedom of the genius, who stresses time and becoming in an era in which Newtonian space and its eternal and immutable laws reigned – is the last, uninterrupted word of the great discourse of Jonathan Edwards.

The motor of the great hostility that surrounded him during his lifetime was not only a reaction to his attack against the use of "means" of sanctification – which he denounced as a human plot to substitute a pure abandonment to God's powerful and merciful design, and therefore, a corruption of true faith and true virtue – rather, it originated in a more radical unease. The Great Awakening of which Edwards was the defender unwittingly constituted a fact that eroded and subverted the dominant Puritan ecclesiology and the consequent Puritan conception of church-state relations in a theocratic union. The exaltation of individual experience downgraded the importance of the Church as institution and the identification of moral religious value with interior emotion and freedom of expression weakened the significance of objective relationships, of authority and government. Even the Puritanism of Cotton relied heavily upon the personal experience that gave witness to the divine election and regeneration that took place; yet, the passion for the objectivity of order and the rational zest for the system integrated the individual event into a context that was established and consecrated, reabsorbing its equivocal centrifugal compulsions.

With the Revivalist Movement, this assumption is diminished, so that the waning of the significance of the institutional Church (Anglican, Congregationalist) marks the progressive affirmation of a religious liberty that favours dissident groups (Presbyterians, Baptists, Methodists: the groups in which Revivalism will take root).

III THE CRITIQUE OF EDWARDS AND THE ONSET OF ANTI-TRINITARIAN THOUGHT

1 *The First Systematic Rationalistic Approaches in Theology*

From a strictly intellectual standpoint, Edwards' conception of freedom found a sharp critic in the works of James Dana of Wallingford (1735–1812), *An Examination of the Late Reverend President Edwards's "Enquiry on Freedom of Will,"* published in Boston in 1770, and *The "Examination of the Late President Edwards's Enquiry on Freedom of Will," Continued*, published in New Haven in 1773, in which two observations stand out. The first notes that, in the analysis of the act of will, Edwards does not take on the crucial problem of the origin or cause by which a certain motive appears prevalent to the will itself. The second recalls the fact that the issue at hand is the person's self-determination, rather than a faculty or property of the person (and therefore Edwards' mechanical determinism is much less sustainable).

CHARLES CHAUNCY AND JONATHAN MAYHEW Yet, the systematic and radical protest against Edwards' entire mental and practical attitude, as well as his Revivalist action, came from Charles

Chauncy (1705–1787), pastor of the First Church (Congregationalist) of Boston, whose grandfather and namesake was one of the most noted presidents of Harvard and an intransigent adversary of compromise. Together with Puritan ideas, the first Enlightenment accents, along with the suggestion of their rationalistic criteria and their naturalistic ethics, found shelter and nourishment in his essays.

The first is a philosophical discourse from 1739, in which he asserts, "As Men are rational, free Agents, they can't be religious but with the free Consent of their Wills; and this can be gain'd in no Way, but that of Reason and Persuasion."[44] In the essay, published in 1741, under the title *The New Creature*, he de-emphasizes, albeit in a cautious way, the value of emotional signs, insisting, rather, on a balanced morality of life. A naturalistic explanation of the phenomena hailed by Edwards is given by *The Late Religious Commotion in New England Considered*, from early 1743.

The most decisive attack came from the voluminous work, also from 1743, *Seasonable Thoughts on the State of Religion in New England*: "The Book is a massive, Johnsonian, indignant work, a source-book for American communal behaviour; learned and dignified, it is monumentally honest. Scholarly to the point of pedantry, and formally Calvinist, it is a classic of hard-headed, dogmatic rationalism."[45] One must be very cautious, says Chauncy, "so far as we are able, to see with our own Eyes, and believe with our own Understanding." And in order to see with his own eyes and to be able to evaluate what he saw in an enlightened way, Chauncy undertook a 300-mile trip, surveying the Revival phenomenon, which he documents: "The Meeting was carried on with what appeared to me great Confusion; some screaming out in Distress and Anguish; some praying; others singing; some again jumping up and down the House, while others were exhorting; some lying along on the Floor, and others walking and talking: The whole with a very great Noise, to be heard at a Mile's Distance, and continued almost the whole Night."[46] Chauncy's conclusion is clear: "The plain Truth is, an enlightened Mind, not raised Affections, ought always to be the Guide of those who call themselves Men."[47]

A "Liberal" revision of the concept of original sin, in the style of John Taylor, can be found in *Twelve Sermons* (1765). In it, he holds that it is not proper to speak of any "imputation" of guilt, but rather that the fall of Adam leaves men "in such a state, as that they will certainly commit sin in violation of the law." The controlled tendency to undermine the intransigent Calvinist affirmation of original sin in a revaluing of human effort was confirmed in the *Sermons*, thanks to their preoccupation with defending the intrinsic value of "good works" even in the unregenerate: placing faith and works in opposition would be "a disservice to religion, and dangerous to the souls of men."[48]

From the doctrinal standpoint, we find his works that most subvert traditional Calvinism at the end of his life: *The Salvation for All Men: The Grand Thing Aimed at in the Scheme of God* (1782), *The Benevolence of the Deity* (1784, although written approximately twenty years prior), and perhaps his most important and influential work in later years, *Five Dissertations on the Fall and its Consequences* (1783). The nucleus of some aspects of the Unitarian Universalist conception of religion are already present, although with prudent expression: in his creative act, God shows his essence as "goodness" and "benevolence"; all of creation is good in that it is an expression of this goodness, man in particular, for whom "original sin" and "hell" are ideas contrary to his very nature.

Chauncy was cautious to not publish *Salvation for all Men*, which was issued posthumously. No such caution was exercised by a good friend of Chauncy, Harvard-educated as he was, Jonathan Mayhew (1720–1766), the pastor of the Boston West Church. In his book, *Sermons*, he openly declares "the monarchy of the universe" in an anti-Trinitarian sense: "The Dominion and Sovereignty of the universe is necessarily *one* and in *one*."[49] And, sharing an Arian position discreetly widespread in England, Mayhew affirms that Christ is not God, but a superhuman being, in that God made him pre-existent to the world with a specific function in creation: it is an error, in Mayhew's view, to invert the biblical expression "son of God" into "God the Son."

Furthermore, in Mayhew, we find the liberal, anti-Calvinistic version of the theme of *The Benevolence of the Deity* energetically expressed, a theme that would remain a classic until the Great War: "What ground is there then to imagine that there is any such kind of justice in God, distinct from, or rather opposite to goodness? Does reason suggest any such thing? No. Do the holy scriptures assert or support it? No: nothing like it. There is, therefore, great reason to think, that this is a distinction only of man's making."[50]

2 *Enlightenment Influence and Puritan Predispositions*

Thus begun, the protest gained consistency in Congregationalist churches as opposition to the basic principles of Calvinism itself, in particular, a "sultanic" conception (as Edwards' position was called) of God's sovereignty and the denial of human freedom and a natural morality. Works of contemporary English theological liberalism had been discreetly disseminated; Edwards' main concern was to debate three authors in particular: Daniel Whitby (1638–1726), Thomas Chubb (1679–1747), and the noted hymnographer Isaac Watts (1674–1748).

Edwards labelled his adversaries as "Arminians," but what had by that time invaded the atmosphere should be identified more generally as an Enlightenment import. The "new science," or "natural philosophy," based on Locke's *Essay* (1690) and Newton's *Principia* (1687) and *Optics* (1704) – which were introduced into Yale in 1714 in a 700-volume collection – had already caused such enthusiasm in Cotton Mather that he suggested that ministry candidates familiarize themselves with Newton, or with William Derham's (1657–1735) *Physico-Theology* (1713): "Be sure, *The Experimental Philosophy* is that, in which alone your Mind can be at all established."[51] This work was smoothing the way for the naturalistic conception that marked *The Religion of Nature Delineated* (1724), by William Wollaston (1659–1724). Thanks to the influence of his works, in Boston, the anti-Calvinist position developed in an ever more naturalistic way and became largely anti-Trinitarian. By the end of the century, all of the Congregationalist ministers in Boston and more than half of those in Massachusetts had become anti-Trinitarian. This spiritual position, so theoretically close to Enlightenment deism, developed a convergence of attention on the ethical factor, in an attitude whose connection to religion was being reduced to a formality.

THE RATIONALISTIC VEIN OF PURITAN EXPERIENCE This outcome of New England Puritanism is not a shock: it isolates and exalts one of the poles of a dualistic tendency that characterized it from the beginning.

On the one hand, Puritanism is determined by a strong perception of the mystery of the Divine, and by its original and absolute transcendence; on the other, it is, as it were, pervaded by a need to rationalize and by a zest for order on a human scale. The hidden God, as such, in his original transcendence, is affirmed in pure faith, conceived of as a grace-filled event uprooted from any human context, "fideistically" understood. Yet, he reveals his perfection to men above all in nature, which is, therefore, his "art" (*techne*); and the order of nature coincides with God's wise working (*eupraxia*) for man. Man possesses an instrument that reads and intellectually reproduces the divine order of things, a means for interpreting natural reality and, therefore, divine communication: logic, understood as the educated and organized method of intuition of the truth in things, according to the Platonizing schema of *Dialecticae libri duo* (1556), by the Frenchman Petrus Ramus (Pierre de la Ramée, 1515–1572), which entered English culture in 1580 through Cambridge and disseminated in New England, above all by Thomas Hooker. "The purpose of Logick is to direct man to see the wisdom of God," in the phrase of Alexander Richardson, the most famous English commentator on Ramus.[52] Logic is, therefore, "art," a reflection in man of the divine *techne* (and "technologia" will become the name of the knowledge developed by this logic); the moral activity illuminated by it is man's *eupraxia*, which corresponds to divine *eupraxia*. The place where the fact of revelation takes place and where the human reply is formed is especially sensitive: it acquires a capital value for spiritual, intellectual, and practical life. Thus, the entire world of faith, if its source is the Bible and theology is its systematic expression, nevertheless, lives the same norms of logic and also is verified in experience: "[Revelation is communicated] in the way of created humane Reason … It is impossible for us to know or understand things, but by some rule of reason or other. Reason is nothing else but the manner of a Being, whereby it is acted upon our Understanding … All things are conveyed to us in a Logical way, and bear some stamp of reason upon them, or else we should know nothing of them. Hence God, to fit his discovery of himself to our manner of entertaining it, takes the Rational or Logical Arguments upon himself."[53]

In the ambiguous tension between a supernatural world fideistically affirmed and an imposing passion for *ratio*, the delicate and profound faith-reason equilibrium found no solid grounding. Indeed, among the "Old Calvinists" of the turn of the century, a "free and catholic spirit" (or liberal spirit) began to insinuate itself more, one by which divine revelation and natural revelation tended to lose their qualitative difference, and an activistic and optimistic humanism expunged every supernatural dimension from ethics. Edwards impassionedly opposed the reductive slide of God's supernatural being and action. It is precisely in the Edwards-Chauncy opposition that the divergent channels that would furrow the soil of American Protestant thought throughout its history were formed: "orthodoxy" against "liberalism" tending towards more radical "secularism."

Yet, it is necessary to note that this reduction was not practised only on the subversive side: the very Edwardsian inheritance in nineteenth-century Revivalist literature would be restrained by a preponderant pietistic anthropocentrism that would take on ever more rationalistic and pragmatic strains, where God's mysterious operation and the experience that verifies it would be constrained within the perimeter of programmed human "means" and within the horizon of their effectiveness in experience.

3 *William Ellery Channing*

The rationalistic and naturalistic ferments encountered fertile soil in the generation of the [American] Revolution. At the dawn of the nineteenth century, one man managed to create a synthesis of the heritage of the second half of the eighteenth century, thereby marking the outlines of what would become the "guiding principles" of the nineteenth century: William Ellery Channing (1780–1842), Congregationalist minister of the Federal Street Church in Boston from 1803 until his death. Pietistic fervour and Revivalist emotion combined in him with a humanitarian moralism that naturalistically reduced the Edwardsian ideal of "disinterested benevolence."

In what was meant to be the preface of an eventual philosophical treatise, entitled *The Principles of Moral Religious and Political Science*, he writes, "The true perfection of man is the great idea of the moral sciences. His nature is therefore to be examined so as to determine its central law, and the end for which all religious and political institutions should be established ... Just views of human nature are, then, all important. In comprehending men ... we have the key to the Divine administration of the world."[54] Enlightenment optimism about human nature gives content to a moral passion that is, therefore, of new inspiration, although it falls within the traditional definition. The essence of virtue, both human and divine, according to Channing, in his famous discourse *Likeness to God*, is benevolence, whose criterion of value is not given so much by having abstract "being in general" as its object as its "social communication." The Spirit of God is given to every man who seeks to do good, and the regeneration of himself that man carries out with the help of the Spirit is contemporary with a "social regeneration": thus Channing supported Abraham Lincoln's work of social reformation, and some of his noted addresses should be remembered in that sense, addresses such as *Slavery* (1835), *The Abolitionist* (1836), and *Duty of the Free States* (1842). Perfection of the individual and social reform or progress are the concomitant possibilities that spring from man's nature. They are real and immediate possibilities, proclaims Channing, with a rhetoric that anticipates the great Social Gospel movement by seventy-five years: "It seems to me that the signs of the times point to a *great approaching modification of society*, which will be founded on and will express the essential truth, that the chief end of the social state is the elevation of all its members as intelligent and moral beings, and under which every man will be expected to contribute to this object according to his ability. The present selfish, dissocial system must give way to Christianity, and I earnestly wish that we may bear our full part in effecting this best of all revolutions."[55]

THE DISCOURSE ON UNITARIAN CHRISTIANITY In the meantime, a true revolution in the heart of Congregrationalist churches carried out its own discourse, entitled "Unitarian Christianity," at Baltimore in 1819 on the occasion of an ordination. It appeared as a manifesto of the entire liberalizing movement. In the first section, the discourse defines the liberal method of scriptural interpretation: "Our leading principle in interpreting Scripture is this – that the Bible is a book written for men, in the language of men, and that its meaning is to be sought in the same manner as that of other books ... We indeed grant that the use of reason in religion is accompanied with danger. But we ask any honest man to look back on the history of the church, and say, whether the renunciation of it be not still more dangerous."[56]

The second part of the discourse registers Christian doctrines from the standpoint of Scripture interpreted in this light. The Trinity is an idea to be repudiated because "whilst acknowledging in words, it subverts in effect, the unity of God." Jesus "is one mind, one soul, one being, as truly one as we are, and equally distinct from the one God. We complain of the doctrine of the trinity, that not satisfied with making God three beings, it makes Jesus Christ two beings, and thus introduces infinite confusion into our conceptions of his character."[57] The new theological systems oppose "purifying, comforting, and honorable views of God ... [and] take from us our Father in heaven, and substitute for him a being, whom we cannot love if we would, and whom we ought not to love if we could." It is, indeed, a dishonour to the Creator to affirm man's total original depravity, or "according to a more modern exposition," the absolute inevitability of evil for man from the very beginning of his agency, and to condemn man and even children out of guilt in similar conditions would be "a wrong unparalleled by the most merciless despotism."[58] Analogously so with the idea that Christ's death took place in order to placate God: "our Father in heaven is originally, essentially and eternally placable, and disposed to forgive." Christ's death cannot substitute us in relation to the Father: "In this way, a sense of the infinite importance and indispensable necessity of personal improvement is weakened, and high sounding praises of Christ's cross seem often to be substituted for obedience to his precepts."[59]

In its final part, the discourse insists, in rationalistic moral terms, on the "nature of Christian virtue, or true holiness," which lies "in the power of forming his temper and life according to conscience … We believe, that no dispositions infused into us without our own moral activity, are of the nature of virtue."[60]

The impassioned affirmation of the commitment to form one's own personality or character as the quintessence of all morality and, therefore, of the value of human life, would be the exhaustive ethical-religious ideal of liberal Christianity for three-quarters of the nineteenth century: "the American creed is optimistic, centered upon Channing's high estimate of human nature."[61]

A serious controversy after Channing's discourse shook the world of New England Congregationalism to the point of a radical division in 1825, when the Unitarians constituted the American Unitarian Association, and 125 churches (the vast majority in Massachusetts) joined. Harvard College found itself completely under the influence of the new current.

IV THE NEW DIVINITY

In the area that remained orthodox, or "Trinitarian," which was most prevalent in Connecticut and the west of Massachusetts, two currents were delineated.

1 The Old Calvinists

The first, which remained faithful to the developments that had become traditional by the beginning of the eighteenth century, especially in valuing the "means" in which God's action could, nevertheless, articulate itself, was known as moderate Calvinists or

Old Calvinists. They tended, according to the line of Puritan history, to "accentuate the element of rationalism, to enlarge the sphere of competence of the natural reason."[62] The Illuminist movement among the clergy found support among the Old Calvinists, and for a certain period of time, the rationalizing tendency and the enthusiasm for "experimental philosophy" of these Old Calvinists and the caution of the illuministic innovators did not allow for an easy demarcation.

Some of those associated with the Old Calvinist movement are Experience Mayhew (1673–1758), whom Chauncy calls "a great theologian," with his *Grace Defended* (1744); Jedidiah Mills (d. 1776); William Hart (d. 1784); Moses Mather (d. 1806); and Moses Hemmenway (d. 1811).

2 *Subsequent Edwardsians*

The second current followed the Edwardsian initiative, by launching the school of thought more strictly known as "New England Theology," which, with modifications, was dominant for almost a century and a half. Its original feature was the emphasis placed on the direct action of God's grace in human activity, and the theology that was developed was often tied to the Revivalist Movement that periodically, as was mentioned above, characterized American Protestant life.

The names of Edwards' immediate disciples and successors within New England Theology constitute a first school known as New Divinity or Consistent Calvinism, and they include a surprisingly rich group of theologians of great worth, most of whom received their formation at Yale College.

The first name to list is that of a personal friend of Edwards and preacher of the Great Awakening, Joseph Bellamy (1719–1790), Congregationalist pastor in Bethlehem, Connecticut. His most noted work is the one that contains four sermons from 1758, entitled *The Wisdom of God in the Permission of Sin*. A new optimism and humanism qualified the basic Calvinist structure of his thought: this world, precisely because God is omnipotent and merciful, is the best of all possible worlds, where the greater glory of God implies also the greatest possible happiness for humanity as such, where the majority are redeemed ("two thirds"), and where the permission of sin assures a situation of wisdom (awareness of human weakness and of the merciful goodness of God) and, therefore, of greater good.

In another of his works, *True Religion Delineated* (1750), Bellamy introduces, for the first time in American theology, Grotius' "governmental" theory, by which the death of Christ was not an expiation required as a tribute to pay to divine justice, but as an "eminent example" of the punishment that the sinner deserves and, therefore, a reminder to the human conscience of the sense of authority of divine law and of the seriousness of the divine government of the world.

In another Edwardsian treatise, we find this theory, which more visibly safeguarded the "benevolence of the divinity" than the idea of the judge to satisfy with a rigid proportion of punishment, capably put to use; it is the book written in opposition to Chauncy's work by Jonathan Edwards, Jr (1745–1801), the second son of Edwards senior, *The Salvation of All Men Strictly Examined* (1790).

SAMUEL HOPKINS Samuel Hopkins (1721–1803) is the leader of the group we are recalling here, whose members were known as "Hopkinsians." A disciple of Edwards, he shared his life and work, (as a pastor in a frontier city, his master was seven miles away, in Stockbridge), and he also inherited his books and manuscripts upon his death. He created an organic exposition of Edwards' teachings in *The System of Doctrines Contained in Divine Revelation Explained and Defended* (1793).

Hopkins' central idea is that of "disinterested benevolence" as the definition of true sanctity, and of sin as self-love, an idea first presented in the book, *Inquiry into the Nature of True Holiness* (1773).

In order to be saved, man must be completely purified of self-love, to the point of being willing to be "damned for the glory of God."[63] Nevertheless, beyond certain accents of rigidity, Hopkins' ethics of benevolence provides a more obvious practicability to the Edwardsian definition. Indeed, for him, "general being," the object of true virtue, is the same as "the totality of beings," acquiring an immediate social connotation, through which regeneration is shown to be love for all beings, in the most existential sense of the word: "Disinterested benevolence is pleased with the public interest, the greatest good and happiness of the whole." Naturally, what is involved in such love is "every being and creature in the system, according to the degree of his existence, worth and capacity of happiness … so far as the good and happiness of each is, or appears to be, consistent with the greatest good of the whole." Moreover, since the self also belongs to this whole, "he must of necessity be the object of this disinterested, impartial benevolence, and his own interest and happiness must be regarded and desired, as much as that of his neighbor, or any individual of the whole society; not because it is *himself*, but because he is included in the whole, and his happiness is worth as much, and as desirable as that of his neighbor, other circumstances being equal. That is not self love; but the same universal, disinterested, impartial public benevolence, which wishes well to being in general."[64] There are concrete practical consequences to this: "This disinterested benevolence regards the interest and happiness of those who are nearest and most in sight, more strongly and tenderly, than of those who are farther off, and more out of sight; and is more affected with the happiness or misery, and good or bad character of the former, than of the latter." Love for one's city and nation is exalted and, thus, attention to "greater public interest."[65]

Because of its obvious concrete implications, this doctrine would offer motivations and stimuli to all the social reform and missionary movements of the first half of the nineteenth century.

Samuel Hopkins also fought vigorously in order to stress the need of grace for good works in the great controversy stirred up by a speech by Jonathan Mayhew entitled, *Striving to Enter in at the Strait Gate* (1761), in which he supported the idea of divine recompense also for the naturally good works of the "unregenerate": Hopkins, who was not an orator, replied with his work, *An Inquiry Concerning the Promises of the Gospel* (1765).

Among the eminent Edwardsians, there is another name to recall: that of Nathaniel Emmons (1745–1840), whose work focused mainly on the struggle to reconcile human responsibility with the absolute dependence of every human gesture, whether virtuous or not, on divine omnipotence. His works were published posthumously in six volumes in 1842, and republished with annexes in 1861–63.

Here, we could also point out, as a significant exponent of evangelical Calvinism inspired by Jonathan Edwards, Isaac Backus (1724–1806), a Baptist minister who was a strenuous supporter of the separation of church and state within a passionate democratic conception of individual freedom lived in the Revolutionary era. He was the author of numerous pamphlets between 1754 and 1789.

V NEW HAVEN THEOLOGY

1 *Convergence and Action of the Orthodox Currents*

The danger of Unitarianism, especially the liberal prevalence at Harvard, just as the common interest in preaching in the west, which was increasing daily, provoked a new rapprochement between the Old Calvinists and the Hopkinsians at the beginning of the nineteenth century.[66]

The majority of the credit for this endeavour goes to Jedidiah Morse (1761–1826), Old Calvinist pastor of Charlestown, who, with this intention, had founded the journal *Panoplist*, in 1805. And thanks to a collaboration with the Hopkinsian Leonard Woods (1774–1854), he was able to bring about the foundation of the Andover Theological Seminary, in 1808. As a bulwark of orthodoxy against any possible Unitarian intrusion, those who taught in the seminary were required to adhere to the Westminster Shorter Catechism and to the so-called Andover Creed, a Hopkinsian summary of belief.

This movement is also tied to the common evangelical commitment to the Revival renewal of the end of the eighteenth and the beginning of the nineteenth centuries. This new wave of Revivalism is known as the Great Awakening, and its greatest impetus is tied to the personality of Timothy Dwight (1752–1817), grandson (nephew?) of the great Edwards, poet and theologian, initially a Congregationalist pastor in Greenfield Hill, Connecticut, and from 1795 on president of Yale College. At Yale, Dwight was able to provoke an exceptional Revivalist fervour, in 1802: "Yale College is a little temple: prayer and praise seem to be the delight of the greater part of the students."[67] Struck by the religiously dissolving action that French Rationalism exercised on American culture, especially after the French Revolution, he concerned himself with giving back vigour to theological vision. For students, he gave a weekly course of doctrinal sermons in a four-year cycle, and thus, as a great master, he expounded his theological vision, published posthumously in five volumes: *Theology: Explained and Defended, in a Series of Sermons* (1818–19). He was an energetic assailant of the "infidels" – as he called the adversaries of orthodoxy – as is evidenced in two of his discourses that were later published, *The Nature and Danger of Infidel Philosophy* (1797) and *The Duty of Americans at the Present Crisis* (1798); nevertheless, he sought to maintain moderate theological positions. One of his favourite themes was the defence of the authenticity of the Bible.

2 *The Revivalist New School*

His concern for making theology better respond to the pressure of the problems posed by the adversaries was inherited by a group of his students, who tangibly modified Hopkinsian Calvinism regarding the *punctum dolens* of free will: it was affirmed as a true capacity to choose, the foundation of true and genuine responsibility. And the Revival movements (of whom Dwight's followers were impassioned champions) would make emotional appeals to this recognized responsibility, as a method of challenging the spread of rationalistic ideas and the recovery of an authentic religiosity. From the beginnings of the nineteenth century, therefore, the Revival phenomenon substantially reduced its claim to be an event of Grace disproportionate to any human dynamic, and tended to recognize itself more and more as a moral boost obtained through emotional techniques, albeit as an instrument of Grace. In this sense, the evolution of the "orthodox" current runs parallel to that of the Liberal Movement towards a moralism which, in the latter, would emphasize *character* formation as a factor of "civic" virtue, and in the former, a devotion that would imitate the divine "benevolence" in an activism of works in favour of the spread of the faith and of a reform of social customs and situations (the well-known benevolent societies).

The new current would be given the name of "New Haven Theology." Its greatest exponents were, in fact, professors of Yale College.

Lyman Beecher (1775–1863), the favourite disciple of Dwight and a powerful Revival preacher, was the most noteworthy supporter of reforming initiatives: "The Unitarians can not be killed by the pen. They depend upon action, and by action only can they be effectively met."[68] His posthumous *Autobiography* (1866) is, indeed, interesting.

NATHANIEL WILLIAM TAYLOR Nathaniel William Taylor (1786–1858) became the most widely known name of the New School (which was later given the name of "Taylorism"), because it was his *Concio ad Clerum* (Advice to the Clergy), a speech given in the Yale Chapel, in 1828, and published during the same year, which aroused the reaction of conservative Calvinists and remained almost as a symbol of the controversy that arose.

The Revivalistic action gave the impression of having managed to contain and hinder the Unitarian attack, and the strict observance Calvinists had more space to become aware of the radicality of the new positions vis-à-vis the older Edwardsian ones. The traditional theses affirmed (as is well known) man's innate corruption, whence came the human will's absolute impotence towards the good; the salvation of some was granted by the inscrutable and sovereign divine choice, which therefore, implied a decree of damnation of others that was just as sovereignly gratuitous. Justice and wisdom were saved by the fact that, in any case, this was the way that the ends of the whole of reality were thus achieved, that is, "the greatest good for being in general" and, therefore, the glory of God. Taylor decisively affirmed the will's fundamental moral capacity, so that man "not only can if he will, but can if he won't." Consequently, sin occurs not because it was mysteriously decreed, but because "such is the nature of *free agency* that God could not wholly prevent its perversion."[69]

On the other hand, the *Concio ad Clerum*, whose theme is the text of Ephesians 2:3, "And were by nature the children of wrath," reaffirms that humanity is morally depraved "by nature," and thus explains: "I do not mean that their nature is *itself* sinful, nor that their nature is the *physical* or *efficient* cause of their sinning; but I mean that their nature is the occasion, or reason of their sinning; – that *such is their nature, that in all the appropriate circumstances of their being, they will sin and only sin*." Taylor makes the comparison with the tree that bears wicked fruit in whatever soil it is planted. It is the human *state* that inevitably provokes evil, but the corruption by which man merits God's wrath: "*it is man's own act, consisting in a free choice of some object rather than God, as his chief good; – or a free preference of the world and of worldly goods, to the will and glory of God.*"[70]

Concio ad Clerum synthesizes the ideas of the whole current by echoing the *Two Discourses on the Nature of Sin* (1826), by Eleazar Thompson Ficht (1791–1871), Dwight's successor at Yale. These discourses constitute the most systematic expression of that school's doctrine.

3 Oberlin Theology: The Exaltation of the Moral Capacity of the Individual in Action

A particular development of Taylorism can be seen in Oberlin Theology, which drew its name from the homonymous college, where the moderate Calvinism of its first president, Asa Mahan (1799–1889), focused attention on the ideal of Christian perfection beginning with his first book, *Scripture Doctrine of Christian Perfection; With Other Kindred Subjects, Illustrated and Confirmed in a Series of Discourses Designed to Throw Light on the Way of Holiness* (1839). The problem was strictly dictated by the spiritual renewal caused by the Revival Movement, and also intended to distinguish its balanced inspiration from the "perfectionist" extremisms that claimed radically antinomian and morally ambiguous positions, by claiming an already realized perfect sanctity. For Mahan, "perfection in holiness implies a full and perfect discharge of our entire duty, of all existing obligations in respect to God and all other beings." The holiness of the Christian can be "perfect in *kind* but *finite* in *degree*, and in this sense imperfect." "Holiness, in a creature," therefore, "may also be perfect, and yet progressive – progressive, not in its nature, but in degree."[71] Holiness is, thus, a real possibility towards which man must grow by obeying the law; therefore, unlike the "perfectionist" currents, one must not presume the abrogation of obligations, the annulment of effort and initiative of the will, substituting "the direct teaching of the Spirit, falsely called, in the place of the 'word.'" Rather, one finds that it is necessary to learn "only in the diligent study of the word, and tries every doctrine by the 'law and the testimony,' expounded in conformity with the legitimate laws of interpretation."[72]

CHARLES GRANDISON FINNEY AND "PERFECTIONISM" The Bible, literally inspired, as word perfectly dictated by God to the individual, and, therefore, the ultimate criterion and directive for the Christian and, at the same time, the proclamation of the need for a "baptism in the Spirit," of God's intense direct action on man, which generates an experience of conversion, is the dialectic that is immanent to the entire opus of the Presbyterian (and later Congregationalist) Charles Grandison Finney (1792–1875), the strongest exponent of Oberlin Theology, leader of the great Revivals that profoundly influenced American social life at the beginning of the nineteenth century. However, the Revival techniques that he used were organized into a rigid methodology that more acutely "expressed his faith in the capacity of man's will to respond to God's just moral demands when clearly and decisively confronted with these demands."[73]

Nothing better signifies the radical distancing from the basic principles of Edwardsian Calvinism than what Finney states at the beginning of his most famous work, *Lectures on Revivals of Religion* (1835): "Religion is the work of man. It is something for man to do."[74]

The conception of divine sovereignty found in Old Calvinism must also be corrected, which "supposed it to be such an arbitrary disposal of events, and particularly the gift of his Spirit, as precluded rational employment of means for promoting the revival of religion." Human will engages its energy in the use of means, and God articulates his intervention through such a use: "Everything goes to show that God has connected means with the end through all the departments of his government – in nature and in grace ... He neither administers [natural] providence nor grace with that sort of sovereignty that dispenses with the use of means."[75] On the other hand, with the same forcefulness, Finney refutes the deistic organization of the God-world relationship: "There is no natural event in which [God's] own agency is not concerned. He has not built the creation like a vast machine, that will go on alone without his further care. He has not retired from the universe, to let it work for itself. This is mere atheism. He exercises a universal superintendence and control."[76] Nevertheless, Finney's God is undeniably more the Creator and Orderer or Governer of the world rather than the Absolute that endows what is human supernaturally and, supernaturally, "enables" it to do the good. As Albert Dod, an intelligent adversary and an old school Calvinist, would object, the action of the Spirit is for him "strictly parenthetical" and "superfluous."[77]

In Finney, theocentric Calvinism slides towards a warm anthropocentrism. "A Revival of Religion is Not a Miracle" is the title of the first paragraph of Lecture I, in de facto opposition to the Edwardsian appraisal of the same phenomena. Indeed, he goes on to explain, "There is nothing in religion beyond the ordinary powers of nature ... When mankind become religious, they are not *enabled* to put forth exertions which they were unable before to put forth. They only exert the powers they had before in a different way, and use them for the glory of God."[78]

It is in this new space of relationship with duty and with God that the energetic appeal to individual initiative is borne witness to: "Sinners ought to be made to feel that they have *something* to do, and that is *to repent*; that it is something which *no other* being can do for them, neither God nor man, and something which *they can* do, and do *now*. Religion is something to *do*, not something to *wait for*."[79] Finney uses the term *cannot-ism*[80] to disqualify Calvinist preaching that, because of man's fundamental incapacity for the good, suggested that the only religious "*doing*" was the awaiting of God's time, which would provoke conversion. Man, instead, can do what he must because divine obligation is always commensurate with the capacity of the individual, who therefore, must strive to be – literally – perfect.

This conception, which Finney developed plainly in his *Lectures to Professing Christians* (1837), goes by the name of "Oberlin Perfectionism," and found dissenters even among the other exponents of the New School, who were more cautious regarding man's ultimate ethical possibilities. A deep humanistic optimism shored up Finney's pietism. He took up the Hopkinsian ideal of sanctity as "disinterested benevolence" (while likely ignorant of its pedigree);[81] he defines its value and urgency in terms of happiness: happiness for one's neighbour, for God, and for the whole universe.

McLoughlin calls such an ethics "cosmic utilitarianism,"[82] whose realization is the aim of an undeniable activism. In making a list of "instructions to young converts," he states, "They should set out with a determination to *aim at being useful in the highest degree possible*. They should not rest satisfied with merely being useful, or remaining in a situation where they can do *some* good. But if they see an opportunity where they can do more good, they must embrace it, whatever may be the sacrifice to themselves. No matter what it may cost them, no matter what danger or what suffering, no matter what change in their outward circumstances, or habits, or employments it may lead to."[83]

In his voluminous work, *Lectures on Systematic Theology* (1846), the fruit of classes taught at Oberlin, Finney affirms that the spirit of all true Christians "is necessarily that of the reformer. For the universal reformation of the world they stand committed."[84] Thus, Finney integrates perfectly into the spirit of social reform proper to his era and he develops its messianic tendencies with great impetus.

From a spur to action, optimism expands to inspire a judgment on history, and fears not to compromise itself in millenarian perspectives: "let us have the United States converted to God, and let all minor questions cease ... If the church will do all her duty, the millennium may come in this country in three years."[85] The conversion of state and society was identified with the conversion of its citizens. "Benevolence" lived by them generates a new atmosphere: salvation and the good of society is not expected from the Church as an organism under the guidance of the clergy, as it was in the theocratic conception of Calvinist tradition, but from the initiative of a regenerated individual. Moreover, Finney's individualism is exalted in the prefiguring of a democracy in which the self-governance of all constitutes the political analogy of the "priesthood of all the faithful" to which his discourse logically led.[86]

The energetic reaffirmation of pietism in Finney has a complex significance. In his individualistic and perfectionist moralism, the dramatic sense of God's incommensurability for man is dampened and muffled and, therefore, so is the religious power of Puritanism, especially the Edwardsian type, just as its ecclesiology is emptied and made banal. Finney would speak of his Church's credo as a "paper pope." On the other hand, such a version of Christianity develops sympathy with the trusting ideal of man and society proper to the intellectual and political vision of his era, which is the era of Jackson. His pragmatism, which recovers experimental efficacy as a criterion for evaluation, takes up again and revives a fundamental feature of the traditional attitude; and his voluntaristic activism, just as his enthusiastic progressivism, mark the passage to a new era in American theological thought. It is an unmitigated optimism that would mark it most clamorously as the typical expression of the entire first part of the nineteenth century, whose new characteristic would be delineated by Whitehead: "That quality was hope – not the hope of ignorance. The peculiar character of this central period was that the wise men hoped, and that as yet no circumstance had arisen to throw doubt upon the grounds of such hope."[87]

VI THE CONSERVATIVE REACTION: MERCERSBURG THEOLOGY AND THE END OF NEW ENGLAND THEOLOGY

1 *Conservative Groups*

The New School achieved a great deal of success among Presbyterian and Congregationalist churches (or "Presbycongregationalists, as they were known after the 1801 "Plan of Union"), especially due to the Revivalist ferment and the benevolent society movement. Conservatives, however, accused the new trends of having abandoned the basic principles of Calvinism, of being Pelagian, and of radically compromising themselves with Liberalism and Unitarianism.

An early noteworthy group of conservatives was the one led by Bennet Tyler (1783–1858), a classmate of Taylor's from Yale, later to become his implacable adversary. Tyler's memorable works include *Letters on the Origin and Progress of the New Haven Theology* (1873).

This conservative group founded the East Windsor Seminary, in 1834, and later, Hartford, as a rival to Yale.

THE CONSERVATIVE "OLD SCHOOL" OF PRINCETON Yet, the stronghold of the Presbyterian Old School – the most conservative current among the Scots-Irish Presbyterians – was Princeton, College and Seminary. A serious and learned trimesterly journal, founded in 1825, the *Biblical Repertory and Theological Review* – later known as the *Princeton Review*, was its authoritative instrument for half a century. Among its most intelligent collaborators was Finney's first severe critic, Albert Baldwin Dod (1805–1845), with his reviews of *Finney's Sermons* and *Finney's Lectures*, in July and October of 1835.

Nevertheless, the most conspicuous name in all of nineteenth-century Calvinist Presbyterian conservatism was the journal's editor, professor of oriental and biblical literature at Princeton Seminary, Charles Hodge (1797–1878).

Hodge's *Outlines of Theology* (1861) and his three-volume *Systematic Theology* (1871–2) were the most widely used textbooks on systematic Calvinism for three-quarters of a century. Hodge was a strenuous, vivacious defender of the principles of traditional theology wherever they fell under attack. He fought energetically against the new attitudes of transcendental philosophy, and he was among the first to see the warning signs of evolutionism in that anticipation of Darwinism, which was the work of Robert Chambers (1802–1871), *Vestiges of the Natural History of Creation* (1844).

Yet, it is within the Calvinist world that his work has meaning. Whereas the Revivalist interest of the New School insisted on issues related to conversion and moral perfection, and favoured the unionistic currents by glossing over differences in theoretical conceptions, Hodge's line of thought stressed the precise contents of the Credo that characterized the ecclesiastical community and, therefore, stressed the doctrinal aspects that were then analyzed and upheld with scholastic rigour. The philosophical framework upon which the theological construction was generally based was Scottish Realism and Reid's common sense, and its content was drawn from the Bible as a reasonably believable historical text, which the quickening of faith in Jesus of Nazareth would lead one to see as the inspired word of God. The Bible, it was held, is for the theologian what nature is for the scientist, and from it, theological work proceeds in an "inductive" way, analogous to that of the scientific process.

This "objective" methodological approach was in opposition to the subjectivism favoured by the liberalizing forms. The specific nature of the Credo also recovered the value of the institutional Church as history and as discipline, vehicle and guarantee of the whole of doctrine and religious life. This value of the Church was vigorously opposed to Revivalistic pragmatism and sentimentalism. Thus, Hodge and the Old School were dogged adversaries of the benevolent societies that carried out missionary and reform activities that originated and developed outside official ecclesiastical structures.*

2 *A Singular Moment of Sacramental Theology in the German Reformed Church*

An exceptional position, which was critical of New England Theology, was that of Mercersburg Theology, with roots in the Old School but with a distinctly different development as the sole relevant branch of systematic theology that was profoundly original with respect to the whole Calvinist intellectual tradition in New England. This phenomenon occurred within the German Reformed Church, mainly through the work of two strong personalities, the theologian John Williamson Nevin (1803–1886) and the historian Philip Schaff (1813–1893).

The German Reformed Church, isolated because of its attachment to the German language, was nevertheless, pushed to establish relationships with the academic life of the old country by introducing a radically new factor into the American cultural horizon. Thus, in 1832, we have Frederick Augustus Rauch (1806–1841) at Mercersburg [Pennsylvania], as professor of biblical literature, formed in the idealism of Heidelberg, which inspired him to write *Psychology or a View of the Human Soul, Including Anthropology* (1840), which would become the philosophical premise of the conception expressed by Nevin, the leader of the school. The latter, although born into the Old School Presbyterian tradition, graduated from Princeton, and was very interested in German thought. Thus, after having taught at Princeton (substituting for Hodge during his years in Germany) and at Western Theological Seminary of Pittsburgh, he was called to Mercersburg in

* Translator's note: Surrounding an issue of this type, connected to the whole theological debate, in 1837 there was a break between the two trunks of American Presbyterianism, roughly corresponding to the areas of influence of the Old School and the New School.

1839. Four years later, the young professor Philip Schaff arrived from Berlin. Schaff, a native of Switzerland and of pietist extraction, had received an education that put him in contact in Tubingen, Halle, and Berlin with all the main attempts to apply the systems of Hegel and Schleiermacher to Church history and to Scripture.

Through the perfect understanding between Nevin and Schaff, Mercersburg Theology vigorously introduced contact with a new intellectual world to America: "In doing so it contributed to a revolution which was completed more than a generation later when, as Schaff and Nevin had predicted, the collapse of New England theology finally opened the way to the tendencies of German thinking."[88]

PRINCIPAL THEOLOGICAL CONTENT If the philosophical arguments upon which the thought of Mercersburg Theology was based were German Idealism and historicism, its theological content, properly speaking, involved the central concerns of the various "High Church" movements of the first half of the nineteenth century. Particularly noteworthy is the influence of the Oxford Movement, especially Newman, Pusey, and Wilberforce: "The Oxford Movement," says Yngve Brilioth, in an observation that strives to highlight the link between pietism (or evangelism) and the sacramental recovery of the High Church movements, "was a rediscovery of the historical mediation of salvation, just as the evangelical movement had been the discovery of the immediate relation of the individual soul to its Saviour ... The question of the historical Church became part of the question of the salvation of the soul."[89]

It can be said that the fundamental theme for Mercersburg Theology is Christ as real "mystical presence" in history. The point of departure is "the great fact of the Incarnation ... This objective act is itself the gospel, in the profoundest sense of the term ... it must underlie and condition all that the gospel can ever become for men in the way of inner experience." However, this point of departure explodes into historical development and continues in a living tradition: "The objective reality from which Christianity springs, the new order of existence which was constituted for the world by the great fact of the Incarnation, must be allowed also to be historical ... But this conception of a supernatural economy having place among men under an objective, historical form, an order of grace flowing from Christ, and altogether different from the order of nature, is nothing more or less than the idea of the holy catholic Church as we have it in the Creed."

The Creed, as a formula in which the original awareness of all these events is fixed, is of great importance. It "is no summary of Christian doctrine primarily for the understanding, but the necessary form of the gospel, as this is first apprehended by faith; a direct transcript, we may say, of what the gospel is to the contemplation of the believer, turned wholly upon the Person of Christ." Theology can only develop as immanence to the Christocentric life of the Church: "It believes in an economy of grace, a sphere of supernatural powers and forces flowing from the historical fact of Christ's birth, death, and glorification, which are themselves present in the world historically (not magically) in broad distinction from the economy of nature; and in the bosom of which only, not on the outside of it, the gospel can be expected to work as the wisdom of God and the power of God unto salvation."[90]

Theology must be essentially ecclesial and, therefore, sacramental. The sacraments are not pure exterior signs: they are facts in which participation in Christ's presence is fulfilled. The first among them is the Eucharist, which Nevin explains as "Real spiritual Presence." In it is established "the fact of a real life-union in the case of the believer with the whole person of Christ, through the force of which the vivific virtue of his true human flesh is carried over in the sacrament particularly into our persons, soul and body, by the power of the Holy Ghost, for our nourishment unto eternal life."[91] For Nevin, the Eucharistic mystery represents the key to all of ecclesial life, and man's salvation is tied to participation in it: "To my own mind, all that is great and precious in the gospel may be said to center in this doctrine. Without it, I must feel that the whole Christian salvation would be shorn of its glory and force. I have no hope, save on the ground of a living union with the nature of Christ as the resurrection and the life. Both for my understanding and my heart, theology finds here all its interest and attraction. For no truth am I more willing to suffer contradiction and reproach, if such be the will of God … The fact that the Christian life holds an actual communication with the humanity of Christ, and that this, in particular, forms the soul of the Lord's Supper, may never be relinquished."[92]

The idea of the Church as "communion with her Head" and as "necessary organ" such that "the revelation of God in Christ becomes effective in the history of the world"[93] led to an emphasis on the importance of the unity of the Church and, therefore, gave Mercersburg Theology an ecumenical concern, as anticipatory and prophetic as it was.

LITERARY PRODUCTION The rich problematic that made the Pennsylvania German school an interesting and unique fact was developed in a copious literary production, particularly in the *Weekly Messenger*, the *Mercersburg Review*, and *Kirchenfreund*.

Among the various tracts and sermons published by Nevin, the following are worthy of note: *The Anxious Bench* (1843), the Revivalist pamphlet *Catholic Unity* (1854), *The Church* (1847), *Antichrist, or the Spirit of Sect and Schism* (1848), *The Doctrine of the Reformed Church on the Lord's Supper* (1850), but above all, his principal work, *The Mystical Presence: A Vindication of the Reformed or Calvinistic Doctrine of the Holy Eucharist* (1846).

In the time of his collaboration in Mercersburg, Schaff wrote many notable works, including *Das Princip des Protestantismus* (1845, the same year as the publication of Newman's *Essay on Development*, with which there are acute analogies), translated a few months later by Nevin under the title of *The Principle of Protestantism as Related to the Present State of the Church*, *What is Church History? A Vindication of the Idea of Historical Development* (1846), *Geschichte der Apostolischen Kirche, nebst einer allgemeinen Einleitung in die Kirchengeschichte* (1851 – the most important work of that period, translated by E.D. Yeomans in 1853 as *History of the Apostolic Church with a General Introduction to Church History*), and *History of the Christian Church from the Birth of Christ to Gregory the Great, 1–600 A.D.*, volume I (1858). Philip Schaff's most noteworthy literary production belongs to the period following the Civil War, when, from 1870 until his death, he taught at Union Theological Seminary in New York. The following works stand out in this second stage of his activity: *Bibliotheca Symbolica Ecclesia Universalis: Creeds of Christendom* (1877); *History of the Christian Church*, 7 volumes (1882–92); *A Companion to the Greek Testament and the English Version* (1893). But his works are numerous: "No other American theological scholar of the century rivaled this production."[94]

Mercersburg Theology constituted a singular enterprise, but its impetus was hindered, as it were, and it did not achieve a lasting presence apart from the liturgical movement it had marked.

3 Final Exponents of New England Theology

It was not the activity of the conservatives and the activities of Mercersburg theologians that halted and demolished the dominant influence of New England Theology. Calvinist doctrine has been the only theology systematically cultivated in the first two and a half centuries of American life: generally traditional, centred on Covenant Theology and the Westminster Confession, confined in inspiration to the themes proper to English Puritanism, despite the use of Dutch, German, and Swiss manuals, like those of Turretinus, Wollebius, Witsius, or Ernesti, for biblical exegesis, within the sphere of an ecclesiastical life tending towards concrete concerns, it had found its humus among the Congregationalists and the Presbyterians of New England and its best problematic impetus in the followers of Edwards. Passing progressively from the secure energy of the early times to the rigour of Edwards and to the pastoral concerns of Taylor and Finney, it was not capable of withstanding the attack of the Liberal Movement.

Even the Revivalist resurgence of 1875–81 of Dwight Lyman Moody (1839–1899) created no cultural expression worthy of note; the same preaching had a rather meagre doctrinal content, focused on an announcement of God's love victorious over any punishment and any hell, and based upon a literal interpretation of the Bible.

In 1880, all of the chairs of Congregationalist theology and many of the Presbyterian ones were held by theologians from the school of Edwards, albeit under various versions. Fifteen years later, all had fallen into the hands of Liberal professors.

Its last authoritative representative was Edwards Amasa Park (1808–1900), until 1881 professor of theology in Andover Seminary, with his "orthodox rationalism," a dogged defender of the old Edwardsian school. He worked until the end of his life elaborating his system, which was, however, never published. His memorable publications include *The Theology of the Intellect and of the Feelings* (1850), *Discourses on Some Theological Doctrines* (1885), and a collection of sermons, the *Memorial Collection*, published posthumously (1902).

3

The Liberal Movement

I ANTICIPATIONS

1 The Transcendentalism of Ralph Waldo Emerson and Theodore Parker

An early premise to the Liberal Movement, which would dominate the American scene from the final decades of the nineteenth century on, was posited by a radicalization of the situation in the Unitarian churches leading to the rise of the Transcendentalist Movement, which a noted historian of American philosophy described as "the flowering of the Enlightenment,"[1] but which, perhaps, would be better to emphasize as a Romantic school of thought.

Ralph Waldo Emerson (1803–1882) and Theodor Parker (1810–1860) are the most famous names, but there are other significant figures, such as George Ripley (1803–1880), Orestes August Brownson (1803–1876), who later converted to Catholicism, James Freeman Clarke (1810–1888), and William Henry Channing (1810–1884), grandson of Ellery Channing, all of whom were Unitarian ministers, although some ultimately renounced their positions.

NEW EPISTEMOLOGY The insufficiency of Lockean sensism, which was the philosophical touchstone for Unitarian teaching, "legitimized" the "religious instincts" according to Theodore Parker, and enthusiastically opened those men to the influence of Kantian idealism, above all, in the Platonically revised and corrected version of the Englishman Coleridge, and of the thought of Schleiermacher. The Transcendent foundation of sentient reality is acquired through a stated experience of direct perception, which would represent the most proper capacity of the human spirit: "The concept of reason proposed by Coleridge, as both a development and surpassing of Kantian criticism implies ... the substantial basis of revelation and of faith, considered by Coleridge as an instrument of metaphysical penetration. This presupposes a concrete basis of qualitative experience, which is its essential content."[2] Theodore Parker affirmed a triple intuitive experience: the direct perception of the Divine, of the moral law, and of immortality. And Orestes Brownson maintained, "We may know that God exists as positively, as certainly, as we may know that we feel hunger and thirst, joy and grief."[3] The gracious "light" with which Edwards founded the awareness of the divine unveiling is here brought back to a potential that defines the essence of the human mind; the supernatural is identified with the supersensory, and that potential, which is common to all, makes everyone equally capable of grasping and expressing the Divine more profoundly than any creed. A universalistic attitude made the Transcendentalists interested in the study of Eastern religions, as is documented in two large tomes by J.F. Clarke, *The Great Religions* (1870, 1883). It evidently disposed them to a relativistic interpretation of Christian doctrine, such as that of Theodor Parker, whose discourse, *The Transient and Permanent in Christianity*, held in his south Boston church in 1841, and his conferences in the Boston Masonic Temple, published as *A Discourse of Matters Pertaining to Religion* (1842), provoked scandal.

DIVINE IMMANENCE The consequence of this epistemology is a conception of radical intimacy between the Divine and the natural, which in Emerson reveals itself more and more as a pantheistic immanence. Nature is "the fabric of God" and, as he writes in his first famous essay, *Nature* (1836), "We learn that the highest is present to the soul of man; that the dread universal essence, which is not wisdom, or love, or beauty, or power, but all in one, and each entirely, is that for which all things exist, and that by which they are; that spirit creates; that behind nature, throughout nature, spirit is present; one and not compound it does not act upon us from without, that is, in space and time, but spiritually, or through ourselves: therefore, that spirit, that is, the Supreme Being, does not build up nature around us, but puts it forth through us, as the life of the tree puts forth new branches and leaves through the pores of the old."[4] The moment in nature in which the "sole spirit" becomes an emergent, aware being is man: "Of the universal mind, each individual man is one more incarnation,"[5] as Emerson says in his *History*, and this Platonizing phrase cannot avoid an ultimate pantheistic interpretation in the final context of his thought, above all, in light of *The Over-Soul*, his most important essay: "In all conversation between two persons tacit reference is made, as to a third party, to a common nature. That third party or common nature is not social; it is impersonal; is God." "The Supreme Critic on the errors of the past and the present, and the only prophet of that which must be, is the great nature in which we rest ... that Unity, that Over-Soul, within which every man's particular being is contained and made one with all other ... We live in succession, in division, in parts, in particles. Meantime within man is the soul of the whole; the wise silence; the universal beauty, to which every part and particle is equally related; the eternal One."[6]

The divine immanence in nature, and its direct intuitability by man, expunges the traditional concept of revelation, and devalues the concept of miracle, as Parker specifies in *God's Revelation in Matter and Mind*: "God, ever present, never intervenes; acting ever by law a miracle becomes needless, and also impossible."[7] Moreover, any exterior authority, from Christ to the Bible to the Church, is eliminated.

OPTIMISM IN HUMANITY AND IN HISTORY The involvement of man in divinity provides motivation for a profound self-assurance on the part of man, as another of Emerson's essays, *Self-Reliance*, proclaims: "We lie in the lap of immense intelligence, which makes us receivers of its truth and organs of its activity."[8] Even where Transcendentalism affirms the Divine in more personal ways, God's infinite perfection, the "cornerstone" of a theological system, according to Theodor Parker, is conceived in continuity with the human experience of values, and his "total love" is thought of in terms of human affection, therefore, according to a naturalistic and rationalistic version of Puritan "benevolence."

An unadulterated optimism permeates such a conception. Moreover, it is expressed, above all, in a vision of man where, especially for Emerson and Parker, sin is interpreted as a mere difficulty inherent to the inevitably evolving mechanism, and regeneration means immanent natural development. Man's regeneration is like the growth of a plant, said Ripley in his *Discourses on the Philosophy of*

Religion (1836): "In both cases, no new properties are imparted, by the operation of external causes, but only the inward tendencies are called into action and clothed with strength."[9]

Optimism, consequently, determines the philosophy of history, according to which evil is destined to be outclassed, and with reformist initiative, social progress is affirmed as something secured through the realization of man's innate divine potential, especially freedom. "Democracy, Freedom," writes Emerson, "has its roots in the sacred truth that every man hath in him the divine Reason."[10] Marcuse rightly notes that "Emerson's generation ... was more enthusiastic than critical and more poetic than theological ... With its leader, that bourgeois saint who was Emerson ... it had turned away from the true dogmas of religion and philosophy so as to face a future in which socialism and democracy, faith, science and life, the Aufklärung and Swedenborg would all be one: an amiable, nebulous optimism."[11]

If the Transcendentalist Movement per se was practically limited to Boston, such that it seemed to be a current within Unitarianism, the web of its motives and promptings has a great reverberation and influence on later American thought. Emerson became almost a symbol, "the characteristic philosopher of the modern sense of American life,"[12] and although a bit emphatic, the observation that a historian of American thought has made regarding his intellectual expression is significant: "To measure the full impact of Emerson's philosophic imagination, to determine all the outcomes of his work would be, in effect, to write the history of American culture since his time."[13]

The Liberal Movement would reveal acute affinities with the Emesonian sensibility, and it would participate with Transcendentalism in essential ideological connotations: God's nearness to the world, as continuity more than contiguity of being and, therefore, the divine immanence to nature and its dynamic,[14] and dogged socially reforming anthropological and historical optimism.

2 *Horace Bushnell's Pedagogical and Christocentric Vision*

There is yet another premise to the Liberal Movement: the new theological orientation overcomes the confines of an internal debate in the Unitarian churches, and its first adherents came from them. It is genetically bound in a more decisive way to the work of Horace Bushnell (1802–1876), a disciple of Nathaniel Taylor at Yale and Congregationalist pastor in Hartford: "It is a hope, cherished by many of the most thoughtful and earnest Christians of our time, that God is preparing the introduction, at last, of some new religious era."[15] The contribution he made to the new era, of which he is the standard-bearer, can be summed up in a dual thematic content: the value of education in the Christian life and Christology.

THE EDUCATIONAL ENDEAVOUR IN OPPOSITION TO THE REVIVAL MECHANISM Bushnell radically disputed the value of the "mechanical system of the revivals," because it conceived the event of the Christian life as a discontinuity and artificial mobilization, misunderstanding the value of the continual development and interior formation that lend consistency to the history of a personality: "Things have come to such a pitch in the churches, by the intensity of the Revival system, that the permanent was sacrificed to the casual, the ordinary swallowed up and lost in the extraordinary, and Christian piety itself reduced to a kind of campaigning or stage-effect exercise ... It was even difficult for the pastor, saying nothing of conversions, to keep alive in Christians themselves any hope or expectation of holy living, as an abiding state, in the intervals of public movement and excitement left to his care; because everything was brought to the test of the Revival state as a standard, and it could not be conceived how any one might be in the Spirit, and maintain a continuance of growth, in the calmer and more private methods of duty, patience, and fidelity on the level of ordinary life."[16]

The normal path of Christian reality is, therefore, not the exceptional pressure of the Revival Movement, but the "continuance of growth" brought about by the education made possible by the presence of the child and the adolescent in the Christian community. That is how Bushnell expresses it in an article with a meaningful title, "The Kingdom of God as a Grain of Mustard Seed": "We hold that children are, in a sense, included in the faith of their parents, partakers with them in their covenant, and brought into a peculiar relation to God, in virtue of it. On this ground they receive a common seal of faith with them, in their baptism, and God on his part, contemplates, in the rite, the fact that they are to grow up as Christians, or spiritually renewed persons. As to the precise time or manner in which they are to receive the germ of holy principle, nothing is affirmed. Only it is understood, that God includes their infant age in the womb of parental culture, and pledges himself to them and their parents, in such a way, as to offer the presumption, that they may grow up in love with all goodness, and remember no definite time when they became subjects of Christian principle. Christian education is then to conform to this view, and nothing is to be called Christian education which does not."[17]

Bushnell overturned the entire dominant position from the Great Awakening onward: the emphasis is no longer on divine initiative, which descends perpendicularly with its gratuitous miracles, free from any antecedent, in order to show itself in man's unforeseen experience of conversion and decision; rather, the emphasis is on the Christian fact as a social reality and historical movement, with its natural rhythm and its natural progress.

This overturning, which paved the way for a new approach that would impose itself more and more throughout the second half of the century, could not be posited without provoking harsh diatribes. His first publication on this topic, *Discourses on Christian Nurture* (1847), was suspended by the editor out of fear. The same year, Bushnell defended himself with *An Argument for* Discourses on Christian Nurture, *Addressed to the Publishing Committee of the Massachusetts Sabbath School Society*, and he also republished two preceding volumes together with other essays under the title *Views of Christian Nurture, and of Subjects Adjacent Thereto*. Many years later, Bushnell renewed the publication of *Discourses* in an enlarged edition, with the title, *Christian Nurture* (1861), which remains his most widely known and influential work to this day.

CHRISTIFORM LIFE AS NEW PRINCIPLE OF KNOWLEDGE The Christocentric concern would mark Bushnell and make him a paradigmatic figure for the thought of the generation that followed him. This concern is documented in his volumes of sermons: *Sermons for the New Life* (1858), *Christ and His Salvation* (1864), and *Sermons on Living Subjects* (1872). However, this concern is developed, above all, in his principal works: *God in Christ* (1849) and its defence *Christ in Theology* (1851), *Nature and Supernatural, as Together Constituting the One System of God* (1848), *The Vicarious Sacrifice, Grounded in Principles of Universal Obligation* (1866), and *Forgiveness and Law, Grounded in Principles Interpreted by Human Analogies* (1874).

An exceptional spiritual experience in 1848 is remembered as the key to his whole theological conception, a personal discovery of Christ as the real point of mediation in which man is given "the form of a divine character" which radically changes him. "Christ, the Form of the Soul" is the title of a sermon inspired by the phenomenon he underwent, published in 1910, together with other writings under the title, *The Spirit in Man: Sermons and Selection*.

His experience brought with it an important epistemological connotation. For Bushnell, religious knowledge is given by an intuitive power that man acquires by joining himself to Christ: "a soul truly given up to Christ, filled with the spirit of Christ, is filled, in virtue of that fact, with a supernatural light; in other words, it is brought into such a close, interior union with the will and spirit of God that it is acted by God, filled with the consciousness of God and, by means of this pure inward experience, lighted up to know the meaning of things."[18] At times, the phenomenon is designated as "knowledge of the heart," and Bushnell's position doubtlessly evokes the Edwardsian doctrine of the "Divine and Supernatural Light" or the "new sense" or the "sense of the heart." Nevertheless, just as evident is the influence of Coleridge, whose *Aids to Reflection* Bushnell read, finding them to be "lucid and instructive," and that of the epistemology of Cousin, with his idea of "spontaneous reason," which was at the time being spread by the enthusiasm of the Transcendentalists.

The intuitive capacity of the "spirit," or of the "heart," which enables man to grasp the religious contents and the meanings of reality, is juxtaposed – analogously to Edwards' low appreciation of the "notional knowledge" of God proper to the "natural" man – to the "knowledge acquired through thought and reflection" or knowledge by "opinion," which, if maintained by an "authoritative force," is designated as "dogma": "When we speak of Christian dogmatics, or of dogmatic theology, we associate the same idea of authority ... understanding some scheme or system of religious opinion, propounded as a guide to others who are theologic pupils or Christian disciples." Opinion or dogma are "dark and feeble in the contrast of spirit and inspiration ... The human soul under sin, or considered simply as unreligious, is necessarily dark, because it is divorced from God, by whose inbeing it was made to have its light. It cannot make light by opinions gotten up in itself. Revolving God's idea, systematizing external cognitions, derived from his works, investigating the historic evidences of Christ, his life, his doctrine – busied in all such ways, it is rather creating darkness than light, until it receives God as an inner light, and knows him by that spiritual manifestation within, which Christ promised."[19]

The skepticism about the renewal possibilities of theology, and the insistence on its subordination to the primacy of the "spirit" and "life" in union with Christ, would pass in a congenial way into the attitude of the Liberal Christianity of the second half of the nineteenth century. Faced with the danger of what "may be called a bondage under the method of science, – as if nothing could be true, save as it is proved by the scientific method," as Bushnell observed in his *Nature and the Supernatural*,[20] what is intuited spiritually grasps reality in its totality, which exceeds the level of nature as the "kingdom of cause and effect."

CHRIST, CENTRE OF REALITY AND IDEAL FIGURE OF MAN With a terminology like that of Coleridge, Bushnell identifies the "supernatural" with personal and free spirituality, with an "inner" world, and affirms total reality as "the grand, universal, invisible system of God" of which Christ is the centre of unity, profound consistency, exhaustive end, and the bearer of the structure of Christianity. Indeed, the Divine is "even more visibly, convincingly, and gloriously expressed in Christianity than he is in all the world."[21] Bushnell insists that it is, thus, necessary to "make out a conception both of nature and of supernatural redemption by Jesus Christ ... which exactly meets the magnificent outline-view of God's universal plan, given by the great apostle to the Gentiles ... Christianity, in other words, is not an afterthought of God, but a forethought. It even antedates the world of nature and is 'before the foundation of the world.' Instead of coming into the world, as being no part of the system, or to interrupt and violate the system of things, they all *consist*, come together into system, in Christ, as the center of unity and the head of the universal plan."[22]

If we wish to better understand this Christocentrism, we must keep in mind that, for Bushnell, the Trinity is not a modality that reveals God: "These persons or personalities are the *dramatis personae* of revelation, and their reality is measured by what of the infinite they convey in these finite forms." In fact, unfathomable and ineffable Absolute Being, in order to provoke our mind to a relationship with it, or to generate in us an awareness of him, must produce himself in finite forms. There is in God "a capacity of self-expression, so to speak, which is peculiar – a generative power of form, a creative imagination, in which, or by aid of which, he can 'produce himself' outwardly, or represent himself in the finite." So, Bushnell concluded, "In these three persons or impersonations I only see a revelation of the Absolute Being, under just such relatives as by their mutual play, in and before our imaginative sense, will produce in us the truest knowledge of God – render him most conversable, bring him closest to feeling, give him the freest, least obstructed access, as a quickening power, to our hearts."[23]

Christ represents the supreme way of God's self-expression: the very Trinitarian personifications emerge in him. He has a more than human personality. The consistency of humanity in Christ leaves Bushnell extremely perplexed; he recognizes that he is not sure if Christ had a human soul. It is his function – the work of Redemption – which, nevertheless, profoundly clarifies his figure. God as he "has produced himself in all the other finite forms of being, so now he should appear in the human"; man would, therefore, be "the truest, most expressive finite type of him." Sin has contorted the relationship, so that "Truth has no longer any living unblemished manifestation in the world; the beauty of goodness lives and smiles no more … the real glory of the Divine, is visible no longer." However, God "will reclaim this last type of himself, possess it with his own life and feeling, and through that, live himself into the acquaintance and biographic history of the world. 'And the Word was made flesh.'"[24] Christ is, thus, divine in that he is the supreme revelation of God, and human in that he reconstitutes the "character," the paradigm or truth of man.

And precisely herein lies "the work of Redemption," in the moral force that Christ exerts on man by renewing the knowledge and terms of his relationship with God. The *vexata quaestio* of the way of conceiving the "vicarious sacrifice," or the redeeming expiation, is resolved by Bushnell according to a conception that attributes a decisive moral influence to Christ's action: "Christ, in what is called his vicarious sacrifice, simply engages, at the expense of great suffering and even of death itself, to bring us out of our sins themselves and so out of their penalties; being himself profoundly identified with us in our fallen state, and burdened in feeling with our evils."[25] The sacrificial terminology of the Scriptures would use depictions with a pedagogical aim, so that the evocation of Christ might have a more morally efficacious effect on man.

In Bushnell, there are hints of an objective version of Christ's expiation, such as the affirmation of the existence of "a cross in God's perfections from eternity"[26] – hints that were taken up again and developed in his final book, *Forgiveness and Law* (1814), where "the work of Christ" is described as really efficacious not only morally upon mankind's attitude towards God, but also upon God's attitude towards men – divine "self-atonement," with the explicit expunging of the idea of expiation as legal satisfaction of God's justice.[27]

Liberal theology would not recognize these final developments, whereas it would enthusiastically welcome the idea of Christ as "moral power of God," which moves man and human history towards perfection; religion would be reduced to purely ethical terms, and the Cross would become a mere example and symbol of natural moral virtues, in whose development the true redemption of the individual and society takes place.

II THE NEW THEOLOGY

1 *Features of the New Current in Theological Thought*

Transcendentalist radicalism, on the one hand, and Bushnellian revisionism, on the other, characterize the climate in which the long discourse of American theological Liberalism develops from the mid-nineteenth century until the beginning of the 1930s.

The term "New Theology" was used by one of the first exponents of this growing movement, the Congregationalist Theodore Thornton Munger (1830–1910), who posited it as the title of the first essay of his book, *The Freedom of Faith* (1833). Munger attempts a description of the features proper to this trend, such as the will to not deny the doctrines contained in the faith of the Church, but also the recognition of the need to mainly use "reason" and to carry out a more historical or "natural" exegesis of Scripture.

The de facto fundamental concern becomes the quest for an interpretation of Christianity that would permit its survival in a world dominated by new philosophies, by scientific development with its positivistic suppositions, in particular, the evolutionistic hypothesis. If, as Paul Tillich states, it is the "situation" that produces a "creative interpretation of existence,"[28] American theological Liberalism is an attempt to face human existence and history under the rich ferment of ideas, assured, above all, by contact with the German cultural world, directly frequented by many exponents of the new thought, and in the urgency produced by the unforeseen industrial technological progress and the consequent urbanization after 1865, that is, after the Civil War. In this attempt, the traditional Christian ideas acted as a working hypothesis that, in their application, would reveal their potential significance, and modern philosophy and science would mediate this verification.

"The substance of our program," asserted the Congregationalist Stearns of Bangor Seminary, reporting on the American situation at the International Congregational Council of 1891, "is to be found now, as always, in the great unchanging facts and truths of Christianity accepted in every age of the church ... So, if we speak of a 'new theology,' we mean that it is new only as a living body is new at each fresh stage of its growth, conserving and fulfilling the one type that runs through all its changes, and that is neither old or new."[29] Yet, such a program, which seems to echo the spirit of faithfulness of St Vincent of Lerins or, at the other end of the arc of the centuries, Newman's intuitions about the "Development of Christian Doctrine," must be implemented with the tools offered by cultural progress, since it is necessary "to be both an intelligent modern and a serious Christian," as one of the most notable liberal preachers, Harry Emerson Fosdick (1878–1969),[30] recalled.

Some more recent studies of American theological Liberalism, like that of Kenneth Cauthen,[31] distinguish between "evangelical Liberalism," which stresses the truth of Christian history as a starting point and seeks a meaning in it that would be acceptable to the modern mentality, and a "modernist Liberalism," which stresses as its starting point modern doctrines and tries to use them in a benevolent recovery of those Christian doctrines thought to have permanent value. Although this example can serve to delineate the vast differentiation in positions, themes, and expressions within the arc of Liberal production, from the most moderate to the most radical, the basic approach to the Christian fact, both in method and aim, is sufficiently homogeneous throughout the various versions that they can be grouped under one name.

REVELATION AS EXPERIENCE The line between theology and religious philosophy was, for the most part, abolished, so that an affirmation such as this became normative: "metaphysics must be the Alpha, and ethics the Omega, of any theology which is rooted in reason and fruitful in life."[32] The epistemology of the new approaches was completely determined by the influence of Schleiermacher and, even more so, Ritschl: the evidence of subjective experience substituted the dictates of an objective revelation, or better, revelation was no longer the supernatural self-communication of truth, but the emergence of meanings within introspection or the affirmation of value judgments within intuition. The American Protestant spiritual world rediscovered a new inflection of the emphasis on experience that had characterized its history. And, in the expression of William Adams Brown, professor of systematic theology at Union [Theological] Seminary in New York, the specific feature of Revivalistic theology seems to be echoed: "It is the connection with experience which gives the work of the theologian at once its dignity and its interest." Theology is not so much a call to systematize teachings that have been authoritatively received or found in Scripture, as the articulation in expressed meanings the wealth of "living convictions, born of experience."

Such a foundation of religious knowledge was judged adequate to safeguard the faith and the intellectual discourse organized around it from any critical attack, and to make them independent of any rational or exegetical scrutiny. Those "living convictions" were, in fact, felt to be able to maintain "themselves in spite of all opposition because of the response which they wake in the hearts and consciences of men."[33]

The affirmation of experience as the exhaustive critical locus and, in particular, the exaltation of the experience of values as the supreme criterion, would, at the turn of the nineteenth and twentieth centuries, also favour an intimate union between theology and pragmatism. Meanwhile, the metamorphosis of the idea of revelation was meant to ultimately clear the path for a radical acceptance of the methods and contents of German "high criticism."

IMMANENTISTIC CONCEPTION If we wish to identify the main factors of the theological vision that resulted from the aforementioned approach, we must focus on two essential points: the conception of the God-world relationship and the conception of the figure of Christ.

Immanentism characterizes the former. From this standpoint, Liberal theology posits itself in terms exactly contrary to the Sovereign God and absolute Lord of Calvinism, which, to one of the most notable representatives of the new climate, seemed to be, in the derivative doctrine of election, "arbitrary": "the ultimate blasphemy of thought."[34]

The range of versions into which immanentism was translated is vast: from positions that specify the concern for distinguishing themselves from pantheistic affirmations to others in which the demarcation lines are impossible to discern. However, one can say that the entire Liberal Movement participates in the idealistic-romantic reaction to eighteenth-century rationalistic deism, in the terms that John Herman Randall highlights: "[That] external deity completely disappeared for the romanticists and idealists: the world was no machine, it was alive, and God was not its creator so much as its soul, its life."[35] God is inner energy, the Spirit that inhabits the universe and determines its dynamism.

Evolutionism seemed to be the scientific proof of this profound God-world symbiosis. Moreover, the optimism towards the future that it opened appeared to be a confirmation of the divine presence at the root of the motion of things, and man, in particular, as *imago Dei*, fraught with a good force that, therefore, excludes any concept of "original depravity" and assures a high esteem for the human aptitude for perfection and fulfilment, and lays the foundation for the historical vision of the certainty of progress.

Liberal immanentism tends to generate a vaguely monistic affirmation of reality, whose first consequence is a nature-supernature relationship conceived without a solution of continuity. "Continuity" is precisely the first and most crucial category in the Liberal rationalization of experience. As John C. Bennett states, "Running through its whole theology there has been the assumption of continuity in the world – continuity between revelation and natural religion, between Christianity and other religions, between the saved and the lost, between Christ and other men, between man and God."[36]

CHRISTOCENTRIC VISION The figure of Christ constitutes, in the most literal sense of the word, the centre of the structuring of Liberal Theology, which affirms this stress by almost claiming the primacy of recovering the importance of Christ, whom the history of theology would have more or less marginalized since the times of the first councils, striving as always to pursue diligently the inner nature of God and to understand man's state before God. It is the "historical Jesus," integrally human, who seems to be rediscovered within a long line of interpretive development that more or less sought to diminish or deny the consistency and coherence of his human reality in explanations preoccupied with saving his exceptionality through extra-natural categories: "Liberalism took another step in the right direction in regarding the humanity of Jesus seriously. The church has always insisted that Jesus Christ was fully man, but it has hesitated to carry out all of the implications of this belief. A subtle docetism has always haunted the theology of the past, even when its more obvious forms were denounced. Liberal thinkers overcame this hesitancy to regard Jesus as fully man and called the attention of the church to the truth that whatever else he was, he was a human being in the fullest sense of the word."[37]

Liberal Christology varies greatly from one author to the other. In the second half of the [nineteenth] century, the predominant positions are Bushnellian, in which Jesus Christ is recognized as something more than a man, according to a type of diminished and confused Arianism: Jesus' consciousness, affirms one of the most notable systematic authors of the New Theology, "was neither that of God nor that of man exclusively, but was that of the unique God-man who was constituted by the Incarnation."[38] At the end of the nineteenth century and in the first decades of the twentieth, it is Harnack's solution that imposes itself.

Be that as it may, there are two points that are shared by almost all authors: the first is given by the rejection of the doctrine of the Incarnation with the specifications given according to traditional categories, as a dichotomy of Jesus' personality and, above all, as a derivative of speculation on the essence of the divine life, illusory because of the unfathomability of this subject. The second is given by the definition of the value and the meaning of the person of Jesus, expressed in the formula "God was in Christ"; in Christ's ethical-spiritual excellence, what God is for man is revealed: "In the perfection of the human is seen the clearest revelation of the divine."[39]

In this sense, for all of Liberalism, Jesus is more than simply the man from Nazareth; he is the only son of God, through whom man reaches God and in whom he grasps the interpretative principle which is decisive for his existence.

Here lies the transformative, "redemptive" power that Jesus exercises on man and history: a moral, paradigmatic power that is irreplaceable mediator for an ideal of humanity in which philosophy and science are close collaborators, mobilizing man and society in a dynamic that evolutionistic doctrine describes as law. Jesus' whole life exercises this function of a restorative influence, by constituting the "work of redemption": the Cross does not have a particular meaning, if not as the conclusive measure of an attitude of life, wherein lies the true value of Christ. Liberal Theology, therefore, clearly maintains a "subjective" doctrine of the reparation carried out by Christ, according to the terminology used by Gustaf Aulen, in his *Christus Victor*.

2 *Systematic Expositions of Liberal Theology*

The most noteworthy and useful books for an overall study of the Liberal theological vision in America are two attempts at a comprehensive and systematic exposition of doctrinal problematics.

The first, in chronological order, is *An Outline of Christian Theology* (1898), "perhaps the most influential book of its kind in American religious thinking."[40] The author, William Newton Clarke (1840–1912), after having been a pastor, was, from 1890 to 1908, professor at Colgate University, and the volume is a result of his lectures there. The "Bible centered on Christ" and "evangelical experience" are naturally the fundamental sources, but Clarke maintains that theology can seek its wellsprings "anywhere." Another of Clarke's notable works is *The Use of the Scriptures in Theology* (1905), as documentation of the diatribe between the evolutionistic conception of the Kingdom of God proper to the nineteenth-century Liberal school and emerging eschatological interpretations.

The second systematic exposition is *Christian Theology in Outline* (1906), by William Adams Brown (1865–1943), an active Presbyterian who went to von Harnack's school in Berlin for two years, and later was a professor at Union Theological Seminary in New York, from 1892 to 1936. He published his text, which is just as well known and utilized as that of Clarke, as a revision of it, transforming it with a more substantial interest in historical tradition: "there is an advantage in relating our modern statements to the older forms about which historic associations cluster."[41] The apologetic line of New Theology is marked by the triple task that Brown assigned to theology: to define and explain Christianity in the terms suggested by the personality of the historical Jesus, with his life and teachings, to identify its value in how effectively this appeal to Jesus Christ influences the ethical change of man and his relationships, and through this verification to achieve, as the explanation and wellspring of that value, faith in the existence of the Supreme Being as "Christiform," that is, as revealed in its personal characteristics by the moral makeup of Christ. It should be noted that Brown was clearly not only "influenced by German Ritschlianism, but also by William James' pragmatism."[42]

An eclectic "comprehensiveness" characterizes Brown's temperament throughout his whole opus. *Christ the Vitalizing Principle of Theology* (1898) reaffirms the Christocentric principle; and again, in

The Essence of Christianity (1902), he explains what in any era and any version of Christianity has always been saved, that is, "the progressive realization, in thought as in life, of the supremacy of Christ."[43] The appeal to Christian doctrine about God inspires wonderful pages in *Modern Theology and the Preaching of the Gospel* (1914), as well as much later in *Beliefs that Matter* (1928). *Is Christianity Practicable?* (1916) is interesting because, by detaching himself from an eschatological concept of the Kingdom of God, he approaches the Liberal futuristic trends that identify that kingdom as a social realization in this world. In *Pathways to Certainty* (1930), he defines an epistemology whereby religious truths can be validated by means of four pathways: authority, reason, intuition, and experience. With *God at Work* (1933), he attempts to approach the most objectivistic themes and interpretations of neo-orthodoxy. Furthermore, in two books, he tackles the problem of the Church, which in his more famous work was only dealt with in a marginal way: *The Church in America* (1922), where he assigns to the Church the task of bringing about "the unifying spiritual influence needed in a democracy,"[44] and *The Church, Catholic and Protestant* (1935), where he ecumenically foresees synthesis in which the two great Christian movements are no longer contradictory but complementary.

3 The Great Liberal Preachers

If Clarke and Brown are responsible for systematizing the corpus of Liberal doctrine, there is a great mass of authors who lent their support to the movement.

The greatest preachers placed themselves at the service of the new speculations: Henry Ward Beecher (1813–1887), who left works particularly of note, such as *Life of Christ* (1871) and *Sermons on Evolution and Religion* (1885); Phillips Brook (1835–1893), whose death was considered a public calamity, and whose publications include *Yale Lectures on Preaching* (1877), *The Influence of Jesus* (1879), *Essays and Addresses* (1892), and many other volumes of sermons, the last of which is *The Law of Growth* (1902); Lyman Abbott (1835–1922), who edited a book worthy of mention, *The Theology of an Evolutionist* (1897); George Angier Gordon (1835–1929), Congregationalist minister for more than forty years at the Old South Church of Boston, lecturer in the major universities, noted for his Trinitarian faith contrary to the general trends and, at the same time, for his impassioned defence of the integrally human reality of Christ, the culture of Plato and the Greek theological tradition, to the point of being labelled "the Origen of our age,"[45] author of numerous and very influential works, the best known of which was *The Christ of Today* (1895), but even more so *Immortality and New Theodicy* (1897), *The New Epoch of Faith* (1910), *Ultimate Conceptions of Faith* (1903; it is the published content of the Lyman Beecher Lectures given in 1902 at Yale University), *Through Man to God* (1906), *Religion and Miracle* (1909), *Aspects of the Infinite Mystery* (1916), and *Humanism in New England Theology* (1920).

In continuity with the aforementioned is the name of Harry Emerson Fosdick (1879–1969), for a long period the eminent preacher in America, leader in the diatribe sparked by the conservatives, known as "Fundamentalists" after 1920. In his autobiography, he wrote, "The fact that astronomies change while stars abide is a true analogy of every realm of human life and thought, religion not least of all. No existent theology can be a final formulation of spiritual truth ... What I have done I would do again and try to do better: believe both in abiding stars and changing astronomies."[46]

His most theologically significant works are from around 1920, thus representing the final phase of Liberal thought and the tension of a lively survival amid a radically changed environment. It is useful to recall works such as *The Meaning of Faith* (1919), with the problem of the nature of God; *Christianity and Progress* (1922), with its emphases on the sinful situation of human nature, exceptionally realistic for a Liberal work; *Adventurous Religion* (1926), with an analysis of the two types of historical Christianity, the essential one, which Christ himself lived, and the one stratified by creeds and theologies, all of which are contingent; *The Modern Use of the Bible* (1924), in which the criterion for grasping the significance of the Bible for today's world is indicated in the celebrated formula "permanent experiences and changeable categories"; in 1938, another work on the Bible, *A Guide to Understanding the Bible*, would be "widely recognized as being one of the best summaries available in English of the results of nineteenth-century critical scholarship";[47] *As I See Religion* (1932), in which he declares that the essence of religion is not belief in certain doctrines or participation in institutions, but individual experience, the subjective psychological event; *The Hope of the World* (1933) and *The Power to See It Through* (1935), with their analysis of the personality as the supreme category of religious and human discourse – "All my thinking starts from and comes back to it. Here it is: the key to the understanding of all life is the value of personality";[48] *The Secret of Victorious Living* (1934), in which there is a recovery of emphasis on the Cross as a sacrifice for mankind, even though the work of redemption lies not so much in expiation per se, as in the impressive and corroborating encounter with the merciful personality of God; and, finally, one should cite *On Being a Real Person* (1943), with its discourse on the difficulties and supports for man's ascesis and behavioural education.

4 *The Contribution of Universities*

Even more than at the pulpit, it is in the university that the most important factors of Liberal discourse are to be found. We will indicate a selection of some of the most important.

THE "PROGRESSIVE ORTHODOXY" OF ANDOVER An active centre of new ideas was the Theology Department of Andover Seminary which, with the intention of adapting Park's traditionalist Calvinism to the new times while remaining orthodox, wound up practically abandoning its Calvinist starting point.

This evolution, especially with regard to the conception of the person of Christ, can be found in a two-volume collection of the works of the professors of the faculty: *Progressive Orthodoxy* (1885) and *The Divinity of Jesus Christ* (1893). The title of Progressive Orthodoxy also applies to the Andover group as a particular school, and it is, at times, used in place of New Theology, more broadly indicative of the Liberal Movement in general. The principal name in the group and editor of the two volumes is Egbert Coffin Smyth (1829–1904), the author of the polemic *The Andover Delenee* (1891).

Some of the most valid Liberal exponents were trained at Andover, such as John W. Buckham (1864–1945), in his latter years professor at Pacific Theological Seminary (now the Pacific School of Religion), whose noteworthy works include *Christ and the Eternal Order* (1906), *Personality and the Christian Ideal* (1909), *Personality and Psychology* (1924), *The Humanity of God* (1928), but, above all, *Progressive Religious Thought in America* (1919), in which the grave experience of war suggests more caution in maintaining the optimism inherited from Andover: "It seemed to many of us who were studying theology and beginning our ministry in the eighties and nineties as if humanity were on the eve of the golden age ... The Kingdom of God appeared to be at hand."[49]

Together with the Andover group, the name of the Congregationalist pastor Newman Smyth (1843–1925) should be mentioned. Smyth, who was invited to take the place of Park in that theological school, was hindered by the partisans of the old school. His strong and influential production reflects the later concerns of New Theology: first, the new religious epistemology introduced by Scheiermacher, based on "feeling" and "intuition," in *The Religious Feeling* (1877); then, the application of the evolutionistic principle to all of theological discourse, in *Old Faiths in New Light* (1879); the problems created for religion by the invading certainty in the ability of science to definitively explain the world, in *The Place of Death and Evolution* (1897), *Through Science to Faith* (1902), and *Constructive Natural Theology* (1913); the efficiency of the Church in a society dominated by technology, in *Passing Protestantism and Coming Catholicism* (1908); finally, the value of the person in social life, in *The Meaning of Personal Life* (1916).

LIBERAL FERMENT IN UNION THEOLOGICAL SEMINARY, NEW YORK Another place in which we find creative support for the new ideas, albeit not in the form of a well-defined group as at Andover, is Union Theological Seminary in New York.

Charles Augustus Briggs (1841–1913) is famous for the serious controversy caused by his inaugural speech upon being appointed to the chair of biblical theology: the speech, published as *The Authority of Holy Scripture: An Inaugural Address* (1891), although rather conservative in ideas, especially on the Trinity and Christology, advocated the new criticism and attacked the dogma of biblical inerrancy. Briggs was forced to abandon his ministry as a Presbyterian pastor, and Union [Theological] Seminary itself broke its ties with the Presbyterian Church.

The central idea of Arthur Cushman McGiffert (1861–1933) – a fervent disciple of Harnack in Germany, and for a quarter-century professor of Church history at Union [Theological] Seminary, and its president from 1917 to 1926 – was the optimistic vision of the Kingdom of God as an earthly endeavour: "The kingdom of God on earth, what does it mean? We answer perhaps glibly enough: the control of the lives of men and of all their relationships one with another and of all the institutions in which those relationships find expression by the spirit of Jesus Christ who has shown us what God is and what he would have this world be."[50] His theological interpretation is well expressed in the collection of his works published posthumously by his son, entitled *Christianity as History and Faith* (1934), while his most-read works are *A History of Christianity in the Apostolic Age* (1897) and *The History of Christian Thought* (2 vols, 1932–33), to this day utilized in theological schools.

The central concern of Eugene William Lyman (1872–1948) – who had the occasion to spend time in Europe with Herrmann and Harnack and later Bergson, Eucken, and Troeltsch – was, instead, to situate a Christocentric theology within the context of a philosophically founded vision of reality. During his long career as professor of philosophy of religion, beginning in 1913 at Oberlin, but above all, from 1918 to 1940 at Union Theological Seminary, he would give a restless response to that preoccupation, which would cause him to move in an unsatisfied way from the metaphysical agnosticism of Kant and Ritschl to pragmatism and later to Whitehead.

His first book, *Theology and Human Problems* (1910), adopts the vision of reality of pragmatism, because it alone can safeguard the evidence of religious and ethical experience, thus, constituting an antidote to scientific materialism; furthermore, by recovering the essential meaning of time as the place where new levels of being emerge, it recognizes with certainty that intrinsic dynamic within reality, that evolution in which is documented and expressed the Immanent Creator Spirit and ethical power which moves man from within, thus developing his personality. Christ, notes Lyman, while reaffirming the liberal principle of "continuity," represents the highest expression of the experience that this dynamic Supreme Presence of man makes in every conscious moment. It is through the growth of this conscience that Redemption takes place, defined as "the process of recovering the sinful personality into a life of God, and of neutralizing the moral wrong done by man to man, through the power of self-sacrificing love."[51] This neutralization, as he optimistically affirms, is assured by the compensating and healing ability of natural or social forces in the evolutionary dialectic.

This optimism is the basis of another address in 1917, published under the title of *The God of the New-Age: A Tract for the Times*: the Kingdom of God is the reality of a democratic society, and the Church must conceive of herself exclusively as an instrument of it. However, the war initially mutes the proclaimed accord between dynamism and good: *The Experience of God in Modern Life* (1918) recognizes that a certain limit impedes divine action in its harmonious aims, and evil is identified as a necessary condition to the cosmic process. Optimism is further reduced in his most complete work, *The Meaning and Truth of Religion* (1933); Lyman faces the epistemological problem whose solution is affirmed in a synthesis of *intuition*, as immediate perception of an objective order of being and value; of *reason*, as the verification of intuitions based on their capacity for coherence; of *faith*, as dedication to the intuited values, necessary for full understanding of religious truth and founded on trust in God as "cosmic moral will." The development of science, and Whitehead's cosmology, are used as confirmations of God as a factor of progress and final causality immanent to the evolutionary phenomena of nature and history. But, this divine immanence is decisively qualified because it must, in part, act in contradiction to nature and man. In the spontaneity of the movements of individual finite realities, particularly in man's freedom, there emerges a resistance to divine influence and to the divine aim. Yet, to the degree in which man responds to God, there is assured the progress towards a human community formulated according to the ideals by which it represents the historical end-point of the divine vision. Lyman's perspective implies a progressive assimilation of human wills to the will of God through work, which is collaboration with it. This integration of the human person with the progressive tendencies of the structure of the whole world is what is meant by salvation. But it is not an automatic salvation, although it is possible and history, indeed, reveals a direction towards it: "our previous study of the new cosmology and of the new interpretations of evolution should not lead us to look for any automatic progress in history nor to conceive progress as something to be easily achieved."[52]

THE RADICALISM OF THE CHICAGO SCHOOL The most radical formulation of the Liberal Movement was that of the Divinity School of [the University of] Chicago, where the influence of the naturalistic pragmatism dominant in that university (the figure of John Dewey) led to the abandonment of any metaphysical concern and idealistic systems and to the adoption of an extremist positivistic modernism with the ever more marked tendency to reduce Christianity in meanings functional to current demands.

The most conspicuous name is most certainly that of the Baptist Shailer Mathews (1863–1941). Beginning in 1894, he taught New Testament history at the University of Chicago, and was later professor of systematic and historical theology in that institution's theological faculty; from 1908 to 1933, he was its dean. The importance of the personality of this author in the American Protestant world is evidenced by the fact that from 1912 to 1916 he was president of the Federal Council of the Churches of Christ in America.

For Mathews, Christianity is more a way of life than of belief; it is not an adherence to dogmas, but a religious and social movement with a historical continuity that begins with Jesus and continues as the Church, albeit through a variety of interpretations and expressions. This is what Mathews energetically shows from his earliest writings: *Social Teaching of Jesus* (1897), *The Messianic Hope in the New Testament* (1905), and *The Church and the Changing Order* (1907).

Seeking a method of appraisal and control of Christian teaching and of its truths beyond systems of formulations, in the famous *The Faith of Modernism* (1924), he defines it as "the use of the methods of modern science to find, state and use the permanent and central values of orthodoxy."[53] "Science" would, thus, be the final criterion in matters of faith. Doctrinal expressions, as he says in *Atonement and the Social Process* (1930), exhaust their meaning as a function of the attempt to formulate a relationship between the person and the social dynamic that nourishes him.

According to this methodological approach, evil and "sin" coincide with the frustration of the personality insofar as its growth is "disorganized," that is, broken apart from the environmental, cosmic, and social environment, above all, because he is hindered in the face of the sufferings inherent to the process of reality or because he turns to already supplanted levels of situations or goods. Salvation is given, above all, as he maintains in *The Gospel and Modern Man* (1910), by the achievement of a new spiritual level that assures a just dynamism beyond the hindrances of struggle and sorrow, and more fully – as is described in *Contributions of Science to Religion* (1924) – by the systematic effort to adapt to the energies of progress in society and the universe which solicit the human personality to undertake the spiritual growth in which the evolutionary process of nature has constituted it. In this sense, the experience of Jesus has supreme value as example, and, in particular, the idea of resurrection "heralds the fact that Jesus, while suffering from others' maladjustment to personality-evolving forces of the cosmic process, triumphed through his own adjustment to those forces."[54] Jesus had affirmed the supremacy of spiritual forces over animal instincts and the blind motions of nature. Indeed, history is a sure path towards the moralization of the human personality and of society: this is the claim of *The Social Gospel* (1909) and *The Individual and the Social Gospel* (1914). It is reconfirmed, without the world situation diminishing his conviction, also in his 1916 work, *The Spiritual Interpretation of History*, according to which "if it be prolonged, will bring the world under the sway of the ideals of Jesus himself," and by pursuing them, men will "be the leaven of that better social order that shall make the world into the kingdom of brothers who, free spirits in the midst of physical forces and economic tensions, are the true children of God the Father Almighty." Moreover, historical perspective seemed to legitimize the following statement: "War is a survival we shall yet outgrow."[55]

The idea of God, which Mathews from the beginning defined as "the Universal Life and Will and Love" or "the personalized Whole,"[56] evolves in a more naturalistic direction in the works of his final period: *The Growth of the Idea of God* (1931), *Immortality and the Cosmic Process* (1933), and *Is God Emeritus?* (1940), and it is tightly bound in Mathews' formulation to ultimate meaning which he gives to cosmic evolution, that is, to the formation and valuing of the personal fact: "the total process in which men are involved is toward personal values,"[57] and God, in a universe understood monistically, is the cosmic whole insofar as it expresses and increases the reality of the person, and his idea is, therefore, formulated according to the conception of the relationship between man and the universe that science generates in society.

Alongside Shailer Mathews, among names such as George Burman Foster (1858–1918) and Shirley Jackson Case (1872–1947), there is the even more radical Gerald Birney Smith (1868–1929), from 1900 until his death professor in the Divinity School at [the University of] Chicago. A convinced advocate of Ritschl's criteria, Smith affirms that historical Christian tradition has the sole task of favouring within our present human experience the emergence of convictions that can concretely influence our current situation and that they be comprehensible to the needs of current culture. His completely relativistic interpretation of Christianity is expressed, above all, in articles in the *Journal of Religion*, of which he was editor, and in the works *Practical Theology* (1903), *Social Idealism and the Changing Theology* (1913), *Principles of Christian Living* (1924), and *Current Christian Thinking* (1928).

Some expressions of the Chicago school completely identified themselves with naturalism and reduced religion to pure humanism, and the study of religion to pure psychology or ethics. Edward Scribner Ames (1870–1958), for thirty-five years professor of philosophy at the University of Chicago, and for fifty years pastor of the University Church of the Disciples of Christ, in his *Psychology of Religious Experience* (1910), stated, "The psychology of religious experience ... is the science which in its developed forms becomes theology or the philosophy of religion."[58]

THE PERSONALISM OF BOSTON AND OBERLIN If the philosophical inspiration of New Theology is mainly Kantian, "personalist" currents influenced by the spiritualism of Lotze also had a strong presence.

The initiator of the Personalist school at the Philosophy Department of Boston University was Borden Parker Bowne (1847–1910), a disciple and friend of Lotze. His thought became the liberalizing ferment in the heart of traditional theology, especially in the Methodist world of which Bowne was a part, to the point of developing an imposing movement. Indeed, at a certain point, the conservative wing of the Methodist Church condemned him as heretical: "In many ways, he became the Socrates of the Methodist church."[59]

His long career teaching philosophy at Boston University (from 1876 until his death) was accompanied by an intense productivity, setting forth the "first complete and comprehensive system of philosophy developed in America which has had lasting influence."[60] Among his most interesting works, from the standpoint of religious conception, are: *Metaphysics: A Study in First Principles* (1882, dedicated to Lotze), *Philosophy of Theism* (1887), *The Principles of Ethics* (1892), *The Immanence of God* (1902), *Personalism, Common Sense and Philosophy* (1908), and *Studies in Christianity* (1909).

In his conception, the sole "being," the only "real thing" that emerges immediately to our awareness is the personal I. The experience of the I is the starting point and offers content to the systematic consideration of reality. Substance is given to other things only as an analogous projection of the experience of the personal I. All of reality is a multiplicity of persons, each of which is an autonomous source of movement and relationship, a law unto itself. Material reality is nothing other than the phenomenon of the appearance of personal activity: "what we call things" are nothing other than a web of relationships subsisting in the mind, and these relationships "are nothing in abstraction from a mind which constitutes and maintains them."[61] The nature of reality is given by personal creativity, which is what truly constitutes things: "those things exist which act."[62]

The experience of the self connotes the fact that the whole of its "external" reference constitutes a "universe," an ordered unity, full of intentionality. The eminent intelligibility of the universe implies a universal regulating mind, and the inexhaustibility of the meaning of its constitutive relationships postulates the infinity of that mind. The intelligence and will of the universe together could be called God; the world is his activity. In particular, God produces an interaction among the multiplicity of people, from which the harmony of the whole intention inevitably springs.

In reducing this interaction that constitutes the cosmos to divine activity, which acts "across individuality," Bowne ultimately denies the independence and, therefore, the self-determination of the human self, with a return to a vision that seems almost Edwardsian. On the other hand, precisely because of the assuredness of the interaction of our human existence, the dynamic of social life and the course of history are essentially "moral." Values have an imperishable consistency or validity, and optimism is an inevitable fundamental consequence. God, therefore, lives in Bowne's system according to the Liberal version of immanence, and his "benevolence" is ultimately interpreted in a polemic with the Calvinism of Edwards: "the God of theology for a long time hardly attained to any real active goodness, such as the thought of ethical love implies. This God, too, was rather metaphysically conceived, and his holiness consisted mainly in making rules for men and in punishing their transgression. He was conceived largely after the fashion of a medieval despot, and the conception of any obligation on his part to his creatures would have been looked upon almost as blasphemy … We see that the law of love applies to power as well as to weakness."[63]

About Bowne, it should be noted, although it is an observation common to all of Liberal literature, that if his optimistic emphasis on the concordance of the Divine with the dynamic of the human phenomenon is a sentimental one, it is never to the detriment of moral urgency. Bowne himself reminds us, not without diffidence towards theology as a speculative system, a diffidence, nevertheless, common to the Liberals in general: "But for the practical realization of this divine presence, logic and speculation can do little for us. This belief must be lived to acquire any real substance or controlling character. This is the case with all practical and concrete beliefs. If we ignore them practically we may soon accost them skeptically; and they vanish like a fading gleam."[64]

Along with Bowne, and because of his Lotzean inspiration, albeit along a different line of development, stands Henry Churchill King (1858–1934), professor (1891) and later president of Oberlin College from 1902 to 1927. Whereas for Bowne the personality is mainly the supreme category of a metaphysical vision, in King, according to a vision more reminiscent of Ritschl, the "primacy of the personal" is, above all, a fundamental category for a structure of values. The key to such a structure is love for Christ: "the love of Christ as a person has, as a matter of fact, proved the mightiest of historical motives to noble living."[65] King's principal work is *Reconstruction in Theology* (1899), which represents the most comprehensive formulation of a "program" of theological renewal according to the canons of evolutionary science and of the philological positivism of biblical criticism. Other works worthy of mention are *Theology and Social Consciousness* (1902), *Rational Living* (1905), *The Ethics of Jesus* (1910), *Religion as Life* (1913), *Fundamental Questions* (1917) and *Seeing Life Whole* (1923).

Along the lines of Bowne's interpretation, the most serious attempt to found a theological system on the personalistic philosophy of Lotze is that of Albert Cornelius Knudson (1873–1953), originally Methodist, a disciple of Bowne at Boston University, and from 1906 professor at its Divinity School. Among his abundant works, the following should be noted: *The Religious Teachings of the Old Testament* (1918), *The Validity of Religious Experience* (1937), *Principles of Christian Ethics* (1943), but, above all, *The Doctrine of God* (1930) and *The Doctrine of Redemption* (1933), which strictly link together from the exposition of his theological vision. This vision represents a fruit out of season, having ripened in times in which Liberalism was already radically put in crisis by new positions.

Knudson confirms the Liberal approach by which "theology is not so much a description of God's redemptive activity as it is an elaboration of man's experience of God."[66] This experience, in its content, marks the existence of the Supreme Person: "Personality in its essence means 'self-hood, self-knowledge and self-direction,' and in these respects it may be either finite or infinite."[67] Even traditional argumentation, even though it is not conclusive as demonstration, is to be esteemed as confirmation of the fact of religious experience, in as much as "the theistic world-view is 'the line of least resistance' for the intellect as it is also for the moral and religious nature."[68] The Infinite Person, ethically perfect, cannot be considered according to the traditional Trinitarian interpretation because it is the fruit of Platonism, which does not posit the personality as the *primum* upon which everything else rests, but subordinates it to essence; the Trinity is a sign that expresses, above all, social values. The physical world's consistency exists only as phenomenon, but it is a direct and continual expression of the divine mind and, thus, profoundly suited to divine ends. Evil in the world is, ultimately, an appearance based upon our ignorance, since "if we know all, as God does, the unideal aspects of the world would not seem so entirely out of harmony with an absolute and holy love as they do now."[69] The concept of salvation is reduced to the psychological reality of a positive attitude towards the intrinsic goodness of the real; and Christ is defined in terms of an example that provokes human responsibility to that positivity. The meaning of Church is to be an instrument of the continuation of that provocation, and Knudson values the sacraments because "they symbolize and mediate the spiritual influence exercised by Christian society upon the individual. In this sense they may be said to represent an objective or superindividual reality," although "it is only in this sense that they do so."[70]

The Lotzean conception of an Absolute Person, who has revealed itself in the world, in the self, and in society, also dominates the work of William De Witt Hyde (1858–1917), [author of] *Outlines of Social Theology* (1895). Professor and president of Bowdoin College for more than thirty years, Hyde was an extremely influential personality in teaching. His other noteworthy works include *Practical Ethics* (1892), *Practical Idealism* (1897), *Sin and Forgiveness* (1909), and *The Five Great Philosophies of Life* (1911).

III THE SOCIAL GOSPEL AND WALTER RAUSCHENBUSCH

Beyond immanentistic and Christological categories, there is another that defines the face of New Theology in its definitive formulations: the social category. It was already discernible in Bushnell, and found its methods in the opposition to the Revivalists. Those who thought that the problem of salvation did not exhaust itself in the phenomenon of individual conference became more and more numerous; they believed that a "redemption" more necessary than the individual one obtained by the Revivals was the redemption of social evils: the Gospel was not only an invitation to charity, but also to justice.

This appeal became the ever more dominant one following the end of the Civil War. The dizzying crescendo of industrialization, and its consequent urbanization, brought with it social unease and class struggle along with the problem of the distribution of goods, or the drama of unemployment and of the miserable living conditions of the urban poor. The Protestant movement of thought and action, which committed itself to trying to solve the inadequacy of the situation, has passed into history with the name of Social Gospel.

The origin of the term can be found in the title of a communally edited monthly, published between 1896 and 1900, in Georgia, through the efforts of hundreds of people who had been mobilized by the prophetic Christian Socialism of George Herron: *The Social Gospel, a magazine of obedience to the law of love*. Spread in this way, the Social Gospel formula was also consecrated in academic usage by the title that Shailer Mathews gave to his volume on the social teachings of Jesus, *The Social Gospel*, published in 1910.[71]

From the very beginnings of the twentieth century, the movement was usually referred to as "Social Christianity."[72]

1 The Social Gospel's Theoretical Inspiration

In its motivations and structure, its theories derive completely from the Liberalism of New Theology.

This observation is undeniable, because a certain part of the vastness of theological Liberalism remained socially conservative for a long time, and those exponents who were sensitive to social issues were at first a minority, albeit an enthusiastic and influential one. Even the churches as such, supported by the wealthy and generally made up of middle-class faithful, did not hide their official antipathy to organizations that defended the rights of the workers. One historian had the following to say about American Protestantism at the end of the nineteenth century: "at the time Protestantism in America achieved its greatest dominance of the culture, it had also achieved an almost complete ideological and emotional identification with burgeoning bourgeois society and the free-enterprise system."[73] Only at the end of the nineteenth and the beginning of the twentieth centuries did the interest fomented by the pioneers of social concern gain general and stable public attention. The churches began to formulate programmatic and socially committed statements, and in 1908, the Federal Council of the Churches of Christ in America, which now includes three-quarters of American Protestantism, adopted the Social Creed – "almost universally adopted by the Protestant denominations of America."[74] In the first two decades of the century, "social preaching" upheld the banner in an almost exclusive way.

As far as theology is concerned, the fundamental orientation of the theories developed within the sphere of the Social Gospel reflects a type of corollary to the Christocentrism and immanentism of New Theology. The ethics of the historical Jesus, in its essence, was understood as a code of social principles that were applicable to any era and were based around the law of love. Furthermore, divine immanence, on the one hand, assured the substantial goodness of man and, on the other, the progressive destiny of history to eliminate the injustice of situations towards an ever greater harmony: in ultimate analysis, sin would be none other than a developmental defect resulting from the prevalence of inertia and selfishness, a defect that social institutions crystallize and tend to perpetuate, whereas an adequate education leads to a breaking up of narrowmindedness and to liberating a more advanced communitarian sense.

The synthesizing idea, the fulcrum of the whole Social Gospel Movement, is the idea of the Kingdom of God as something that can be realized on earth, as a historical possibility. The figure of Jesus, as venerated and interpreted according to the spirit of Harnack, was credited with the intuition of a philosophy of history full of optimism, in which a permanent ideal in the American Protestant religious tradition – the Puritan idea of the "Sovereignty of God" and of a Christian society – converged with the Revivalistic idea of the Kingdom of Christ,[75] the naturalistic anthropology of the Englightenment,[76] and confidence in the definitive meaning of evolutionistic theories and the programs of science.

2 *Significant Exponents*

Among the most distinctive figures in the Social Gospel Movement are the Lutheran John Henry Wilbrandt Stuckenberg (1835–1903) of Wittenberg College, whose *Christian Sociology* (1880) was the first formulation of "social theology"; Josiah Strong (1847–1916), with his main publications *Our Country, its Possible Future and its Present Crisis* (1885) – which constituted one of the most famous contributions of the whole movement's history: *The New Era or the Coming Kingdom* (1893) and *The Next Great Awakening* (1920); George Davis Herron (1862–1925), with his radical socialism and his exalted messianism, and with his more controversial books *The New Redemption: A Call to the Church to Reconstruct Society According to the Gospel of Christ* (1893), *The Christian Society* (1894), and *The Christian State* (1895); Richard Theodore Ely (1854–1943), who integrated evangelical principles into economic science (of which he was a well-known professor at Johns Hopkins University) and whose most significant publications for the history of the Social Gospel are *Social Aspects of Christianity and Other Essays* (1889) and *The Social Law of Service* (1896); Francis Greenwood Peabody (1847–1936), "probably the first teacher of social ethics in the United States,"[77] with *Jesus Christ and the Social Question* (1900).

However, the personalities who "did more ... to direct the mind of the churches toward the social problem than any of their contemporaries"[78] were Gladden and Rauschenbusch, one at the beginning and the other at the end of the flowering of the movement.

3 *Washington Gladden, "Father" of the Social Gospel*

Washington Gladden (1836–1918), a Congregationalist minister seized by the Liberal mentality thanks to Bushnell's influence, marks the beginning of the enormous literary production of the Social Gospel, with the publication of the conferences he gave to the unemployed and the businessmen of Springfield in a book entitled, *Working People and Their Employers* (1876). In it, he posits the fundamental theme among all the interests of Social Christianity, the relationship between capital and labour. The outlines of his approach are as follows: "Now that slavery is out of the way, the questions that concern the welfare of our free laborers are coming forward; and no intelligent man needs to be admonished of their urgency. They are not only questions of economy, they are in a large sense moral questions; nay, they touch the very marrow of that religion of good will of which Christ was the founder."[79]

COOPERATION: THE EVANGELICAL FORMULA FOR THE SOLUTION TO SOCIAL EVILS In the same work, a formula that would technically solve the problem is highlighted, a formula that would become the watchword for the whole Social Gospel: "The subjugation of labor by capital is the first stage in the progress of industry; the second stage is the warfare between labor and capital; the third is the identification of labor and capital by some application of the principal of cooperation. This is what we are coming to by and by. The long struggle between these two conflicting interests promises to end by uniting them, and making the laborer his own capitalist."[80] In substance, Gladden asserts, "cooperation is nothing more than the arrangement of the essential factors of industry according to the Christian rule, 'We being many are one body in Christ, and every one members one of another.' It is capital and labor adjusting themselves to the form of Christianity; and, like every other outward symbol, is a false deceitful show, a dead form, unless filled with the living spirit of Christianity itself."[81]

The same problem, and the same diagnosis, form the content of Gladden's best-known work, published exactly sixteen years later (1886), in which he makes the same affirmation of the immediate therapeutic capacity of evangelical principles when applied to social ills: "Christianity is a law, as well as a gospel. And the Christian law, faithfully preached, as the foundation of the gospel, will put an end to all this trouble."[82]

Cooperation also means the possibility that entire industries be managed by workers, and it requires that monopolies be taken over by the government; but it does not imply the abolition of private property, which is, indeed, indispensable for the normal development of the human personality and for the fecundity of society – as he sustains in *Christianity and Socialism* (1905).

Other works will echo and apply the same content: *Tools and the Man: Property and Industry under the Christian Law* (1893), *Social Facts and Forces: The Factory, the Labor Union, the Corporation, the Railways, the City, the Church* (1897), *The Social Salvation* (1920), *The Church and Modern Life* (1908), and *The Labor Question* (1911).

Gladden demonstrated the coherence of his own social commitment in 1905 when, as moderator of the National Council of the Congregational Churches, he vociferously opposed accepting a gift of $100,000 for missions, offered by John D. Rockefeller of the Standard Oil Company: his passionate arguments against "dirty money" are collected in *The New Idolatry and Other Discussions* (1905).

THEOLOGICAL THEMES Much of Gladden's literary production is focused on interpreting New Testament doctrines as motivations for his social commitment. His central concern was, naturally, that of showing how the fundamental Christian doctrines could be reconciled and, indeed, with great advantage for their meaning, with modern science and evolutionistic theories; such is the case with *Burning Questions of the Life that Now Is and that Which Is to Come* (1889).

In the first place, biblical criticism has diminished the value of the sacred texts by eliminating the doctrine of "infallibility," as he explains in *How Much is the Bible Worth?* (1891): "[The Bible] is not infallible historically ... It is not infallible scientifically ... It is not infallible morally ... Not to recognize the partialness and imperfection of this record in all these respects is to be guilty of a grave disloyalty to the kingdom of the truth."[83] Divine immanence provides a new univocal applicability to the concept of revelation, as Gladden clearly emphasizes in *How Much is Left of the Old Doctrines?* (1899): "Surely if God is in this world, he must be revealing himself to us in all its laws and forces, and therefore all ordered knowledge of the world must be tributary to that great unifying revelation wherein faith and knowledge are no longer twain, but one."[84]

Christ represents the summit of what is, nevertheless, manifested in "every good man." Jesus is the supreme expression of human perfection. And the recognition of this excellence of Christian reality is a revelation that can be experienced, as described in *Present Day Theology* (1913): "[This is how] present-day theology undertakes to find out what it ought to think about Christ. It does not go to the councils or the creeds or the philosophers. It finds confusion and darkness in all these speculations. It goes directly to Jesus Christ himself ... The present-day theology proposes to put this teaching of Jesus to the test of life. And by this purely scientific experiment it verifies his claims. It finds that those who open their minds to his teaching and their lives to his spirit, who become identified with him in thought and feeling, do find peace of mind, strength to resist temptation, courage and hope and moral vigor. In short, they find that fellowship with Jesus brings God into their lives, brings into their lives that practical power to help and to deliver which we call God. There is no speculation about this, it is an actual experience."[85]

Salvation lies in feeling helpful and ethically vigorous. And, from the individual, this salvation flows back onto society and its structures. The Kingdom of God advances concretely and irresistibly, as Gladden wrote in 1895, in *Ruling Ideas of the Present Age*: "The thought of this world is gradually being freed from superstition and prejudice; the social sentiments are being purified; the customs are slowly changing for the better; the laws are gradually shaped by finer conceptions of justice."[86]

The relationship between Church and Kingdom of God is discussed in *The Church and the Kingdom* (1894), in which the author insists on the obvious version of the Social Gospel, which defined the Church as an instrument of the good of society in which the Kingdom of God is realized: "we may say that the kingdom of God is the whole social organism so far as it is affected by divine influences ... humanity is one body with many members. Every organism is the produce of one coordinating life force; and the vital principle of this social organism is the life which is in Christ ... Now I do not think that the word 'church' can be very well stretched to cover all this. I do not believe that politics and business and art and literature are properly departments of church life ... The kingdom of heaven is the entire social organism and its ideal perfection; the church is one of the organs – the most central and important of them all – having much the same relation to Christian society that the brain has to the body."[87]

4 *Walter Rauschenbusch: The "Most Convincing" Theoretician*

If Gladden was named "father of the Social Gospel," Walter Rauschenbusch (1861–1918) was called by Reinhold Niebuhr its "most celebrated exponent."[88] His education was marked by Baptist individualism, but his encounter with the problems that plagued the lives of workers in his New York parish – where he carried out his pastoral activities from 1886 to 1897 – awoke in him a lively social concern. He immediately joined with friends in publishing a monthly review aimed at discussing "the interests of the working people of New York City," "from the standpoint of Christian-socialism."[89] The journal *For the Right* had a brief life (1889–1891), but its social passion would develop into a systematic expression that assigned to Rauschenbusch "the central place in an important chapter in American church history."[90] Numerous trips to Europe awakened in him an interest in economics and, above, all theology in Germany – by which he acquired a deep affinity for the thought of Ritschl, Wellhausen, and Harnack – and sociology in England – where he was the guest of the leaders of the Fabian Socialist Movement, Sidney and Beatrice Webb.

Rauschenbusch's enormous influence is due, above all, to his books, even more so than to the reputation he acquired through his academic activity at the Rochester Theological Seminary, beginning in 1897, especially as the chairman of Church history which position he held from 1902 until his death: his entire opus was characterized by a historical interest.

Two works, one at the beginning and the other at the end of his publishing career, represent the expressive cornerstone of his thought: *Christianity and the Social Crisis* (1907) and *A Theology for the Social Gospel* (1919).

HISTORICAL REVISION AS POINT OF DEPARTURE The first book was, against all predictions, enormously successful (six editions in less than two years), and skyrocketed the author to the leadership of the Social Christianity Movement and to the forefront of national public opinion: "It could not have such an impact had Americans of this era supposed that widespread 'spiritual unrest' was the concern only of clergymen ...The popularity which came overnight to Walter Rauschenbusch was evidence that Americans from all walks of life – not just the clergy –recognized he was responding to a central dilemma that had developed in American cultural and intellectual life."[91]

Christianity and the Social Crisis could be defined as a reappraisal of the essence of Christianity within the context of its entire history until the present day. This historical revision moves from the recovery of the "religion ethical and therefore social" of the Hebrew prophets to a description of "The Social Impetus of Primitive Christianity" and to a clarification of "Why has Christianity Never Undertaken the Work of Social Reconstruction?" reaching the point, therefore, of indicating "The Present Crisis" and, by determining "The Stake of the Church in the Social Movement" delineates "What to Do."

However, the historical revision is, as it were, the cue for the discovery of the second chapter, "The Social Aims of Jesus," out of which emerges the core idea of the book and of Rauschenbusch's entire system of thought: the idea of the "kingdom of God on earth" as the essence of the message that encompasses the entire meaning of the figure of Christ. "Jesus began his preaching," he writes, "with the call: 'The time is fulfilled; the kingdom of God is now close at hand; repent and believe in the glad news.' The kingdom of God continued to be the centre of all his teaching as recorded by the synoptic gospels. His parables, his moral instructions, and his prophetic predictions all bear on that." The meaning of this passage was obvious to his audience. It pertained to the hope of the people for "changes in the course of its history," even if it were through a final catastrophe.[92] But Jesus brought decisive corrections to the popular conception, above all, in terms of the way in which the Kingdom would come about: "While they were waiting for the Messianic cataclysm that would bring the kingdom of God ready-made from heaven, he saw it growing up among them. He took his illustrations of its coming from organic life ... Jesus had the scientific insight which comes to most men only by training, but to the elect few by divine gift. He grasped the substance of that law of organic development in nature and history which our own day at last has begun to elaborate systematically." Thus, through slow, seedlike communication to individuals, Jesus aimed towards society's change: "He knew ... that a new society would have to nucleate around personal centres of renewal. But his end was not the new soul, but the new society; not man, but Man."[93] A social reality was already present in act, that is, the Kingdom of God preached by Jesus: "If he put his trust in spiritual forces for the founding of a righteous society, it only proved his sagacity as a society-builder. If he began his work with the smallest social nuclei, it proved his patience and skill." The most subversive error that one could commit in transmitting the message would be to dissolve it into the concern for the individual salvation of the soul in the hereafter: "But Jesus never fell into the fundamental heresy of later theology; he never viewed the human individual apart from human society; he never forgot the gregarious nature of man. His first appeal was to his nation."[94]

The whole ethics of Jesus has meaning only in terms of this vision of the Kingdom: the moral being is the same as the social being. Thus, the only law is love, the force that eminently generates social good. Thus, one can understand the difference between Jesus and Jewish institutionalism, a difference that is replicated now in the dialectic between the recovery of the genuine idea of the Kingdom affirmed by Jesus and ecclesiastical institutionalism: "[For the Jews of his time] the written Law inherited from the past was the supreme thing; to Jesus the better human life to be established in the future was the supreme thing."[95] Wealth was evil if it was not used for society, the new and just society that would assert itself in the world and which Jesus was inaugurating: not an ascetic preoccupation, but a "revolutionary awareness" dictated Christ's words, the awareness of a profound revolution that would involve all of the aspects of human life in a harmonic event that evolutionary history would ensure beyond present resistance or the Cross. It is important to recognize, Rauschenbusch insists, "that Jesus was not a mere social reformer. Religion was at the heart of his life, and all that he said on social relations was said from the religious point of view. He has been called the first socialist. He was more; he was the first real man, the inaugurator of a new humanity. But as such he bore within him the germs of a new social and political order."[96]

Primitive Christianity had been aware of the great occasion and engaged in a mission to bring about this new order. Now, after so many centuries, for the first time in history, the clear awareness of the significances of Christ's work and, therefore, of the urgency of the "new apostolate" bursts forth: "The championship of social justice is almost the only way left open to a Christian nowadays to gain the crown of martyrdom. Theological heretics are rarely persecuted now. The only rival of God is mammon."

Rauschenbusch notes that his vision does not carry with it a utopian illusion; the author recognizes that "there is always but an approximation to a perfect social order. The kingdom of God is always but coming. But every approximation to it is worth while."[97]

Yet, the dialectic of this paradox, which parallels the moral situation of the individual, by which man makes "it a duty to seek what is unattainable," is, in the end, in complete and final seriousness, broken and surmounted by Rauschenbusch. What determines and characterizes his message is not the tension, the struggle, and the precariousness within that dialectic but, rather, the enthusiastic affirmation of the possible result: "And sometimes the hot hope surges up that perhaps the long and slow climb may be ending … Since the Reformation began to free the mind and to direct the force of religion toward morality, there has been a perceptible increase of speed. Humanity is gaining in elasticity and capacity for change … The swiftness of evolution in our own country proves the immense latent perfectibility in human nature … Perhaps these nineteen centuries of Christian influence have been a long preliminary stage of growth, and now the flower and fruit are almost here."[98]

FINAL THEOLOGICAL SYSTEM Rauschenbusch's final book, *A Theology for the Social Gospel*, undoubtedly represents the most mature and important statement of the history of the whole movement.

This work is a compilation of the "Taylor Lectures," given at Yale in April 1917, when the United States was involved in the war whose outbreak struck a mortal blow against the liberal philosophy of history. But the certainty of a more just realization of things human remained untouched and exuberant, trustful of "the fraternal ethics of democracy" and resting on the advent of "social common sense."[99] The Liberal analysis of the figure of Christ and his religion remained sure of itself (and, more so than in his other writings, references to Schleirmacher and Ritschl abound), almost as if the eschatological interpretations of Wrede, Weiss, and Schweitzer were totally without importance; Rauschenbusch eliminates them from his dialectic as an ideological product of a bourgeois theological mentality "constitutionally incapacitated for understanding any revolutionary ideas, past or present,"[100] which are, therefore, bent to ascetic and eschatological understandings.

What he had pre-established with this work is clarified in his initial statement: "We have a social gospel [movement]. We need a systematic theology large enough to match it and vital enough to back it."[101] After three introductory chapters, in which the provocation to the theological revision implicit in the movement is affirmed, as well as the difficulties in attempting this rejuvenation and the Christian authenticity of the themes produced by the Social Gospel, the discourse then organizes itself around two basic themes: in the first part, sin, and in the second, the Kingdom of God on earth.

In his conception of the nature of sin, Rauschenbusch follows the line of thought common to all the liberals: sin is man's failure to live up to the ideals of conscience, a failure that is provoked by instinctivity, ignorance, and inertia. The ideals constitute a vision marked by a higher, more inclusive and, therefore, more "social" standpoint; sin is rightly defined as selfishness, in which "we frustrate our possibilities; we injure others; we disturb the divine harmonies"; sin impedes and ensnares, and places the expansive dynamism of relationships among beings in contradiction. Sin becomes guilt in the true sense of the word "in the degree in which intelligence and will enter": in any case this does not touch the "meaning" of the personality, it is not a corruption of the human being; it is an incorrect relationship, which is "against God," insofar as it is against humanity. The theological idea of sin as "rebellion against God" is a version born out of the sociological situation proper to monarchical institutions: this individualistic privacy in the conception of the man-God relationship overturned by the mentality of the democratic era, which provides a more objective and comprehensive definition of sin as rupturing social harmony; indeed, for the Liberal immanentistic vision, "God is not only the spiritual representative of humanity; he is identified with it."[102]

But Rauschenbusch's most significant contribution centres precisely on the most difficult aspect of sin, the problem of the "sin of origin," so much so that certain historians speak of him as the restorer of the concept of original sin.[103] Liberal Theology had often hastily identified the doctrine of the fall of Adam as a prescientific version of the Darwinian idea of the struggle to evolve from the animalistic level to that of a moral personality. The importance that Rauschenbusch contributed to the problem lies in the fact that he saw the sole expression of dogmatic tradition in a "solidaristic" conception of man. By recovering aspects that could already be seen in Brown and other Liberals, but giving them space and incomparably broader development, Rauschenbusch boils down the idea of original sin to the social transmission of bad influences. Each social group strives to advance its own interests by justifying them and imposing instruments of their affirmation: through decisive influence on individuals and reciprocal pressure, social groups radically determine the character of the entire human situation: "Theology has not given adequate attention to the social idealizations of evil, which falsify the ethical standards for the individual by the authority of his group or community, deaden the voice of the Holy Spirit to the conscience of individuals and communities, and perpetuate antiquated wrongs in society. These social idealizations are the real heretical doctrines from the point of view of the Kingdom of God."[104] These generate the forms for their own affirmation and tend to impose them, that is, to convert them into institutions of the established social order. Thus, this adulteration penetrates the organism of the succeeding generation. "The life of humanity," says Rauschenbusch, inspired by Schleiermacher's *Der Christliche Glaube*, which he cites at the end of the most brilliant chapter of the entire book, chapter IX, "The Kingdom of Evil," "is infinitely interwoven, always renewing itself, yet always perpetuating what has been. The evils of one generation are caused by the wrongs of the generation that preceded, and will in turn condition the sufferings and temptations of those that come after ... Our theological conception of sin is but fragmentary unless we see all men in their natural groups bound together in a solidarity of all times and all places, bearing the yoke of evil and suffering."[105]

Thus, one can find in the world and its history the web of evil and sin to be an intense and complex interplay of "super-personal forces" which, like monstrous "composite personalities," create within society what could rightly be called the "Kingdom of Evil," no longer imagined in terms of Satan and his demons, but identified with experiential factors that can be recognized and analyzed, and defined in terms of "our growing sense of racial unity,"[106] that is, of profound "continuity" between the individual and the human community and among all the moments of its realization. And scientific confirmation of the profound reasons behind its explanation, following the methodological concern particular to Liberal Theology, is given by citing "the amazing regularity of social statistics ... The statistics of social morality are the pulse-beat of the social organism. The apparently free and unrelated acts of individuals are also the acts of the social group. When the social group is evil, evil is over all."[107]

Nevertheless, there is the capacity for salvation in the human being, which is the possibility to discern the Kingdom of Evil and to cause it to evolve into the Kingdom of God: this is the them of the second part of Rauschenbusch's book. Salvation begins in the individual as an event that transforms his egocentrism into an attitude in which provocation and determination are given by God, that is, by the common good: "God is the all-embracing source and exponent of the common life and good of mankind. When we submit to God, we submit to the supremacy of the common good. Salvation is the voluntary socializing of the soul."[108] The energy that makes this transformation possible is faith, radically qualified within the context of these thoughts: "It is not so much the endorsement of ideas formulated in the past, as the expectancy and confidence in the coming salvation of God ... It is faith to assume that this is a good world and that life is worth living. It is faith to assert the feasibility of a fairly righteous and fraternal social order."[109] This faith, "miraculous power of the human personality," is irresistible in its capacity for communication and mobilization. Thus, through the person's spirit of devotion, it makes what is the lynchpin of history's drama possible: the conversion of even the "super-personal" factors, changing selfish agents into instruments of service and cooperation. Here is the Kingdom of God, which is none other than the "commonwealth of co-operative service" and, as a consequence, "humanity organized according to the will of God."[110]

This idea is the central thesis of Christian theory, and based on it, theology must revise all of its doctrines and be organized around it. Rauschenbusch, in defining his most original contribution in chapter XIII, affirms that Christian history has lost this "marrow of the gospel" and substituted it with faith and devotion in the Church, impatiently identifying the means with the end. Moreover, the ill-fated consequences are numerous: contact with authentic Christian discourse has been lost, so that "traditional theology and the mind of Jesus became incommensurable realities";[111] Christian ethics, in particular, has been emptied of its prophetic content and its revolutionary energy, replaced by the emphasis on fidelity to the ecclesiastical institution and even the political version of its affirmation in the world; hence, a conservative image and a reactionary attitude, a devaluation of worldly life, by which "religious value is taken out of the activities of the common man and the prophetic services to society"; the salvation of the individual has no relationship with the issue of the salvation of society; and, finally, Christian discourse becomes existentially obtuse, because "the Kingdom of God breeds prophets; the Church breeds priests and theologians."[112] The sensibility awakened by the social movement joined to biblical criticism have awakened the authentic passion of Christ for the Kingdom of God. The categories of this reality are catalogued as a "social order which will best guarantee to all personalities their freest and highest development," as "a progressive reign of love in human affairs," as "the free surrender of what is truly our own, life, property, and rights," and finally, as "unity of mankind."[113]

The capillary genesis of such a reality, which constitutes the meaning of history, lies in the attitude of the person who, by overcoming egoism, is opened to the vision of himself and of his work as a function of the social order. In order to mark this step, the terms of conversion and justification, of sanctification, but above all, regeneration, with an emphasis similar to that of Revivalism. It is a typical experience (and the explanation aligns coherently with the well-noted criteriological line), in which the influx of the new meaning of relationships and flourishing of the impetus to solidarity establish a "repentance" which is assimilated to the "vicarious suffering" of Jesus Christ, but which, above all, constitutes the event of the miraculous power of God: "The passive and active resistance of the

Kingdom of Evil at every stage of its advance is so great, and the human resources of the Kingdom of God so slender, that no explanation can satisfy a religious mind which does not see the power of God in its movements. The Kingdom of God, therefore, is miraculous all the way, and is the continuous revelation of the power, the righteousness, and the love of God ... It is the energy of God realizing itself in human life ... By accepting [the Kingdom of God] as a task, we experience it as a gift."[114]

A certain ambiguity, if not outright contradiction, can still be noted in this work's use of the formula "Kingdom of God." In a strict sense, what Rauschenbusch identifies as "Kingdom of God on earth" is not, as has already been observed, a utopian perfection that solves every problem, but the *referring* of societal structures and organizations to Christian categories. He considers this to be possible, and even near to completion, and its task is to facilitate, in a stable way, the overall struggle for the evolutionary approach to the ideal of the common good; since man, in Rauschenbusch's diagnosis, is determined by "superpersonal" forces, that is, by social institutions, if these are Christianized, this will solicit to the maximum degree the dynamic of transformation that must take place in each individual so that good will be consummated in the world: "Every new being is a new problem of salvation."[115] The dialectic of conversion is always maintained in the person; therefore, in history as well, dialectical tension towards perfection is never eliminated: in its broadest and most comprehensive sense, the Kingdom of God must be conceived of as "always coming, always pressing in on the present, always big with possibility, and always inviting immediate action."[116] The optimism of Rauschenbusch seems to suspend the dialectic as regards the evolution of social forces, at least in their radical approach.

His system of thought will reveal this as its weakest point, and events would push the new generation to point that out. Yet, in its central intuition, the social dimension of Christian experience, it would continue to be one of the most influential expressions in the history of American Protestant thought.

OTHER WORKS For the fiftieth anniversary of the death of Rauschenbusch, a fortunate discovery in the archives of the American Baptist Historical Society made possible the publication of an extensive manuscript, one whose writing dates to a 1913 conversation in which Rauschenbusch confides: "All this time I began to have a desire to write a book. I had six books in mind – I still have – but I didn't know which one to write ... I decided, however, to write a book on the social questions for the Lord Christ and the people. This was a dangerous book and I entered upon my task with fear and trembling. It was part of my Christian ministry, a religious book to me. Three times I started and each time I was compelled to stop in the middle on account of work. When I went back to my book, I found each time I had out-grown the book."[117] Indeed, in *The Righteousness of the Kingdom*, Rauschenbusch's fundamental theme is already impetuously present, the nucleus of which is the idea of Christianity as a revolutionary fact in human relationships (chapters 1 and 2), of Christ as a force that determines such a revolution (chapter 3), of the New Law as equality, non-violence, and solidarity (chapter 4), of religiosity as commitment to action (chapter 5). One can also find a determination to struggle against the dominant traditional conception of a Christianity detached from the world, a Christianity that "asks for a 'pure gospel' and means a disembodied spirit that haunts churches but never ventures out into the market and the stock exchange and the real estate office."[118]

Alongside the other major works of Rauschenbusch can also be placed *Christianizing the Social Order* (1912). In this book, Rauschenbusch evokes the discovery of the idea of the Kingdom of God as "the first and most essential dogma of the Christian faith," as the ultimate category where all the aspects of human interest are led to a unity: "So Christ's conception of the Kingdom of God came to me as a new revelation ... the perspective of life shifted into a new alignment. I felt a new security in my social impulses ... I now know that I had history on my side. But in addition I found that this new conception of the purpose of Christianity was strangely satisfying. It responded to all the old and all the new elements of my religious life. The saving of the lost, the teaching of the young, the pastoral care of the poor and frail, the quickening of starved intellects, the study of the Bible, church union, political reform, the reorganization of the industrial system, international peace, – it was all covered by the one aim of the Reign of God on earth."[119] The optimism of his conception of history reaches its boldest expression in statements that are among the most quoted of Rauschenbusch: "The largest and hardest part of the work of christianizing the social order has been done," and family, church, school, and politics founded on democracy are cited as the Christianized areas of social life. Thus, all action must be centred on "the unchristianized portions of the social order," that is, the areas of business, industry, and commerce.[120]

In short, it can be said that, in *Christianizing the Social Order*, the identification of religious destiny with social evolution, and of Christian content with the ways of worldly structures is exemplified. At the end of the work, the author declares in a significant way: "In looking back over the field traversed in this book, it may seem to some as if our argument had fallen away from the high religious ground taken at the outset and had sagged down to the level of mere economic discussion. That impression would be superficial. This is a religious book from the beginning to end. Its sole concern is for the Kingdom of God and the salvation of men. But the Kingdom of God includes the economic life; for it means the progressive transformation of all human affairs by the thought and spirit of Christ."[121]

Feeling the lack of an almost "catechetical" synthesis of broad appeal, Rauschenbusch edited a manual, *The Social Principles of Jesus* (1916), organized into twelve chapters of biblical passages with commentaries.

The whole passionate religious inspiration that animated the figure, the thought, and the action of the professor from Rochester, and which had impelled him to promote a type of spiritual and cultural sodality, "The Brotherhood of the Kingdom," is documented in a volume of prayers that achieved a good deal of fame: *For God and the People: Prayers of the Social Awakening* (1910). The title takes up the term that marked the greatest phenomena of religious fervour of the two preceding centuries, but it also sums up the radical metamorphosis that had taken place.

IV REACTIONS TO THE LIBERAL MOVEMENT: FUNDAMENTALISM AND HUMANISM

1 *Traditionalism*

Faced with the New Theology, traditionalism had not found great voices to come to its defence, with the exception of some names from the Princeton School, who carried on the position of Charles Hodge. Among the most conspicuous, the following should be noted:

Archibald Alexander Hodge (1823–1886) of Princeton, known for his interventions in the controversy on biblical criticism; Benjamin Breckinridge Warfield (1851–1921), teacher of New Testament at the Western Theological Seminary (Pittsburgh), intelligent and developed defender of biblical inerrancy, widely renowned in conservative Calvinist spheres; and Augustus Hopkins Strong (1836–1921), Baptist, president of Rochester Theological Seminary, author of a *Systematic Theology* in three volumes (1907–09, in the final edition), summed up in *Outlines of Systematic Theology* (1908).

THE FUNDAMENTALIST MOVEMENT In 1910, following conferences between the various Protestant denominations, there began the publication of a series of twelve short volumes, entitled *The Fundamentals: A Testimony of the Truth* (1910–12). The patronage of two wealthy laymen made possible a vast circulation (2,500,000 copies) of the pamphlet. In it, the following were held to be basic truths of the faith, so much so that all those who denied them were qualified as non-Christians: the virgin birth of Christ, his physical resurrection, the inerrancy of the Bible in every particular, the vicarious redemption, and the imminent physical second coming of Christ. The movement, which acquired the name "Fundamentalist" based upon the title of the pamphlet, developed particularly in the immediate postwar years of 1920 to 1925, as an urgent need to save historical Protestantism, giving new value to traditional biblical exegesis and condemning the modernistic application of modern scientific methods to the interpretation of Scripture and of religious experience in general. Evolutionism, in all its applications, was particularly condemned. The most famous Liberal preachers, such as Fosdick, suffered bitter attacks; dogged efforts were put forth to make the Fundamentalist creed official in the different denominations.

The most significant controversies broke out among Presbyterians, causing schisms and the formation of Westminster Theological Seminary in opposition to Princeton Theological Seminary, where the less rigid personages ultimately prevailed, and among the Disciples of Christ, among whom two opposing bi-weekly publications sprang up: the Liberal *Christian Century* and the Fundamentalist *Christian Standard*.

The theologian of greatest validity among Fundamentalists was the Presbyterian John Greshan Machen (1881–1937): notwithstanding the fascination he held for the school of the Ritschlian Wilhelm

Herrmann during the year he spent in Germany, Machen reacted with a serious recovery of traditional terms.

He is noted, above all, for his *Christianity and Liberalism* (1923). He keenly and strongly attacks Liberal Theology's immanentism, the substitution of sentimental intuition for objective revelation, the elimination of sin in anthropology, and utopian optimism in the vision of history. He called Liberalism or modernism "a totally diverse type of religious belief, which is only the more destructive of the Christian faith because it makes use of traditional Christian terminology." What he wishes to demonstrate, above all, is that the definition of Christianity can solely be determined by those elements that offer an objective analysis of the documents that reflect its origin: "At the foundation of the life of every corporation is the incorporation paper, in which the objects of the corporation are set forth ... So it is with Christianity ... It is conceivable that Christianity may now have to be abandoned, and another religion substituted for it; but at any rate the question of what Christianity is can be determined only by an examination of the beginnings of Christianity."[122]

Machen also defends the fundamentalist thesis in *The Origin of Paul's Religion* (1921), *The Meaning of Faith* (1925), and *The Virgin Birth of Christ* (1930).

Other conservatives were able to join the attack on Liberalism to a labour of systematic construction done with a positive method that was more open in its evaluation of what was new: as, for example, the Baptist Edgar Young Mullins (1860–1928), with his works *Axioms of Religion* (1908) and *The Christian Religion in Its Doctrinal Expression* (1917), while in *Christianity at the Crossroads* (1924), he scolds Liberalism for so reducing Christianity according to a purely rational schema that it diminishes it to the level of any other religious phenomenon in human history.

2 *Humanism as Dominant Climate*

The Chicago School had represented the maximum sliding of Liberal idealism towards a Humanistic naturalism by which science was the only method of truth, the evolutionistic principle was the unquestionable criterion of any realistic approach to reality, the optimistic vision of man and faith in progress indisputably obvious, and God – when that word was used – was conceived of as a pure immanence. This Humanism became the dominant climate in American universities, especially between 1920 and 1930, when, in the euphoria of an unprecedented economic prospect, it seemed evident that human initiative could achieve all of the goals of human desire.

In terms of the "God" reality, the Humanists assumed a doubly distinct position.

The first group affirmed an essentially agnostic standpoint: science is the sole source of objective truth; God is not the object of science: he can neither be denied nor affirmed. The sole strength on which man must count in order to transform, build, and achieve fullness is that which he finds in himself. The development of this strength within the self is true religion, affirms Curtis Williford Reese, of Chicago's Lincoln Center: "religion is the natural functioning of a normal person in the effort to achieve a full, a free and socially useful life in ordinary circumstances."[123]

The others, instead, attest to clearly materialistic positions that deny God. The most valid expression of this current is found in the work, *Common Faith* (1934), by John Dewey. In this work, God is identified with "all the natural forces and conditions – including man and human association – that promote the growth of the ideal and that further its realization."[124] Here, the "ideal" is that collection of goals that lived experience cause to flash within the self's imagination, as a happy integration of its being in a necessary connection of dependence on the good of the society in which the self is articulated. Naturally, religion is merely devotion to these ideals and the attention to their development, according to the definition of Albert Eustace Haydon, the radical exponent of the Chicago School, for whom religion is "the shared quest of the good life."[125]

THE "MANIFESTO" In 1933, the journal the *New Humanist* published a "Humanist Manifesto," which, in fifteen theses undersigned by thirty-four noted personalities of the cultural, editorial, and educational worlds, established the essential terms of what Charles Francis Potter (1885–1962), founder of the First Humanist Society of New York, considered "belief in a new religion called Humanism."

The seventh thesis specified the concept of "religion" in the following terms: "Religion consists of those actions, purposes and experiences which are humanly significant. Nothing human is alien to the religious. It includes labour, art, science, philosophy, love, friendship, recreation – all that is in its degree expressive of intelligently satisfying human living. The distinction between the sacred and the secular can no longer be maintained."[126]

All of the humanistic trends were in agreement in rebuking the Liberal theologians for an incoherence that stopped them from drawing out the consequences of the premises that they themselves adhered to: the Liberals did, indeed, recognize science as an absolute value, and yet, they sought the light in an extra-scientific field; they recognized evolution in a continual indefinite progress as indisputable, and yet, they established as unsurpassable outdated paradigms such as the Bible or Christ. Potter, in his humorous and expressive way, would say, "The modernists have fallen between two stools in trying to sit on both."[127]

4

Realism

I DISTRUST OF THE SOCIAL GOSPEL: EMPIRICAL TRENDS, "NEO-ORTHODOXY"

1 The "Realistic" Signals of Social and Political Events

What eventually defeated the idealism of the Social Gospel was not its opponents from the right or from the left, but history itself. It was the First World War that brought to the forefront its illusory and utopian character. The Great Depression of a decade later revealed the incurable unease into which the force of events had plunged such optimism. The Second World War marked the definite collapse of utopia. Thus, "Since 1914 one tragic experience has followed another, as if history had been designed to refute the vain delusions of modern man."[1]

Scientific naturalism had rebuked the Liberal theologians for not being consistent in their dutiful trust in science as the sole criterion of truth and the sole secret of happiness for mankind: they contaminated pure fidelity to science with the relics of obsolete superstitions. Humanism had made optimism regarding the forces of reason into an absolute. Yet, by now its appeal was in too open a contrast with reality for it to find the enthusiastic followers which fifty years earlier the demands of science had found among Protestant theologians: "During the thirties," wrote John C. Bennett, "the chief theological lesson that I learned has now become a commonplace; it was the inadequacy of the optimistic views of man and history which I had taken over uncritically from an earlier theological liberalism."[2] Perhaps there is no more significant proof of the change in mood than the statement contained in Fosdick's famous article, "Beyond Modernism," published in the *Christian Century*, 4 December 1935: "the watchword will be not, Accommodate yourself to the prevailing culture! but, Stand out from it and challenge it! ... we cannot harmonize Christ himself with modern culture."

On the other hand, a pure and simple return to conservative orthodoxy was not possible. The outlines of a new and extremely varied movement of currents began to form, all of which fell under the common heading of Realism. They juxtaposed themselves to the idealism that had made up the Liberal system, reduced the level of romantic subjectivism, and recognized within reality the presence of a "datum" that imposes itself on human action as an unsurpassable limit and which human reason will never be able to manipulate according to its own immanent ideals with freedom in unlimited progression. In particular, they stressed the imposing seriousness of Evil. At the same time, the positive word in diagnosing evil is sought decisively in a foundation beyond the self, beyond human society and nature, at least as it appears; that is, in a foundation "too deep to be shaken by the earthquakes that shatter the dreams of idealists."[3]

The problem about whose solution the "realists" were divided, even radically, is how to reach this objective foundation, and how to build a theology upon it. The different standpoints at the origin of the new Realist Movement are reflected in the symposium *Religious Realism*, edited by Douglas Clyde Macintosh in 1931.

2 *Empirical Realism*

One initial current was that of *empirical* realism. In its inspiration, it is linked to the experimental method with which William James, in his *Varieties of Religious Experience* (1902), had sought to demonstrate the validity of theism. James had an enormous influence on contemporary American religious experience. The standpoint from which he had approached the religious phenomenon was congenial to the American temperament, which was inclined towards individualism, desirous of learning from the facts of experience, and sensitive to the practical nature of consequences and applications. Thus, "psychology of religion became the pearl of great price for which we were willing, if need be, to barter away all other theological disciplines."[4] James' influence per se does not divide the thinkers we are about to examine from the Liberals: his influence on them had been great from the beginnings of the twentieth century. But the authors catalogued in what we call the "empirical current" can be distinguished by a radically non-subjective intentionality and by an interest that is not psychologically descriptive. The method they followed could be described as "scientific consideration of religious experience," so as to grasp the fundamental constant, and the objective determinants of the dynamism towards good, which, in their view, constitute the essence of religious life.

THEOLOGICAL EPISTEMOLOGY IN DOUGLAS CLYDE MACINTOSH The works of Douglas Clyde Macintosh (1877–1948) were well known in that sense. A graduate in theology and philosophy at the University of Chicago, from 1902 to 1942 he was professor of theology and philosophy of religion at Yale.

His epistemological concern from the beginning to the end of his career appears in *The Problem of Knowledge* (1915) and *The Problem of Religious Knowledge* (1940); in *The Reasonableness of Christianity* (1925), he carries out an apologetic labour; and in *Personal Religion* (1942), his final book, he also touches on the theme of the Church. Yet, his principal work remains *Theology as an Empirical Science* (1919), whose program is reiterated in the long essay that Macintosh contributed to the volume *Religious Realism* (1931).

Macintosh holds that "it is possible to relate theological theory to that acquaintance with the divine which is to be found in religious experience at its best, as the physical and social sciences, with their theories as to the nature of things and persons, are related to our common human acquaintance with things and persons in sense and social experience."[5] An "empirical theology" distinguishes itself from religious psychology in that the latter is interested in the internal states of consciousness, therefore, experience as a phenomenon to describe, whereas the former is interested in the "thing experienced," that is, the object marked out by experience itself. Just as in every science, the basic presupposition of theological science is that the object of any research be real and that some knowledge of it be possible. Thus, "on the basis of knowledge of God through religious experience, one can scientifically assume *that* God is, although he may have as yet very little knowledge as to *what* God is."[6]

God as an objective existing reality is the concern that dominates Macintosh's research, highlighted in this statement during his debates with Feuerbach: "Better a God that is unknowable than a knowable God that is unreal."[7] Indeed, Macintosh tends to define God in a way that does not allow for doubting him, that is, based on that supreme aspect of human experience which is the striving for values and which generates the only "sane" (!) attitude: "moral optimism," understood as "a fundamental attitude of confidence in the cosmos, together with a full sense of man's moral responsibility" or "confidence that ultimately the universe is on the side of the highest values" by which "moral optimism is an act of self-maintenance on the part of the spiritual life of man."[8] From this standpoint God, says Macintosh, thereby inserting himself into the long American Protestant tradition regarding the essence of the Divine, is "a benevolent Power sufficiently in control of the universe to guarantee an ultimate adequate harmony of virtue and happiness" or a "Factor which can be depended upon for conservation of the highest values for persons of good will, in spite of anything the forces of nature can do."[9]

Macintosh, therefore, seeks to discover within the phenomenon of religious experience those "data" that point to the immediate "product" of divine activity, and that, thus, constitute divine "revelations" to man. Finally, the statement that "the God that man needs exists ... can be taken as a very general working hypothesis, from which more specific working hypotheses may be deduced. This whole body of theory will be scientific in the sense that is it is being scientifically tested, and, we may believe, progressively verified";[10] thus "theological laws" can be established, the "constants" of the God-world and God-man relationships.

THE NATURE OF GOD IN HENRY NELSON WIEMAN The problem of God also dominates the works of Henry Nelson Wieman (1884–1975). Wieman received his doctorate in 1917 at Harvard, where he fell under the influence of the idealistic religious philosophy of William Ernest Hocking, after having studied for two years in Jena and Heidelberg, and from 1927 to 1947 he taught philosophy of religion in the Divinity School of the University of Chicago.

Wieman's intent was to maintain himself rigidly within the confines of scientific experimentalism, as he energetically sustains in the book, *Is There a God?* (1932), which also contains essays by Macintosh and the humanist Max Carl Otto. Prior to this, he had written *Religious Experience and the Scientific Method* (1926), *The Wrestle of Religion with Truth* (1927), *The Issues of Life* (1930); later, he wrote *Normative Psychology of Religion* (1935, in collaboration with Regina Westcott

Wieman), *The Growth of Religion* (1938, in collaboration with Walter Marshall Horton), *The Source of Human Good* (1946), *The Directive in History* (1949), and *Man's Ultimate Commitment* (1958).

For Wieman, human values are not a "product" of human effort and activity, as Humanists à la Dewey would like, but fundamentally dependent upon a cosmic principle that is a connecting and evolutionary force: God is "whatever in truth operates to save man from evil and to the greater good no matter how much this operating reality may differ from all traditional ideas about it."[11] This cosmic principle is revealed in events. God could also be called "the undefined and unexplored totality of what is best as it emerges sequentially in concrete situations where choices must be made."[12]

In any case, the cosmic principle absolutely cannot be conceived of as a personal characteristic; it is an aspect of nature, specifically nature as creative wellspring of historical events, immanent to events themselves: "The only creative God we recognize is the creative event itself."[13] It is something absolute because its dynamism is limitless, and cannot be determined by human aspirations or human activity.

Despite the immanentistic-naturalistic reduction of the concept of God, Wieman's oeuvre, with its rigorous appeal to a cosmic principle, an objective reality that is the source of values, constituted for many Liberals the precious aid in overcoming the subjectivism inherent in Liberalism and Humanism. "Wieman was my Barth," wrote the editor of the *Christian Century*, Charles Clayton Morrison.[14]

THE "EMPIRICAL" EVOLUTION OF PERSONALISM IN EDGAR SHEFFIELD BRIGHTMAN An interesting synthesis can be found in the thought of Edgar Sheffield Brightman (1884–1953), who held the [Borden Parker] Bowne chair at Boston University from 1925 to 1953. He attempted to integrate personalist ontology into the dominant empiricist framework. At the beginning of his *A Philosophy of Religion* (1940), he critically states, "The keynote of the book is experience,"[15] and it is also the key to his whole system. It is impossible to step outside of experience, and outside of experience there is nothing: "it is the present consciousness which is the sole possible starting point, and the sole possible source of evidence for any statements about the absent."[16] By probing experience, hypotheses emerge, whose verification cannot occur through the experimental scientific method, but with reason, with thought, that is, in as much as it applies as the ultimate criterion, the principle of the "coherence" of every hypothesis with the other hypotheses and with experience as *totum*. This does not amount to an abandonment in extremis of the empirical method, because "to demand coherence is to demand full attention to all the facts of experience, to neglect none, in short, to 'save the appearances,' as Simplicius said in his commentary on Aristotle's *De coelo*."[17]

Upon these epistemological premises and critiques, Brightman bases his conception of religion in many works, the principal ones being (in addition to the one cited above) *Religious Values* (1925), *The Problem of God* (1930), *The Finding of God* (1931), *Is God a Person?* (1932), *Moral Laws* (1933), *Personality and Religion* (1934), *The Spiritual Life* (1942), *Nature and Values* (1945), and the third part of the volume *Person and Reality: An Introduction to Metaphysics* (1958), edited by his successor in the Boston chair, Peter Anthony Bertocci.

In terms of experience, God is known as wellspring and meaning of values, their source and redeemer; the quest for God is "a search for the purpose of life and for an unfailing source of eternal value."[18] If one keeps in mind that a "person is a conscious self able to develop ideal values,"[19] one understands how to affirm that God is person, "the unbegun and unending energy of the universe is conscious rational will."[20]

However, the experience of values is complicated by the problem of evil.

Now, it is true that "the problem of evil admits no final, no completely enlightening solution";[21] the need to formulate the most coherent hypothesis in light of the person's experience remains. And this seems to be that of the *finite God*: "No possible experience could reveal unlimited and absolute power."[22] God is perfect vision of the ideal and perfect actual energy (i.e., perfect will); this is what is essential to the concept. But God's dual perfection is conditioned by a "datum" that is structurally inherent in it, which in every moment allows the divine will to have limited possibilities of ideal action, finite possibilities in an infinite evolution and progression; this is what is essential to the coherence of the concept of God with experience. Therefore, "[God's] perfection … consists in his [infinite] perfectibility," and we are forced to recognize "a duality of nature at the very eternal heart of things, in which the active is indeed in control, but maintains its control with struggle and pain."[23]

3 "Neo-orthodox" Realism

EUROPEAN IMPORTATION AND AMERICAN CHARACTERIZATION Of decisive importance for American theological thought was the importation and diffusion of the European theological existentialism in the 1930s. Barth appeared on the scene in 1928 with a translation, *The Word of God and the Word of Man,* by Douglas Horton (1891–1968) of *Das Wort Gottes und die Theologie.* The discussion was fuelled in 1929 by Brunner's *The Theology of Crisis.* Kierkegard's works found an excellent translator and popularizer in Walter Lowrie, one of the pioneers of the new trend, whose *Our Concern with the Theology of Crisis* (1932), which followed Wilhelm Pauck's *Karl Barth: Prophet of a New Christianity?* (1931), engaged him favourably, albeit critically, with the radical change of theological accent. Anti-Liberalism in Paul Tillich's non-Barthian version was welcomed in American literature with H. Richard Niebuhr's translation of the volume *Die religiöse Lage der Gegenwart,* with the title *The Religious Situation* (1932). The new Swedish school of G. Aulen and A. Nygren, with its Lutheran relevance, was fortunate to find an interpretation through *Swedish Contributions to Modern Theology* (1939) by Nels Ferré.

It is Liberal immanentism that is dramatically contested as a religiously ineffective and naively adopted presupposition: "Where liberal theology saw the goodness of God as continuous with the highest human goodness and the fulfillment of life as gradual sanctification and as the conservation of value, neo-orthodoxy is more concerned with the discontinuity between God's goodness and human sin, and visualizes the relationship of the eternal to history as a dialectic one in which God as the End fulfills man's desires and expectations only by disappointing the in their corrupted form."[24]

The absolute transcendence of God, the reality of sin, and the consequent judgment on human nature, and justification and salvation only through Christ returned to being the dominant ideas, and they characterized the new movement in open opposition to other trends. In *The Faith We Declare* (1939), Edwin Lewis applied the European term "neo-orthodoxy" to the new movement, even though its American exponents did not feel themselves to be exactly defined by it.

Indeed, a characteristically American re-elaboration assured that the issue was not a mere echo of European positions. Barth proclaimed absolute contrast, absolute "discontinuity" between God and creatures, between faith and reason, between revelation and experience. The American temperament and culture negated this rigid contrast. "We do not share the absolute act of accusation against human nature,"[25] said John Bennet. American thought would anxiously seek points of contact between the two poles of the natural and the transcendent. Thus, more than Barth, Americans found Brunner to be comprehensible; in his *Natur und Gnade* he had admitted the existence of an *Anknüpfungspunkt* [point of contact] between time and eternity, with the consequent introduction of a natural theology. Brunner would also teach at Princeton and various other universities in the United States.

Nevertheless, Americans and Europeans held in common the substantially dialectical conception of the nature-transcendent relationship and the fundamental categories in such a dialectical vision, even if profoundly and distinctly reworked. What for empirical theology is given by inductive observation and experimental proof, for neo-orthodoxy is given by "faith" and "revelation."

SIGNIFICANT AUTHORS A number of quite compelling and diverse authors give proof through their works of the birth and self-assertion of this new current.

In addition to the aforementioned Walter Lowrie (1868–1959) and Wilhelm Pauck (1900–1981),* George Warren Richards (1869–1955), in *Beyond Fundamentalism and Modernism: The Gospel of God* (1934), is among the first to take up the banner of the topics that Barth and Brunner had caused to echo throughout Europe.

Edwin Lewis (1881–1959), English by origin, and from 1916 to 1951 instructor at the Drew Theological Seminary, in his *A Christian Manifesto* (1934), energetically documents his movement beyond the Liberal positions of his first book, *Jesus Christ and the Human Quest* (1924); whereas *A Philosophy of the Christian Revelation* (1940) and *The Creator and the Adversary* (1948) represent the mature fruit of his thought.

* Translator's note: The latter should also be remembered for his work *The Church against the World* (1935), a precise diagnosis of the situation of the Church "in bondage to capitalism" (p. 128) written in collaboration with H. Richard Niebuhr and Francis P. Miller.

The spiritual odyssey from Liberalism to Neo-orthodoxy is particularly well documented in the evolution of the thought of Walter Marshall Horton (1895–1966), professor of systematic theology at Oberlin, from his book on "empirical" theology *Theism and the Modern Mood* (1930) or from *A Psychological Approach to Theology* (1931) to *Realistic Theology* (1934), where the new themes are sympathetically recovered. This final viewpoint also inspired historical essays, *Contemporary Continental Theology* (1936) and *Contemporary English Theology* (1938), and above all, the Christological study *Our Eternal Contemporary* (1942). After the "Eugene Lyman Lecture," given at Briar College in Virginia in 1952 and titled *Liberalism Old and New*, Horton concerns himself with establishing a balance between the words of the Gospel and modern demands which neo-orthodox "hegemony" risks neglecting. His final systematic synthesis, *Christian Theology: An Ecumenical Approach* (1955), is based upon the ideal of this balance: "Conservative attachment to the eternal Gospel and liberal adaptation to modern needs and problems are not mutually inconsistent but equally necessary concerns. Without the first, Christianity becomes lost in its environment; without the second, its message does not reach the world for which Christ died … essential Christianity keeps both concerns in fruitful tension and commerce with each other."[26]

In John Coleman Bennett (b. 1902 [d. 1995]), from 1943 professor of ethics at Union Theological Seminary, the impetus towards social and political ethics harkens back to its Liberal origins. Yet, in his most noted works, his discourse is dialecticalized from the awareness of man's involvement in evil, limit, and egotism, and by the tremendous ambiguity that evil creates in human groups and in history: [see his] *Social Salvation* (1935); *Christian Realism* (1941), with a vigorous appeal to the need for valuing the concrete historical facts of Jesus' life in order to affirm the prophetic force of his message; *Christian Ethics and Social Policy* (1946); and *Christian and the State* (1958).

CHRISTIAN VALUES AND FUTURE IN THE INVESTIGATIONS OF HELMUT RICHARD NIEBUHR The relationship between Christianity, historical moment, and social future inspires the themes and content of the best works of Helmut Richard Niebuhr (1894–1962), one of the most serious and interesting figures of post-Liberal theology for some pastors of the Evangelical and

Reformed Church, and from 1931 to 1962 professor of theology and Christian ethics at Yale.

His 1924 doctoral dissertation at Yale University was on "The Philosophy of Religion of Ernst Troeltsch"; and inspired by Troeltsch, Weber, Tawney, Harnack, Müller, and Gooch,[27] he starts off by facing the problem of the socio-cultural significance of American Christianity. In *The Social Sources of Denominationalism* (1929), he seeks to "discover the nature of the relation of religion to culture and to throw light on the complexity of American Christianity by examining the influence of social forces on faith and by tracing the sociological pattern of race, class and sectional interests as it manifested itself in the denominations."[28] Yet, this work, despite becoming a classic of American Protestant historiography, does not satisfy him: "Though the sociological approach helped to explain why the religious stream flowed in these particular channels it did not account for the force of the stream itself"; in particular, "while it could deal with the religion which was dependent on culture it left unexplained the faith which is independent, which is aggressive rather than passive, and which molds culture instead of being molded by it."[29]

In *The Kingdom of God in America* (1937), he identifies in the ideal of the Kingdom of God, albeit in different varieties, the specific aspect of faithfulness to the Reformation in American religious history. "As a religious movement the Reformation was characterized above all by its fresh insistence on the present sovereignty and initiative of God,"[30] and the idea of the Kingdom of God was the sign and figure of that actual sovereign initiative.

With *The Meaning of Revelation* (1941), Niebuhr's interest deepens into the analysis of the most general dimensions and essential categories of Christian reality, above all, those that have to do with "the relations of the relative and the absolute in history," upon which the author pronounces his methodological position: "We are aware today that all our philosophical ideas, religious dogmas and moral imperatives are historically conditioned and this awareness tempts us to a new agnosticism. I have found myself unable to avoid the acceptance of historical relativism yet I do not believe that the agnostic consequence is necessary."[31]

The Christian fact as such, as meaning that concretely lies within the historical context, is the topic of another of his well-known works, *Christ and Culture* (1951). The phenomenon of faith constitutes the Christian fact in history: "This faith has been introduced into our history, into our culture, our church, our human community, through this person and this event ... On the basis of that faith we reason; and much that was unintelligible on the ground of faithlessness or faith in the little gods who are not trustworthy is now illuminated ... it forms the basis for our reasoning in culture; for our efforts to define a rational justice; for our endeavors after rational political order; for our attempts to interpret the beautiful and true. It does not form the only basis; for our faith our loyalty, our confidence is small, as we forever lapse into faithlessness – even in those regions where it has won some victory over our thoughts. In that faith we seek to make decisions in our existential present ... To make our decisions in faith ... is to make them in view of the fact that the world of culture – man's achievement – exists in the world of grace – God's Kingdom."[32] *Radical Monotheism and Western Culture, with Supplementary Essays* (1960) is almost a specification of the preceding discourse: the significance of living faith for society, above all, in terms of political community and in terms of scientific activity.

Niebuhr was also very interested in problems of education and pastoral activity, and along these lines the following works are noteworthy: *The Ministry in Historical Perspectives* (1956, in collaboration with D.D. Williams), *The Purpose of the Church and Its Ministry* (1956, in collaboration with D.D. Williams and James M. Gustafson), and *The Advancement of Theological Education* (1957, in collaboration with the same authors).

One posthumous volume collects articles, sermons, and essays, and is precious in terms of a definition of the author's ethical conception: *The Responsible Self: An Essay in Christian Moral Philosophy* (1963).

Above all, two figures emerge, who with their stature dominate not only the Neo-orthodox Movement, but all of contemporary American theology: Reinhold Niebuhr (brother of Helmut Richard) and Paul Tillich, both of German origin. The former, born in America, reveals a formation and spirit that are integrally American, characterized by a particular sensitivity to historical-ethical-social issues and by the profound predominance of the "pragmatic" concern; whereas the latter, who immigrated to America to escape Nazi persecution with an already mature and fruitful cultural formation, shows a more systematically logical temperament and a more metaphysical preoccupation.

II REINHOLD NIEBUHR

1 *The Origin of His Intellectual Position: A Lived Experience*

Reinhold Niebuhr (1892–1971) is the recognized leader of the true revolution in American Protestant thought in an anti-Liberal direction in the 1930s. The Social Gospel formed part of the overall spirit of an era: "Modern men of all shades of opinion agreed in the belief that historical development is a redemptive process ... Though there are minor dissonances the whole corpus of modern culture learned to sing the new song of hope in remarkable harmony. The redemption of mankind, by whatever means, was assured for the future. It was, in fact, assured by the future."[33] Niebuhr's oeuvre is a passionate and systematic struggle against such a presupposition and environment. If the influence of European theological existentialism is undeniable, a clear originality marks it from the outset, whose inspiration and whose key tendencies are formed and delineated in the experience he lived as a pastor in the Bethel Evangelical Lutheran Church in Detroit. A remarkable resemblance to the genesis of Rauschenbusch's social passion produces a radically contrasting attitude. The diary of those years (1915–28), published in 1929 with the title *Leaves from the Notebook of a Tamed Cynic*, documents his dramatic observations: the results of the Ford organization, acclaimed as the evident confirmation of the futuristic theories that the Social Gospel seemed to consecrate theologically, were obtained through the sacrifice, exploitation, and brutalization of the masses of workers; selfishness, self-deception, and cruelty infiltrated every program and action. A vision of human nature was sown in him that had a profoundly tragic and contradictory character at every level, together with the demand for a type of thought that would hold fast to real life in order to have the possibility of having an impact on it.

2 *The Development of His Discourse*

Niebuhr's vast discourse evolves and becomes more precise as if by means of successive thematic accentuations, which can be summed up in three periods in a long itinerary: initially, there dominates an ethical-social thematic by means of a diagnosis of the human condition involved in relationships and expressed through them; in the second period, in which he produces his principal work, he deepens his anthropology by focusing on an analysis of what is human per se, both in terms of structure and original situation; and finally, the conception of history dominates his concerns.

His first book, *Does Civilization Need Religion? A Study in the Social Resources and Limitation of Religion in Modern Life* (1927), "was still safely within the Social Gospel presuppositions,"[34] with the identification of social progress with man's redemption, and the mechanism of correspondence between ideal engagement and worldly realization. He asserts that a "merely realistic analysis of any given set of facts is ... as dangerous as it is helpful. The creative and redemptive force is a faith which defies the real in the name of the idea, and subdues it."[35] Yet, the disconnect between ideal and practice is already acutely, although discretely, marked out: in the face of daily life, Christian ethical norms are always somewhat foolish,[36] and the relation between the absolute and history is not one of simple harmony, but rather one of tension and contrast.

In the year following this first publication, Niebuhr went from the parish in Detroit to the chair of applied Christianity at Union Theological Seminary in New York, and the features of his ethical vision matured rapidly. In 1930, with the Forbes Lectures, published in 1932 under the title of *The Contribution of Religion to Social Work*, he was already openly questioning the spheres of action of the law of love that religious idealism unreservedly proclaimed as a panacea.

In the same year of 1932, he released *Moral Man and Immoral Society: A Study in Ethics and Politics*. The stir it caused in the United States was compared to that of Barth's *Römerbrief* in Europe. Many years later, Albert C. Outler, professor of theology at Southern Methodist University in Dallas observed, "The tragic discrepancy between the personal and the social dimensions of ethical behavior seems now a commonplace in contemporary theology – but it wasn't in 1932! Niebuhr did not invent the notion, but he did sense its 'ripeness' – and this book about it still remains a sort of turning point in 'the new theology' in America."[37] The inevitable reality of evil is affirmed and documented, contrary to every optimism that does not see the existential impossibility of passing from the knowledge of the good that the individual has to its realization, an impossibility that is inexorably evident in the collective sphere. Neither ascesis in the name of the Gospel law of love, as the Social Gospel dreamt of, nor scientifically imparted education, according to the confident secularism of John Dewey, is capable of assuring a wise and perfect social structure and, therefore, of simply being translated into the ideal political tool for a peaceful guidance of society. In the area of social relationships, egoism unleashes its uncontrollable virulence, which only force, "power," can challenge: "an uneasy balance of power would seem to become the highest goal to which society could aspire."[38] The kingdom of power is quite distinct from the kingdom of brotherhood and love: "It would therefore seem better to accept a frank dualism in morals than to attempt a harmony between the two methods which threatens the effectiveness of both."[39]

Realism in the socio-political conception of Niebuhr reaches its extreme in *Reflections on the End of an Era* (1934). For a "tolerable society," the formula is that of an "equilibrium of power"; what is necessary is political theory that is radical "not only in the realistic nature of its analysis but in its willingness to challenge the injustice of a given social system by setting power against power until a more balanced equilibrium of power is achieved."[40] This is the moment in which Niebuhr feels the attraction of Marxism, and he prophesies catastrophe, thereby completely overturning the liberal philosophy of history that rested on the inevitability of progress: "the end of capitalism will be bloody rather than peaceful."[41] But, Niebuhr's approach remains vigilant and critical: "There are indications that communism will substitute a mechanistic collectivism for the mechanistic individualism of a bourgeois civilization … In this, as in some other respects, communism is too much the child of capitalism and lives too much by a precise negation of the vices of the latter to bring real peace and happiness to mankind."[42] Moreover, it is at the extreme horizon of this universal negativity that the final chapter of his book takes the path of Christian hope by elucidating the kernel of Christian dialectics and apologetics: "When the hard realities of history have once again dissipated the utopian dreams of the present the emphasis of classical religion upon the experience of grace will find its way back again into the moral and religious life of the race."[43]

In 1935, *An Interpretation of Christian Ethics* radicalized the analysis of the moral possibilities of man as such: "The ethical demands made by Jesus are incapable of fulfillment in the present existence of man"; "The full dimension of human life includes not only the impossible ideal, but realities of sin and evil which are more than simple imperfections and which prove that the ideal is something more than the product of a morbidly sensitive religious fantasy. Anything less than perfect love in human life is destructive of life. All human life stands under an impending doom because it does not live by the law of love."[44]

A volume of marvellous sermons, *Beyond Tragedy: Essays on the Christian Interpretation of History* (1937), anticipates the terms of that "dialectic of existence," which for Niebuhr bear the content of the Christian discourse and in whose definition and proclamation the entire meaning of the Christian presence in history lies.

The place where that dialectic is most powerfully developed and balanced is in the Gifford Lectures, given by Niebuhr at Edinburgh in 1939 and 1940, and published in two volumes in 1941 and 1943, respectively, with the title *The Nature and Destiny of Man: A Christian Interpretation*.[45] This masterpiece of Niebuhr's is the lynchpin to his entire investigation, because in the first volume, *Human Nature*, he systematically expresses an idea of man and, thus, genetically clarifies the ethical and social conception already featured in the central theme of his prior works; whereas in the second volume, *Human Destiny*, he brings forth what is at once a corollary and fulfilment, positing the initial terms of a vision of history, which he will define and document in later studies, among which the principal ones are *Faith and History: A Comparison of Christian and Modern Views of History* (1949),[46] *The Self and the Dramas of History* (1955), and *The Structure of Nations and Empires: A Study of the Recurring Patterns and Problems of the Political Order in Relation to the Unique Problems of the Nuclear Age* (1959).

3 *Theological Conception of Man and History*

Niebuhr deduces an overall vision of human nature, its existence or "situation," its history from an existential analysis whose elements are found fully enunciated in biblical-Christian revelation.

ESSENTIAL EPISTEMOLOGICAL AND HERMENEUTICAL FACTORS IN HIS THEOLOGICAL CONSTRUCTION The principal instrument in that analysis, as well as in his biblical interpretation is the idea of *myth* or "better … to avoid the skeptical connotation of the word 'myth,'"[47] the idea of *symbol*. In fact, the entire problem of reality can be boiled down to the time-eternity relationship. Now, "the relation between the temporal and the eternal is dialectical. The eternal is revealed and expressed in the temporal but not exhausted in it. God is not the sum total of finite occasions and relationships. He is their ground and they are the creation of his will. But, on the other hand, the finite world is not merely a corrupt emanation from the ideal and the eternal. Consequently, the relation of time and eternity cannot be expressed in simple rational terms. It can be expressed only in symbolic terms. A rational or logical expression of the relationship invariably leads either to a pantheism in which God and the world are identified, and the temporal in its totality is equated with the eternal; or in which they are separated so that a false supernaturalism emerges, a dualism between an eternal and spiritual world without content and a temporal world without meaning or significance."[48] Myth or symbol are "facts" into which the dimensions and ultimate meanings of existence are incorporated. There cannot be defining formulae, because that would be a rationalization of a particular point of view, and they would empty the transcendent terminus: they are historical cues in which man grasps the truth of his striving tension towards the transcendent that makes up his structure and his destiny. That the meaning of everything, the meaning of universal history, should be determined not by "recurrences and forms to which all historical phenomena conform," according to rationalistic demands, nor by "the endless development of human power and wisdom," according to modern evolutionistic demands, but instead emanate "from the core of a particular historical event," is the paradox that human culture treats as a scandal, the "'scandal of particularity' (*einmaligkeit*)."[49]

The confirmation of this fundamental phenomenon for man is what makes up the experience of *revelation*. The meaning of human existence, on the strength of its relationship with eternity, which is documented in its indefinite capacity for surpassing itself, the characteristic of its dynamism, can only come from "beyond" each and every moment of existence itself, from what is beyond time, from God: revelation is precisely "the invasion of the self from beyond the self."[50] And since reason is the faculty that apprehends and knows contingent, temporal entities, the perception of this communication of meaning by the eternal demands another type of power of apprehension, the one belonging to the spirit as man's capacity of relating to the transcendent: this capacity for apprehension of the spirit is actualized as *faith*.

This intuition of the ultimate meaning of existence is an experience that is renewed in every believer: in this sense revelation continues "in our own day."[51] But the events upon which faith draws and in which the connotations of its object are specified are specific moments in history, in linear connection, forming a history within history, the *Heilsgeschichte*. The intuitive believer, thus, maintains the "primacy of direct experience," but in Niebuhr, more than in all of mainstream American Protestant theology, this is structurally anchored to history. The Hebrew people with its prophets, Jesus, and the early Christian community were the first believers: the event of faith sprang forth in them through precise experiences. Divine revelation is bound to and exhausted in them in their concrete features: indeed, with them the meaning of what is finite is definitively clarified. They constituted the most profound existential experiences in an absolute sense. Each and every contact of man with God must reference those particular experiences and take possession of them. They are, therefore, the historical experiences that not only establish the origin of the faith, but also limit the history of revelation in a strict sense. The source events of faith conclude with the Cross and Resurrection of Christ. Yet, the "revelation of God … is not completed until man is able, by faith, to apprehend the truth which is beyond his apprehension without faith." Therefore, the "revelation of Christ is not completed until the little Christian community surveys the whole Christian epic."[52]

Revelation, in its original definition as the eternal meaning of the contingent that manifests itself in certain historical events, ends with *the early Christian community*. Myth and symbol are, therefore, the expressions with which the community "elaborates" and "completes"[53] the fact that reawakens the miracle of faith and in which the mystery of Revelation comes true: "miracle" and "mystery," because they are not the fruit of a rational process and, thus, they are also "gift of grace."[54]

Through the experiential recovery of the significance of myth, *the believer* of all times organically prolongs within himself the primitive event with its immanent vision of man and history.

Essence, existence, and human history are radically described in their makeup by the two elementary myths of Adam and Christ.

THE PARADOXICAL STRUCTURE OF THE HUMAN FIGURE AND EXISTENCE AS SIN It is in the *myth of Adam* that the paradox that constitutes the unity of the human person is marked out, the human person as "organic relation"[55] between an element that Niebuhr calls "creature" or "nature," and that substantially means man's finiteness and the determination or "givenness" of his forms, and another element indicated by Niebuhr as *imago Dei* or "spirit" or "freedom," "capacity for and affinity with the divine,"[56] whose characteristic is the phenomenon of the fact that the human self, despite being immanent to the situation in which it is relativized, is never definitively within it because it possesses an irreducible energy of going beyond itself, of "indefinite transcendence."[57] The structural tension between these two factors is expressed and realized as "will": more precisely, the will is the function of freedom insofar as, pushed by the urgency of the ideal, it manipulates the self as datum, as contingent determination; the will is the executive, "existentializing" aspect of freedom.

It is in the use of the will that the human tragedy plays out. In fact, the infinite is the meaning, the measure of freedom, and pure love is its adequate law. But the realization of freedom in existence mortifies and inevitably denies the ideal, and love is reduced to egocentrism. By means of an innate and mysterious "defect," which the myth of Adam connotes with the idea of "original sin," freedom in act is not pure "will of God," but in giving in to the "anxiety of freedom" it is reduced to "self-will," that is, to an egocentric affirmation of a finite, limited being. Therefore, as essence will is freedom, as act it is denial of it. Sin is man's "wrong use of his freedom and its consequent destruction."[58]

The inevitability of the contradiction within the will exists, paradoxically, side by side with the personal imputability of sin. It is an aspect of the will, and the will is the organ that expresses freedom; freedom is the antithesis of necessity. So, despite the presence of the "original" character of evil in the will, this must not be attributed to a necessity of human nature, but it is something extraneous to its essence and which happens in the will's determination. Man is, therefore, responsible. The content of such a judgment is motivated by man's psychological experience: Viewed from the outside, "sin may seem to be the necessary consequence of previous temptations."[59] However, the interior experience of sin destroys this deterministic explanation; interior experience always connotes the presence of a certain type of conscious dishonesty. The "feeling of remorse" and the "phenomenon of repentance" are proofs of this connivance.

The paradoxical dialectic between the inevitability and the imputability of evil is what provides all the drama of the human condition. What is proper to human acts and the historical instant is denial, failure according to the etymological connotation of lie and disappointment. The universality of this law is absolute. It is absolute for individuals, for whom "there is no justification in the revelation for any good man."[60] It is absolute for any collective existence and any human social manifestation; and it is significant that this law can be documented to the degree that a human place is called to carry meanings: "the claim of ultimate and absolute validity is always involved in religion."[61] Religion qua religion is always idolatrous. Moreover, not only is every individual or collective being subject to the law of human defeat, but every human theoretical expression: "There is ... no pure ethical norm in history; nor any hope of history gradually purifying itself so that it will achieve this norm."[62]

JUSTIFICATION AND SANCTIFICATION: POSSIBILITY AND MEANING OF HISTORY Nevertheless, the unfulfilled realization of the ideal, of the eternal, of the absolute, is not a total and definitive "condemnation" of temporal acts. In the *Christ myth*, the human condition is revealed with definitive clarity, and a valid conception of history is founded. In the *Cross,* the Divine, which is the norm of freedom, affirms itself as the point of comparison that shows the deficiency of history and becomes the "judgment" on it. The idea of the sovereignty of God that dominates the Bible is completely within this intuition: "The most obvious meaning of history is that every nation, culture, and civilization brings destruction upon itself by exceeding the bounds of creatureliness which God has set upon all human enterprises ... God is revealed in the catastrophic events of history as being, what each individual heart has already dimly perceived in its sense of being judged: as the structure, the law, the essential character of reality, as the source and centre of the created world against which the pride of man destroys itself in vain rebellion."[63]

Yet, this aspect of God's dominion in human history is not the extreme. One connotation of the symbol of the Cross reveals that the ultimate value of God for man is that of *forgiveness*: "human history stands in contradiction to the divine will on any level of its moral and religious achievements in such a way that in any 'final' judgment the righteous are proved not to be righteous"; and yet, the "good news of the gospel is that God takes the sinfulness of man into Himself."[64] Forgiveness exhaustively signifies God's power "over" man, the power that God has to surpass his own justice and to continually absolve with his infinite capital the inevitable debt of every human action, the power to tirelessly fill the void that is at the heart of every existential moment: "The revelation of the Atonement is precisely a 'final' word because it discloses a transcendent, divine mercy which represents the 'freedom' of God in quintessential terms: namely God's freedom over His own law."[65]

The perception of the Cross as "God who forgives" is the grace of "justification." This must not be determined based upon preconceived theological schemas, but based upon the individual's existential experience. Man, beyond his contrite recognition of his own unfulfilled realization, perceives the ideal and, therefore, God, as still "his," as still a value "for him," as something permanently attractive: in a certain true way man experiences justice as a new intentional possession. One could say that by faith man possesses justice as "sentiment," not "as act." The act corrupts this sentiment, this attitude of interior aspiration: and the dialectical process that governs human existence goes on. It is, therefore, a newness of life that remains at the root of the self without managing to translate itself completely into reality, just as the infinite transcendence of the spirit remains at the root of the self without managing to be completely realized. But, in that new intentional contact with perfection, with the Divine, a power of going beyond flows back into man and a new tension and a new capacity for action are developed: "the justification by faith is a release of the soul into action."[66]

Thus, the historical agent experiences himself as a continuous impulse to live up to the ideal: "The goodness of Christ must be embodied in the stuff of history."[67] Newness of life is found in the phenomenon of the renewed engagement of the whole self with reality, the recovery of the unity of the self and unity of the self with reality, the recovery of the possibility of action and the intensity of action; this is the grace of God's power "within" man or the grace of "sanctification."

In the Christ myth, this is all connoted in the sign of the Resurrection, indicator of the positive dimension of history that, thus, appears as "a realm of endless possibilities of renewal and rebirth."[68] Every human action is a striving towards the ideal and, thus, an approximation to it. Every historical reality, thus, incarnates a bit of the absolute, a bit of the good; the distinction between good and evil in existence and in history is not vain, and the moral struggle is proclaimed to be full of meaning. The definition of that meaning belongs to a transhistorical judgment (the Last Judgment myth), but its fulfilment takes nothing away from existence, of which every aspect will be preserved, integrated into the harmony of the whole (myth of the Resurrection of the flesh).

4 *Application to Particular Topics of Study*

The dialectic of historical humanity, suspended between ideal and realization, between the deficit and consistency of the value of every endeavour, illuminates particular topics of Niebuhr's other works through his "awareness of the moral precariousness of historical striving combined with his moral resoluteness about the immediate issues."[69]

In the 1940 work, *Christianity and Power Politics*, he denounced the naïveté of a pacifism which, by claiming that an ideal could be realized, in fact, reduced the resistance to evil. Niebuhr seeks almost what is a theology of war. War is a judgment of God on sins, it is a decision for freedom, for the Church, for democracy, therefore, for God himself. God's action in the world is not limited to revealing himself in the conscience, but is also carried out in events and, therefore, through human engagement.

In *The Children of Light and the Children of Darkness: A Vindication of Democracy and Critique of Its Traditional Defenders* (1944), this most complete Christian meditation specifies his judgment on Marxism, which "does not understand that even universalized property may become the instrument of particular interest ... Its failure to understand the perennial and persistent character of human egotism in any possible society, prompts it to make completely erroneous estimates of human behavior on the other side of a revolution."[70]

The keen observations that fill *Discerning the Signs of the Times: Sermons for Today and Tomorrow* (1946) focus on the grave error of modern culture, "which fondly assumed that the kind of 'objectivity' of which the natural sciences boast may be easily transferred to all historical, political and social judgments," and document how such an assumption "rests upon a disregard of the partly conscious and partly unconscious dishonesty involved in the error of social and historical judgments."[71]

The same accusation against society's claim of the impartiality and certainty of "scientific analysis," particularly as proclaimed by Dewey, is taken up again in the first and second chapters of *Christian Realism and Political Problems* (1953), while in other pages, he tirelessly appeals to the ambiguity and illusions of the social and political programs that fight to control our moment of history.

One of the categories of Niebuhr's perception of history, categories directly derived from the existential dialectic that frustrates all ideals and only leaves their presumption and expectation, is that of *irony*: "[Christian faith's] interpretation of the nature of evil in human history is consistently ironic ... the whole drama of human history is under the scrutiny of a divine judge who laughs at human pretensions without being hostile to human aspirations. The laughter at the pretensions is the divine judgment."[72] The main target of his brilliant ironic judgment is the illusory figure of an ideal America, casting light on incoherencies and contradictions in the moralizing and evolutionary role in the world that the United States thought to be its function in history. This is the inspiration of *The Irony of American History* (1952), *Pious and Secular America* (1958), and *A Nation so Conceived: Reflections on the History of America from Its Early Vision to Its Present Power* (1963).

5 *Value of the Figure of Niebuhr*

In Niebuhr, the main accents of American Protestant theological discourse re-emerge in a new and balanced synthesis: the imposing profile of Edwards' absolute and sovereign God, the Hopkinsian ideal of pure disinterested benevolence, the Revivalistic energy in the appeal to conversion, the Liberal sensitivity to making the Christian fact comprehensible and pertinent to modern culture, social urgency.

In Niebuhr, however, Protestant anthropological pessimism suggests a conception of the structure and meaning of human life with a dialectical coherence that cannot be found in Edwards. It is significant that Niebuhr demythologizes that idea of an America as the place where the Kingdom of God is manifested, which, in varied inflections and hues had animated the spirit of the breadth of American history, beginning with the most rigid Puritanism and ending with the euphoric sentiments of the Social Gospel.

Along the "tortuous path ... in adjusting the original Protestant heritage of individualism and perfectionism ... to the present realities of a highly technical and collective culture,"[73] Niebuhr carried on the inspiration of the Social Gospel in a certain way, albeit with an interpretative approach to the Christian fact that was ultimately still Liberal. He recovered the entire traditional Protestant anthropology that had been frustrated by the preceding generation, and from it developed a coherent idea of history in which the clear affirmation of pessimistic realism eluded its passivity and gave it a dynamic and interventionist direction. He, thus, originated an expression of Christian thought that this full of biting criticism, ready to point out the ambiguity and limits of each and every position and, at the same time, to energetically provoke engagement with every situation.

On the final page of his final book, *Man's Nature and His Communities: Essays on the Dynamics and Enigmas of Man's Personal and Social Existence* (1965), in which he intends "to summarize, and to revise previously held opinions," in a beautiful synthesis, Niebuhr delineates the categories in which his eminently pragmatic temperament has summed up his conception of human life: "the law of love is indeed the basis of all moral life ... it can not be obeyed by a simple act of the will because the power of self-concern is too great, and ... the forces which draw the self from its undue self-concern are usually forces of 'common grace' in the sense that they represent all forms of social security or responsibility or pressure which prompt the self to bethink itself of its social essence and to realize itself by not trying too desperately for self-realization."[74] Social and political commitment, although contingent in force and precarious in results, are therefore, the function that resolves the essential tension between divine and universalizing agape and anxious egocentrism.

Thus, Niebuhr had a very broad echo and impact also in social and political journalism, whereas in the history of American Protestant theology perhaps no figure after Edwards has equalled his influence and played such a decisive role in the spiritual world to which he belonged.

III PAUL TILLICH

1 *European Origin and Temper*

The brothers Reinhold and Richard Niebuhr introduced Paul Tillich (1886–1965) to the American theological world. Pastor of the Evangelical Lutheran Church of Brandenburg, after the First World War he passed into academic life and taught theology at Berlin and

Marburg and philosophy at Frankfurt, where he lost his chair in 1933 due to his anti-Hitler positions. He accepted an invitation from Reinhold Neibuhr, who at the time was touring Germany, and at the end of the year, Tillich became the Charles Briggs Graduate Professor of Philosophical Theology at Union Theological Seminary in New York. His name was, however, well known in America thanks to a translation and presentation that Richard Niebuhr had made in 1932 of his work *Die Religiöse Lage der Gegenwart* (1926) in an edition titled *The Religious Situation*.[75]

Tillich's intellectual makeup was completely generated and defined in his native country. The historical awareness of Romanticism and Idealism, especially in their incarnation in Schelling's philosophy of nature (the work he did for his 1911 doctorate at Breslau and for his licentiate in theology in 1912 at Halle were both on Schelling), mark the first influence, which will later be opened up by his readings of Kierkegaard and in his contacts with Heidegger, his colleague at Marburg, and with Husserl. His lively interpretation of the link between Christian categories and cultural forms, a feature of the teachings of Martin Kähler with his "theology of mediation," permanently inspired Tillich's theological approach. Art and literature, depth psychology, and sociology in the rich expressive tensions of the pre- and post-war German world offered provocations to that relationship without which religious discourse is deprived of meaning and impact. A 1919 contribution, "Über die Idee einer Theologie der Kultur,"[76] identifies the formula, "theology of culture," which can characterize the need that dominated all of Tillich's intellectual labour. In particular, the synthesis between religious values and social interest committed Tillich very concretely to being one of the leaders of the "German Socialist Religious" movement.

The titles of his works until 1933 testify to the complex interests of the author. Some are pamphlets, including *Masse und Geist* (1922); *Kirche und Kultur* (1924); *Das Dämonische: Ein Beitrag zur Sinn deutung der Geschichte* (1926); and *Hegel und Goethe: Zwei Gedenkreden* (1932). Others are well-developed works, including *Das System der Wissenschaften nach Gegenständen und Methoden* (1923), the abovecited *Die Religiöse Lage der Gegenwart* (1926), *Religiöse Verwirklichung* (1930), and *Die sozialististische Entscheidung* (1933).

The over one hundred articles and essays of the German period testify to the mature consistency of his thought. His American oeuvre would expand and elaborate into a magnificent organism the inspiration, topics, and lines of development that are already present in them. Thus, his first two books published in America, *The Interpretation of History* (1936) and *The Protestant Era* (1948), recover many writings from 1922 on, and his main work was arranged and begun during the time of his teaching at Marburg. The structure of his intellectual dynamism is qualitatively European, and this explains the comparison that critics have at times drawn between Tillich's structure of thought and the systematic nature of Thomism: "[Tillich's] mind has a generous comprehensiveness peculiarly his own. May he be the new Aquinas who will find a place within his system for the truth in all our contending theological schools."[77] G. Weigel, after the publication of *The Protestant Era*, commented: "There is something Thomistic about this brilliant thinker, not in the sense that he subscribes to the more characteristic Thomistic theses – he rejects many of them violently – but in the sense that he is moved by the same feeling for unity and completeness in his vision of the real."[78]

The figure of Tillich, thus, emerges outside the natural lines of the American Protestant theological tradition and, despite the fact that most of his production belongs to his émigré period, ultimately, it is that of a European thinker.

2 *Correspondence with the Features of American Discourse*

Nevertheless, no other spiritual position or intellectual discourse could better enter into a suitably intense dialogue with Liberal American theology in its "realist" or "neo-orthodox" conversions than that of Paul Tillich.

In accepting the fundamental inspiration of European dialectical theology, it was the declared intention of the new American theologians to not resign themselves to merely repeating, but to testify to biblical truth in a synthesis that would be appropriate to their own temperament. "Empirical temperament" was how they defined it, with a fundamentally pragmatic and psychological tendency that made them distrustful of any absolutist position and of any theological and dogmatic framework "not born from the light of experience and criticism."[79] In particular, as noted earlier, they did not share the absolute opposition that dialectical theology established between Grace and nature. Indeed, it is their characteristically American effort that clarifies the bridge between the two poles: "Revelation *and* reason, revelation *and* experience say the same thing for American theology. Precisely this 'and' against which Barth struggles, is the American synthesis."[80] Tillich's position is in agreement with this type of dialectical unity, and it is that demand for pragmatic verification that his "experiential method" would value.

Tillich's cultural framework made him exceptionally ready to dive into the rich openness to contacts with the whole world that characterized the possibilities of the American situation, and to integrate dialogue into it.

Thus, Tillich is a master within the world of American Protestant thought and is accepted as tremendously suited to the urgencies and accents proper to that world. In conscious contrast to the "kerigmatic" theology of Barth, Tillich insists on the "apologetic" nature of his thought. The word of revelation cannot be, as in the Barthian position, a stone that has fallen from heaven to man's earth. It is an answer to the need of man as man, and it is grasped within the particular situation in which that need lives. It, thus, starts with the analysis of the human condition as recognized in a given cultural and civilizational moment and speaks through the intellectual tools proper to that time. Thus, a theology can never claim a final definition, but as one step among the many that man takes in the quest for his meaning, documents a contingent way of approaching revelation. The apologetic approach is, therefore, on the "boundary"[81] between philosophical investigation and theological development: "as a theologian I tried to remain a philosopher, and conversely so."[82]

3 *First American Publications*

The long series of his American publications testifies, in a fascinating way, to the tension of this dialectic in the adventure of a profound thought.

In the first of these books, *The Interpretation of History* (1936), Tillich states that the basis of his system is a philosophy of the meaning of being. In attempting to give consistency to the relationship between philosophy and theology, he affirms that "the presupposition of success of this attempt is, of course, that the theonomous character of knowing be acknowledged; that is to say, that thinking is rooted in the absolute as the foundation and abyss of meaning."[83] With a concept already spoken of in *Das System der Wissenschaften*, Tillich defines theology as "theonomous metaphysics," in that by overcoming a purely rational interpretation of experience, it grasps divine self-revelation in the "depths" of experience itself.

In the essays that make up *The Protestant Era* (1948), what dominates is the concept of God as absolutely unconditioned and, therefore, absolutely inexpressible, whose existence emerges to human consciousness solely in the immediateness of existential intuition that takes place in faith. Protestantism is the true religion precisely because it is essentially "protest" against any attempt to give to something finite, conditioned, the devotion and recognition that are due only to what is unconditional and absolute. Man's supreme duty is the ever-ready obedience to that design of the good and the true that cannot be identified by absolute norms, but that can be found in the soul that is ready to grasp, in an essentially variable situation, the unforeseeable requests of the transforming divine presence. The Christ of the Cross is the supreme example for man, and is the symbol of the relationship between man and God, thanks to his obedience precisely at the point in which his dreams and ideals are frustrated.

Tillich's Christology, like that of Niebuhr, is Nestorian: Christ is not God, but in him *is revealed* what God is for man.

4 *His Principal Work*

In 1951, the first of three volumes of *Systematic Theology* (which would be completed in 1957 and in 1963)[84] was released.

THE "METHOD OF CORRELATION" The grandiose organism of Tillichian theology as systematic interpretation of the contents of the Christian faith follows what is called a "method of correlation." This method is the consequence of the typical situation in which theological discourse is posited; it is solicited by "an a priori of experience and valuation"[85] that implicitly conditions it. An ultimate and primordial intuition about reality impels and nourishes the later theological theorization, which, at a certain moment, can become aware of its intuitive basis, but cannot neutralize it because it is precisely from it that it draws its origin and sustenance. The intuition of the "mystical" a priori coincides with the criterion of the Christian message.

Thus, a circular *Geisteswissenschaft* is created: the Christian message, assumed courageously and critically by the theologian (the aforementioned coincidence is affirmed as the fruit of existential choices and risks, rather than of logical evidence), generates a dialectic with the problematic demands of lived reality. The "theological circle" is to be understood as an ellipsis whose foci are the problem of existence and the theologian's response.[86]

The forms of this relationship define the method of correlation, whose initial aim is "to seek a theological method in which method and situation are related."[87] The questions that existence poses are compared to the solutions that theology offers by examining the Christian message originally assumed by it. Between question and answer, between situation and message, there is an indissoluble bond: while, on the one hand, the analysis of the existential condition is influenced by the theological solution because the form of the existential problem is determined by the totality of the system and by answer given within it, on the other hand, the answer is revealed solely as ultimate content, whereas its form comes from the existential problem. The method of correlation, thus formulated, seems to be a valid tool for bringing about the challenging rapprochement between the Christian message and the modern world because "it makes an analysis of the human situation out of which the existential questions arise, and it demonstrates that the symbols used in the Christian message are the answers to these questions."[88]

PHILOSOPHY AND THEOLOGY: RELATIONS The articulation of this method also clarifies his conception of the relationship between philosophy and theology. The task of philosophy is to investigate the existential situation, delineate its problems, and ask for solutions. Philosophy is an analysis of reality that is more descriptive than constructive; and it is also laboriously developed out of an original intuition of being, through an attitude of detachment and of generalization; it uses pure reason and seeks the definition of the universal logos. Theology tries to build the ultimate answer to the human problems that are thus marked out: "Only those propositions are theological which deal with their object in so far as it can become a matter of ultimate concern for us … Our ultimate concern is that which determines our being or non-being. Only those statements are theological which deal with their object in so far as it can become a matter of being or not-being for us."[89]

The specific differences between the philosopher and the theologian can be recognized, above all, in the fact that the cognitive attitude of he theologian is eminently "committed" to his own faith, whereas the cognitive attitude of the philosopher is characterized by a detachment and an attempt at objectification. Second, whereas the philosopher is equally interested in any historical event whatsoever for what it may say regarding the ultimate structures of being, what constitutes the source and object of knowledge for the theologian is instead "the Logos 'who became flesh,'" that is, "the *logos* manifesting itself in a particular historical event" and that is revealed not through "common rationality but the church, its traditions and present reality."[90] Third, both the philosopher and the theologian, "even when they speak about the same object, they speak about something different." If, for example, they deal with the problem of history, the philosopher will seek to penetrate its nature and define its limits, he will enter into ontology and into the logic of being and non-being: "The philosopher deals with the categories of being in relation to the material which is structured by them." The theologian, instead, "relates the same categories and concepts to the quest for a 'new being.' His assertions have a soteriological character":[91] if he investigates history, he will seek the nexus that binds the structures of life at the creative depths of being, and he will formulate the victory of being over non-being in terms of nature's participation in salvation history.

Nevertheless, a profound convergence qualifies the positions of both philosopher and theologian. The philosopher, like the theologian, "exists," and despite his attempt at objectification, he cannot avoid, in the concreteness of his existence, asking for an answer to the anxiety of non-being that afflicts his daily life. Philosophy draws its *eros*, its passion and its creativity, from an ultimate motive that as such is implicitly theological: "[The philosopher] is a theologian in the degree to which his existential situation and his ultimate concern shape his philosophical vision. He is a theologian in the degree to which his intuition of the universal *logos* of the structure of reality as a whole is formed by a particular *logos* which appears to him on his particular place and reveals to him the meaning of the whole. And he is a theologian in the degree to which the particular *logos* is a matter of active commitment within a special community."[92]

On the other hand, the theologian seeks to cause the universal validity of his object to emerge. He is critical of every expression of it, and while on the one hand, he accepts the various historical formulations of the Christian message, on the other, he denies them as not exhaustive or as ambiguous.

The philosopher and the theologian, precisely because of this convergence, live an acute dilemma: the detachment required by every honest theological labour risks destroying the commitment to the faith, and the conflict between the intention of universal becoming and the destiny of remaining particular characterizes every philosophical existence. It is in such a dilemma that both the limit and the greatness of their labour both reside.

STRUCTURE OF HIS OEUVRE The method of correlation, which suggests the overall dialectic of Tillich's discourse, also determines his individual works. "Reason and Revelation" and "Being and God" are the two "parts" into which volume I [of *Systematic Theology*] is divided. The discussion begins with the structure and deficiencies of reason and the fact of revelation's victory over them, then follow the structure and the contradictory nature of existence in being and divine being's triumph over them.

Volume II, titled *Existence and the Christ*, offers an analysis of existential alienation, that is, of the "fall" within existence from a state of harmony, or "essence." Christ as the "New Being" is the mediating and resolving figure, since in him is inaugurated a new reality in which existential alienation finds peace.

In volume III, in the first section (part IV of the entire work), entitled "Life in the Spirit," he discusses human existence in its present state, which is neither essence in its imperturbable perfection, nor existence in its inexhaustible contradiction, but concrete life with its ambiguities and, at the same time, with a foretaste of the truth, immanence in its material makeup in which some of the truth shines through. "Life" is expressed in various forms (morality, culture, religion), and the divine Spirit manifests itself as their ultimate foundation. The traditional Trinitarian symbol is a sign of that foundation, "the threefold manifestation ... as creative power, as saving love, and as ecstatic transformation."[93]

In life, however, history is the "the most embracing dimension, presupposing the others and adding a new element to them." "History and the Kingdom of God" is the title of part V of the work: "A theological discussion of history must ... deal with the structures of historical processes, the logic of historical knowledge, the ambiguities of historical existence, the meaning of the historical moment. It must also relate all this to the symbol of the Kingdom of God, both in its inner-historical and in its transhistorical sense."[94] This symbol marks the final repose of human anxiety and the fulfilment of human reason's quest.

5 *Minor Works*

Although Tillich's themes are exhaustively dealt with in his main work, a reading of his books that anticipated or documented and developed certain aspects of those themes is of great interest. In 1951, there appeared a clear and fascinating study of the psychological condition of modern man who had become insecure in the autonomy he had achieved: *Courage to Be*. Tillich analyzes the various forms of anxiety of death, of meaning, of guilt. Anxiety, pressed to its ultimate consequences, becomes desperation, and in this extreme situation a way out is once again found. In fact, "The paradox of every radical negativity, as long as it is an active negativity, is that it must affirm itself in order to negate itself. No actual negation can be without an implicit affirmation ... The negative lives from the positive it negates."[95] Upon it is founded the "courage to be," the courage to accept in the face of the negativity that threatens existence: "Courage is the self-affirmation of being in spite of the fact of nonbeing."[96]

In 1954, in *Love, Power and Justice: Ontological Analyses and Ethical Applications*, he defines power as "the drive of everything living to realize itself with increasing intensity and extensity" or the "self-affirmation of life overcoming internal and external resistance."[97] Power creates a balance whereby expansion does not become violence but a productive force, by means of the intervention of love, "the drive towards the unity of the separated"[98] or the estranged, and of justice, which regulates the various forms that being assumes in its concrete expressions. The interplay of love, power, and justice, examined in the individual, in groups, and in history, reveals a latent conflict. The concepts recall each other in essence, but in existence they separate and enter into conflict. Unity is established in Being itself, which reveals itself as love, and which, in a certain sense, is already present within history: "In this way, the power and justice of being in a social group is dependent on the spirit of the community, and this means on the uniting love which creates and sustains the community."[99]

A slim volume of eighty-five pages, *Biblical Religion and the Search for Ultimate Reality* (1955), marks out the difference between biblical religion, which is concrete and anthropomorphic, and the more rational and abstract forms that characterize the Greek culture inherited by us and modern science. Both forms of thought can encounter each other at the level of a common interest in what transcends finite existence, that is, for the foundation of every being.

In the same year in which the second volume of his major work was released, *Dynamics of Faith* (1957) accuses the distorted way in which the faith is presented of being the cause of the contemporary world's ignorance of it: "Faith is the state of being ultimately concerned," and precisely for this reason, "it demands the total surrender of him who accepts this claim, and it promises total fulfillment even if all other claims have to be subjected to it or rejected in its name."[100] But faith is not static tranquility: "If faith is understood as belief that something is true, doubt is incompatible with the act of faith. If faith is understood as being ultimately concerned, doubt is a necessary element in it. It is a consequence of the risk of faith ... The doubt which is implicit in every act of faith is neither methodological nor skeptical doubt. It is the doubt that accompanies every risk ... One could call it the existential doubt ... It does not question whether a special proposition is true or false. It does not reject every concrete truth, but it is aware of the element of insecurity in every existential truth. At the same time, the doubt which is implied in faith accepts this insecurity and takes it into itself in an act of courage. Faith includes courage."[101] Faith, understood correctly, that is, as "ultimate concern" lived in the risk of existence – and the man of today has particular need of this faith that does not rest, but rather values the anxiety of time and posits itself as the possibility of man's integration with himself and his peers – "cannot be undercut by modern science or any kind of philosophy ... Faith stands upon itself and justifies itself against those who attack it, because they can attack it only in the name of another faith."[102]

A collection of essays on varied themes (philosophy, aesthetics, psychology, and science) is *Theology of Culture* (1959). Its connecting thread is the attempt to define "the way in which Christianity is related to secular culture," and Tillich notes how this "has always been in the center of my interest."[103] This attempt is based upon the basic assumption that "in all preliminary concerns, ultimate concern is present, consecrating them."[104] The relationship between religion and culture is, thus, a dialectical one, in which each of the two terms needs the other in order to define itself: "Religion as ultimate concern is the meaning-giving substance of culture, and culture is the totality of forms in which the basic concern of religion expresses itself. In abbreviation: religion is the substance of culture, culture is the form of religion."[105]

As testimony to his visit to the Far East, *Christianity and the Encounter of the World Religions* (1963) is concerned with comprehending what there is in common between Christianity and the other religions and what may be the basis for a dialogue between the world's great faiths, as Tillich begins and exemplifies through the relationship with Buddhism: the future will not see conflicts between religions, but between all religious movements and secularism and communism.

The same year another collection of essays, many already published, *Morality and Beyond*, confirms the basic point that man's moral attitude has meaning only if seen in the context of his ultimate reference, his relationship with God.

Three books of sermons enter the index of volumes published by Tillich, almost all dictated in college and seminary chapels: *The Shaking Foundations* (1948), *The New Being* (1955), and *The Eternal Now* (1963).

5

Recent Trends

1 NEO-LIBERALISM

During the Second World War a Neo-liberal trend had manifested consistent renewal. In it, there came together also personalities who were initially active in the Neo-orthodox orbit. The contents of a symposium, published in 1942 by David Everett Roberts (1911–1955) and Henry Pitney Van Dusen (1897–1975), provides excellent documentation in this regard: *Liberal Theology: An Appraisal.* Human nature and human reason are defences against that "veiled … glance of agnosticism"[1] for which Willard Learoyd Sperry of Harvard University would scold Neo-orthodoxy in his *Religion in America* (1946).

Among the more significant names, Charles Clayton Morrison (1874–1967) must be remembered, beyond the role he played in the *Christian Century*, the most characteristic and influential periodical in the dialogue on Church life and the theological debate in the twentieth century, edited in Chicago, for his ecclesiological and ecumenical concern and his publications in that regard: *What Is Christianity?* (1940) and *The Unfinished Reformation* (1953).

Henry Pitney Van Dusen, president of Union Theological Seminary from 1945 to 1963, recently gave a critically sympathetic synthesis of the fundamental categories of the Liberal tradition in *The Vindication of Liberal Theology: A Tract for the Times* (1963).

Lotan Harold De Wolf (b. 1905 [d. 1986]), former professor of systematic theology at Boston [University] and, later, dean of that department at Wesley Theological Seminary, exemplifies in a clear summary exposition a systematic discourse on Christian themes interpreted with the Liberal mentality, in *The Case for Theology in the Liberal Perspective* (1959); and he also gives us the best manual of recent Liberal theology with *A Theology of the Living Church* (1953).

Yet, the Liberalism of the turn of the century has decisively passed on to evaluating the new appeals. While remaining firm as a theological method and in biblical criticism, it seeks the outlines of a system that can integrate the elements of truth that emerged from the Neo-orthodox Movement. The best example of such an attempt at balance is the Rauschenbusch Lectures of Daniel Day Williams (1910–1973), at the University of Chicago, published with the title *God's Grace and Man's Hope* (1949). In them, Williams stresses how redemptive action is confirmed by the reality of moral progress, in the existence of the individual and of society; and the biblical message regarding the form of divine activity towards human destiny is related to the dynamic vision of nature and history offered by the new philosophical currents.

2 THE CONTINUITY OF FUNDAMENTALISM

Fundamentalism continues in conservative circles, at times with its old intransigence, as can be seen in *The New Modernism* (1946) by Cornelius Van Til (1895–1987), and with unaltered methods, as is documented in the collection of Christological works of B.B. Warfield, edited by Samuel G. Craig (1874–1960), under the title *The Person and Work of Christ* (1950).

The traditionalist discourse finds its point of reference in the widely read bimonthly *Christianity Today*, which posits itself as an alternative to the liberal the *Christian Century*. Its editor, Carl Ferdinand Howard Henry (b. 1913 [d. 2003]), is the author of *Fifty Years of Protestant Theology* (1950), notable also for the consideration given to Neo-orthodox and Neo-liberal trends.

Among the best expressions of the current legacy of Fundamentalism is Edward John Carnell (1919–1967) of Pasadena Theological Seminary, with his balanced works *An Introduction to the Christian Apologetics* (1948) and *The Case for Orthodox Theology* (1959).

3 ECUMENICAL THEOLOGY

The ecumenical movement found intense adhesion on American soil, both in the pragmatic version of *Life and Work* and in the more strictly doctrinal version of *Faith and Order*.

In response to the "cooperativistic" concerns dictated by the urgency of action and effectiveness in a non-Christian world – which was the motivation for so much of the activity of the pioneers of the Social Gospel like Josiah Strong – the great apostle Charles Henry Brent (1862–1929), American Episcopalian bishop in the Philippines, had introduced the idea of communion among the various denominations as necessary for a "completeness" of Christian life and expression. At the Oxford Conference of 1937, John A. Mackay (1889–1983), later president of Princeton Theological Seminary, developed Brent's idea in the concept of an "Ecumenical Church" as a reality endowed with "inherent and objective unity," while during the same year, Princeton inaugurated the first chair of "Ecumenics" as the "science of the universal Church conceived as worldwide missionary community in its nature, in its functions, in its relations and in its strategy."

In that sense, the intensification of the ecumenical concern directly or indirectly gave rise to a recovery of the essential ecclesiological themes, which had been scarcely valued by the dominant theological doctrine of the eighteenth, nineteenth, and early twentieth centuries, with few exceptions, above all, in the Lutheran camp with Samuel Simon Schmucker (1799–1873) and his prophetic *Fraternal Appeal to the American Churches: With a Plan for Catholic Union, on Apostolic Principles* (1838), or at Mercersburg, particularly with Schaff, or among the Episcopalians with the noteworthy *The Church Idea: An Essay Toward Unity* (1870), by William Reed Huntington (1838–1909).

The abundant literature that accompanied the concretization of the ecumenical interest marked a historical concern, together with an attempt to identify the principles it implied, in Kenneth Scott Latourette (1884–1968), *Toward Christian Fellowship* (1938); William Adams Brown (1865–1943), *Toward a United Church: Three Decades of Ecumenical Christianity* (1946); Walter Marshall Horton (1895–1966), *Toward a Reborn Church: A Review and Forecast of the Ecumenical Movement* (1949); Leonard Hodgson (1889–1964), *The Ecumenical Movement* (1951).

The essence of an ecumenical Church is tentatively sketched out in the works of Theodore Otto Wedel (1892–1970), *The Coming Great Church* (1945); Norman Victor Hope (b. 1908 [d.1983]), *One Christ, One World, One Church: A Short Introduction to the Ecumenical Movement* (1953); Christopher Glover, *The Church for the New Age: A Dissertation on Church Unity* (1956); Winfred Ernest Garrison (1874–1969), *The Quest and Character of a United Church* (1957); Nils Ehrenström (1903–1984) and Walter G. Muelder (b. 1907 [d. 2004]), *Institutionalism and Church Unity* (1963). The biblical foundation is sought in Clarence Tucker Craig (1895–1953), *The One Church in the Light of the New Testament* (1951).

New Ecclesiological Sensibility

But the ecclesiological sensibility, as it were, reawakened, freed, and increased by the ecumenical spirit, has found insistent expression also not directly and immediately finalized towards the ecumenical movement. The phenomenon is found among the various currents of thought. Particularly significant in that sense is the recovery of the theme by Liberals, as has been documented in C.C. Morrison and L.H. De Wolf.

Some notable examples of ecclesiological studies are Nels F.S. Ferré (1908–1971), *The Christian Fellowship* (1940); Donald George Miller (1909–1997), *The Nature and Mission of the Church* (1957); Paul Sevier Minear (b. 1906 [d. 2007]), *Images of the Church in the New Testament* (1960); John Knox (b. 1900), *The Church and the Reality of Christ* (1962); Lewis Mudge (b. 1929 [d. 2009]), *One Church: Catholic and Reformed – Toward a Theology for Ecumenical Decision* (1963); Claude Welch (b. 1922 [d. 2009]), *The Reality of the Church* (1958); Lewis Howard Grimes (1915–1989), *The Church Redemptive* (1966); and William Klassen (b. 1930), *The Forgiving Community* (1966).

Of notable interest is the revision of John Robert Nelson (b. 1926 [d. 2004]), *The Realm of Redemption: Studies in the Doctrine of the Nature of Church in Contemporary Theology* (1951).

4 ATTEMPTS TO REBUILD THEOLOGY WITH THE AID OF NEW CATEGORIES

Theology and Process Metaphysics

The process metaphysics of Alfred North Whitehead (1861–1947) and Charles Hartshorne (1897–2000) seemed to offer a more open possibility of building a foundation or a rational interpretation of the faith, thus, suggesting formulations that were no longer bound to Kantian or existentialist frameworks, nor to the traditional metaphysical concept of God as timeless and changeless being.

In his works, *Man's Vision of God and the Logic of Theism* (1941), *The Divine Relativity* (1948), and *A Natural Theology for Our Time* (1967), Charles Hartshorne expresses the idea of a God who, essentially love, is completed in the relationship with the freedom of his creatures; this is the dynamic of which the reality of the universe would consist: "Process theologians believe ... that the Christian knowledge of God has analogues in our knowledge of the world and of other persons. The task is to see how the Biblical faith is to be interpreted in relation to the kinds of experience which contemporary man has of his world, and to the evolutionary historical picture of the life of nature and of human existence ... only in relation to a more adequate scientific, philosophical and theological understanding of nature can the contemporary man's questions about God be given meaningful answers."[2]

One work carried out in this intellectual climate is *A Christian Natural Theology: Based on the Thought of Alfred North Whitehead* (1965), by John Boswell Cobb Jr, professor of systematic theology at the Southern California School of Theology. According to Cobb, from Whitehead's philosophical framework one can deduce that God "is an actual entity who envisages and orders the realm of eternal possibilities. He adds himself to the world as the vision of ideal possibility, from which every new occasion takes its rise, thereby ensuring a measure of order and value in a situation that could otherwise be only chaotic and indeed could achieve no actuality at all. The world, in its turn, reacts upon him so as to affect the way which he, in his turn, acts upon it."[3]

Another interesting document on Cobb's thought is *The Structure of Christian Existence* (1967).

One of the most important names in contemporary American theology was certainly influenced by Whitehead's theories. Nels Fredrick Solomon Ferré (1908–1971) was concerned with finding a discourse suitable for the conception of God, founded on reason and on faith. His position constitutes a very personal synthesis, in which accents of Neo-orthodoxy and traditional themes like that of the Thomistic "analogy" are revisited. Faith casts further light on the God of reason, to whom the limitations of existential processes must be attributed, and thus, divine reality is finally identified with a higher order of being, a sovereign power beyond all conditionings, that transcends the entire world of experience and its motion, and yet, is actively bound to it through the creative operation that is continually determined by the dynamic element that constitutes the essence of its nature, that is, *agape*, and by which it will, ultimately, be saved. Among Ferré's many works, in addition to the aforementioned, we should draw attention to *Reason and the Christian Faith*: vol. I, *Faith and Reason* (1946), and vol. II, *Evil and the Christian Faith* (1947); *The Christian Understanding of God* (1951); *Christian Faith and Higher Education* (1954); *Christ and the Christian* (1958); *Reason and Religion* (1963), and *The Living God of Nowhere and Nothing* (1967).

Some Christological essays also borrow their interpretive point of view from process philosophy. In much of the Protestant world, criticism on early Christianity has changed the meaning of the terms of the problem of Christology: "It is not two 'natures' which have to be related; but two 'histories.' There is the history of our human existence with its fate, its freedom, and its course of events. In this history stands the real person, Jesus of Nazareth, who is just as truly 'historical' as any other. There is also the history of God's creative and redemptive dealing with men which has come to its climax in the history of Jesus. It is these two histories which we have to relate to each other. When we look for God's redemptive action it is not supernatural existence but personal meaning which concerns us."[4] Whitehead's and Hartshorne's doctrines have demonstrated themselves adaptable to being an intellectual framework upon which to base a study of the image of Christ in that sense: this is what is documented in *Word Incarnate: A Study of the Doctrine of the Person of Christ* (1959), by William Norman Pittenger (b. 1905 [d. 1997]), an Anglo-Catholic at the General Theological Seminary in New York, whose notable works also include *Christ and the Christian Faith* (1941) and *Rethinking the Christian Message* (1956).

Theology and Heidegger's Categories

Heideggerian categories are referenced in the structuring of the theology of John Macquarrie (b. 1919 [d. 2007]), professor of systematic theology at Union [Theological] Seminary, as he himself attests to in his *Principles of Christian Theology* (1966): "For many philosophical categories employed in this book I am indebted to the writings of Martin Heidegger. As it seems to me, his way of philosophizing and the concepts he has developed provide the basis for a viable twentieth-century philosophical ('natural') theology, and can be used further for the articulation and elucidation of the whole body of Christian truth in a contemporary way."[5]

Also worthy of note is Macquarrie's study on the value of theological discourse, *God-talk: An Examination of the Language and Logic of Theology* (1967).

Theology and Analytical Philosophy

Wittgenstein's analytical philosophy determined many of the dialectical concerns of the Lutheran William Hordern, a graduate of Union Theological Seminary and later president of Lutheran Theological Seminary in Saskatoon (Canada), mainly in his study on the Christian experience of God, *Speaking of God: The Nature and Purpose of Theological Language* (1964). The absolute unknowability of the mystery of God does not take away the ontological significance of the language that references it: "To say that 'God is' is to make a dramatic statement about the nature of reality, it is ontological." He continues: "The Christian faith stands or falls with certain specific statements about reality – 'God was in Christ,' 'God is love.' Insofar as Christianity makes such statements it is committed implicitly to certain ontological affirmations ... In this case, far from being indifferent to ontology, Christianity has its own ontology to offer."[6] Hordern takes up themes that are dear to neo-orthodoxy, but he prefers to refer to his current of thought as "new reformation," as in his work, *The Case for a New Reformation Theology* (1959).

An Augustinian Inspiration

The inspiration of St Augustine lives again in the basic arrangement of *Christian Apologetics* (1947), by the Anglican (Episcopalian) Alan Richardson (1905–1975): revelation is illumination; in the light of faith man recognizes truth, and that light permits reason to organize the interpretation of the world; theology has the task of verifying how much the standpoint of the faith is more suitable to the facts and factors of the real than the alternative hypotheses.

5 TRENDS IN ETHICAL THEOLOGY

In the field of ethical theology, the positions can be summed up in a double categorization that the philosopher William K. Frankena defines as *act-agapism* and *rule agapism*.[7] Paul Ramsey (b. 1913 [d. 1988]), of Princeton University, an excellent student of Christian ethics, refers to the first attitude as that in which "we are to tell what we should do in a particular situation simply by getting clear about the facts of that situation and then asking what is the loving or the most loving thing to do in it"; the second attitude, instead, seeks to identify "what we ought to do, not by asking which *act* is the most loving, but by determining which *rules of action* are most love embodying."[8]

Ethics of Law

Without doubt, Ramsey belongs to the second group. In his *Basic Christian Ethics* (1950), he had sustained the centrality of sacrificial love as the ultimate norm, and the profound detachment of that love from any egocentric connotation: "The commandment [of love] requires the Christian to aim at his neighbor's good just as unswervingly as man by nature wishes his own. Thus Christian ethics draws its standard *from man* only by inverting it."[9]

Ramsey's other publications document the necessity that the loving ideal be translated into structures and be articulated in norms: *Christian Ethics and the Sit-In* (1961), *Nine Modern Moralists* (1962),[10] *The Limits of Nuclear War* (1963), and above all, *Deeds and Rules in Christian Ethics* (1965), where he reproposes the issue with clarity: "The fundamental question concerning the Christian life is whether from agape there comes any instruction concerning the moral life, or any formative influence productive of a Christian style of life."[11]

Situation Ethics

Act-agapism corresponds to the approach that has been otherwise formulated as "situation ethics" or "context ethics."

In the structure [proposed by] Paul Louis Lehmann (b. 1906 [d. 1994]), of Union Theological Seminary, in *Ethics in a Christian Context* (1963), the decision that produces the morality of the act in its origin goes beyond any restricted individualism, because its formation takes place in the context of the Christian community, and for this reason, Lehmann speaks of *koinonia ethics*: "There is no formal principle of Christian behavior because Christian behavior cannot be generalized," but it is through the life of the Christian community that we are able to view our neighbor as neighbor; thus, *koinonia* is a "laboratory of maturity," and within it "conscience acquires ethical reality and the power to shape behavior through obedient freedom."[12]

The genetic process of the moral decision is clearly individualistic in Joseph Fletcher (1905–1991), teacher of social ethics at the Episcopal Theology School of Cambridge (Massachusetts), who became one of the leaders of the Situation Ethics Movement – or the New Morality according to the formula he adopted – with his book *Situation Ethics: The New Morality* (1966). Christian ethics is not "a scheme of living according to a code but a continuous effort to relate love to a world of relativities through a casuistry obedient to love."[13] Fletcher also speaks of his position as that of a "neocausistry," where "Love Is the Only Norm," "Love and Justice Are the Same," and "Love Justifies Its Means," as the titles of chapters IV, V, and VII of this work stated. Thus, "If a lie is told unlovingly it is wrong, evil; if it is told in love it is good, right."[14] The best synthetic expression of the radical conception that Fletcher has of the moral fact is perhaps the formula he uses in a 1959 article: "*The indicative* [of the situation] *plus the imperative* [of love] *equals the normative*. What is, in the light of what love demands, shows what ought to be."[15]

Fletcher's other work that should be remembered is *Moral Responsibility: Situation Ethics at Work* (1967).

6 RADICAL THEOLOGY

For some years now, a new movement has risen up that bears a sensational aspect that has also brought it to the forefront of European attention, giving rise to a vast literature. This is called Death of God Theology or Radical Theology.

Its approach is dictated by the presupposition that theology cannot avoid speaking within the experiences and terms of the culture of its times. In making note of the Barthian total disconnect between the expression of the faith and worldly experience, between theology and culture, Tillich had made the juncture between these two his typical centre of interest; and numerous attempts at connecting the pole of Christian discourse with that of philosophical language have characterized American Protestant thought of the 1950s and 1960s as this last chapter has exemplified. But, for Radical theologians, modern culture must impose form and content on theological interpretation. Now, today's culture is characterized by "an awareness predicated on the uselessness of God, whether he exists or not."[16] Dietrich Bonhoeffer, whose influence on this new theology is quite keen, noted in his *Letters*: "Man has learned to cope with all questions of importance without recourse to God as a working hypothesis ... But for the last hundred years or so it has been increasingly true of religious questions also: it is becoming evident that everything gets along without 'God,' and just as well as before."[17]

Thus, the best description of Radical Theology's point of departure is the one formulated by the author most representative of the movement, Thomas J.J. Altizer (b. 1927): "we must recognize that the death of God is a historical event: God has died in *our* time, in *our* history, in *our* existence. Insofar as we live in our destiny, we can know neither a trace of God's presence nor an image of his reality."[18]

Altizer, adjunct professor of religion at Emory University, had begun by working in the field of history of religions with his *Oriental Mysticism and Biblical Eschatology* (1961) and *Mircea Eliade and the Dialectic of the Sacred* (1963). In oriental mysticism, the tension between the sacred and the profane is resolved according to the law of "coincidence of opposites" in a reabsorbing of the profane into the image of original totality. In Christianity, the idea of an Incarnate Word overturns the dynamic of resolution and affirms God's otherness that had been erased by his entering into the temporal process, with the "flesh" coinciding with God's life. God "loses," "empties" himself of independent reality, "dies" by sacrificing himself for his creature, who is thus liberated from a foreign and alienating authority: this is the basis of Altizer's most noted work, *The Gospel of Christian Atheism* (1966).

Once again, the impossibility of believing in a transcendent divinity "beyond" the world and of recovering traditional theological themes is affirmed by William Hamilton (b. 1924 [d. 2012]), professor of systematic theology at Colgate Rochester Divinity School. In one of his notes, he distinguishes "soft" radicals from "hard" radicals: the former are anxious about the forms of the Christian religious message (institution and language). For the latter, instead, "It is not a loss of the idols, or of the God of theism. It is a real loss of real transcendence. It is a loss of God."[19]

In his book *The New Essence of Christianity* (1961), he states, "We need to reduce the area of what is believed and to lay claim upon it."[20] Love for mankind, based upon the example of Jesus, "a man for others" is the essence of Christianity.

Hamilton also published a small work, *The Christian Man* (1961), but the reference to personal experience, which characterizes and makes his discourse in on the "fragments" of Christianity that are still capable of recovery lively, is documented above all, in the collection of essays – generally previously published articles – in collaboration with Altizer and published with the title *Radical Theology and the Death of God* (1966).[21]

The reduction of Christianity to the ethics of the "historical Jesus" also marks the thought of Paul Matthews van Buren (b. 1924 [d. 1998]), who initially taught at Austin Episcopalian Seminary and, later, at Temple University in Philadelphia. The work that established him within the triad of Radical Theology is *The Secular Meaning of the Gospel* (1963), where, in utilizing the philosophy of language as his tool, he seeks to describe how the very use of the word "God" is without meaning, if not deceptive: "the problem now is that the *word* 'God' is dead." All "God-statements" ought to be translated into "man-statements."[22] His position is further illustrated in *Theological Explorations* (1968).

Together with the aforementioned three authors, the name of Gabriel Vahanian (b. 1927 [d. 2012]) of Syracuse University is often cited. But the book that made him famous, *The Death of God: The Culture of Our Post-Christian Era* (1957),[23] is not a program of Godless theology, but is, instead, a documentation of the cultural situation of our era. It could even be labelled as critical of Radical Theology in that it affirms the reality of the Divine in Tillichian terms as "totally other," beyond and unassailable by any cultural fact, and insofar as he is opposed to the idea of a Christianity without God, or with Christ in the place of God. This is what he holds in *Wait without Idols* (1964) and *No Other God* (1966).

Harvey Cox and "Secularization"

The discourse that made Harvey Gallagher Cox (b. 1929), associate professor of church and society at Harvard Divinity School, famous cannot immediately or adequately be assimilated to that of the "death of God" theologians. With his best-seller *The Secular City: Secularization and Urbanization in Theological Perspective* (1965) and with *God's Revolution and Man's Responsibility* (1965),[24] he has perhaps become the most lucid exponent of that trend known as "theology of secularization," which originated as an expression within the Anglo-Saxon Protestant world, but which also garners great interest on the European continent and among Catholics. Leslie Dewart (1922–2009), [for example], is a Canadian Catholic who gave an original contribution to this "theology" with *The Future of Belief: Theism in a World Come of Age* (1966).

Secularism, according to Cox's definition, "implies a historical process, almost certainly irreversible, in which society and culture are delivered from tutelage to religious control and closed metaphysical world views." He specifies, "Secularism arises in large measure from the formative influence of biblical faith on the world, an influence mediated first by the Christian church and later by movements deriving partly from it."[25] Human freedom that dominates reality, the historical process, the uninterrupted flow of worldly affairs as the sole mode of encounter between God and man and as the entire horizon of human interest, the commitment to the contingent as the place of the continual creative determination of values, pragmatism as the supreme criterion of truth and of approach: these facts create the structure that informs the "secularist" mentality.

Two connotations of this should be particularly emphasized, in that they seem to bring together the aspects that are most energetic and characteristic of the strongest American theological expression of the nineteenth century.

The first reconfirms the rootedness of the spirit that gave rise to and animated the Social Gospel Movement: the Kingdom of God coincides with the "secular" ideal and its advent is the humanizing of the world; the final event is the coming to being of the "City of Man"; the Church "is where the shape and texture of the future age come to concrete visibility,"[26] and its action in the world is vibrantly synthesized as "cultural exorcism," that is, of liberating the forces of human progress and fulfilment. Cox identifies those emerging ideals in certain outcomes of social struggles, renewing the methodological approach with which Rauschenbusch canonized examples taken from the social victories of his era.[27]

A second connotation affirms the historicization of all values. This involves the seriousness of the contingent responsibility, as well as the precariousness and eminent capacity for improving the way that responsibility formulates its creativity. Any absolute is an idol, the "graven image" forbidden by the Sinai Covenant: "The persistent protest against idols and icons which runs through the history of biblical faith provides the basis for a constructive relativism";[28] "a certain degree of healthy relativism provides the philosophical basis for a pluralist society."[29] According to a genesis that is not built on anthropological analysis like that of Niebuhr or in Tillich, but which is affirmed as a pure reading of the Bible and of history, it is the very relativistic emphasis present in Neo-orthodox Theology that is offered as extremely pragmatic wisdom.

The "Death of God" Theology appears as the most consequential attitude, the most coherent accent in the Secularization Movement. From the standpoint of historical phenomena, it seems to be the revenge of an exasperated Liberal spirit against the *kerigma* of Neo-orthodoxy. This was in response to an angst and a sense of desperation that, although dominant between the two world wars, have evaporated, and their pessimism corresponds to a past devoid of meaning for us. The death of T.S. Eliot on 4 January 1965, in Hamilton's view, can be taken as the sign of the end of what Saul Bellow called "the Wasteland Era."[30] It is as if man had emptied the dimension of the Ultimate, and he feels completely free and available to his present circumstances. It is the resurrection of the optimism of the Social Gospel that rested its hermeneutics on the paradigms of science and boiled the whole Christian ethical content and the meaning of the advent of the Kingdom of God to the commitment to transform social structures. But, all of the formal elements which Liberal Humanism lingered over have been expunged from the "new optimism": "This," concludes Hamilton, one of the leaders of the New Theology most influenced by the Social Gospel, "is not an optimism of grace, but a worldly optimism I am defending. It faces despair not with the conviction that out of it God can bring hope, but with the conviction that the human conditions that created it can be overcome, whether those conditions be poverty, discrimination, or mental illness. It faces death not with the hope for immortality, but with the human confidence that man may befriend death and live with it as a possibility always alongside. I think that the new optimism is both a cause and a consequence of the basic theological experience which we today call the death of God."[31]

But, on a deeper level, such a theology manifests itself as a more up-to-date – and paradoxical – version of the Protestant spirit in its characteristic qualities that was brought forth by its most prominent exponents.

According to the Tillichian view, this spirit is in essence "protest" against any defining identification of – and therefore, against each and every type of pressure to render static – the Divine and its activity. Radical Theology goes so far as to exterminate the very word "God," and the historical forms of those identifications, to the point of a general disputation against the historical structures that bear those identifications.

According to the Barthian view, the Protestant spirit is the affirmation of the "tangential" nature of divine intervention in the world: the existential moment is the true place of personal vocation in its irreducible and unprogrammable newness. For Radical Theology, the role of the biblical and Gospel message is exclusively that of determining an ethical attitude, or impetus, that makes one capable of grasping within the historical present the sole authentic divine provocation to the value and construction of meaning.

For Radical Theology, since the redemptive influx extends throughout worldly reality, which is in the process of becoming, the presence of Christ is identified with present experience, and being Christian is identified with the responsible reaction to the demands and imperatives that are contingent on this experience: "From the point of view of radical Christianity, the original heresy was the identification of the Church as the body of Christ ... the radical Christian points the way to the presence of the living Christ in the actuality and fullness of history."[32]

Within the context of such a conception, the exorbitance of immediate factual experience, which tends to qualify the criterion of American religious thought, completely absorbs any consistency of the Divine into itself, emptying it in a strange "kenosis" and becomes the "tomb" of every divine "otherness," the antithesis to Puritanism and the radicalization of Liberal immanentism.

And, in line with the Protestant negation of the existence of an already redeemed historical reality, there is a consequent denial of a new ontology communicated to man, therefore, the disavowal of a "supernatural" structure within history, through which all of history is destined to be redeemed and into which all of history is destined to be integrated. With a radical conversion of meaning, Christ and the Church are affirmed as pure sign and function of human becoming, the novelty of Christianity has the aim of affirming the consistence of the world, and worldly reality is not destined to the "overabundance" of "another" communication.

Yet, the final value of such an approach could be energetically positive and be communicated as the expectation of the resurrection of God from the depths of his creation, truer and more concrete than the "limit" towards which Tillich cast connections from the various forms of human culture without a clearly formed and secure point of arrival. Jesus Christ is often appealed to as the figure who catalyzes the whole process, and it is his centrality in the conception of life and history that is the greatest patrimony of the late nineteenth century and the early twentieth, from Bushnell to Rauschenbusch, that Radical Theology holds onto. And, in this sense, profane responsibility assumes a religious dimension and a prophetic tone, such that "being a Christian means a distinctive way of being in the world,"[33] thus continuing, in a radically different version, the original ideal.

APPENDICES

APPENDIX ONE

Aspects of the Conception of History in Reinhold Niebuhr*

[Ludwig Marcuse wrote,] "When reality is confused with the ideal, the latter masks the former. America became (in the nineteenth century) the incarnation of the Declaration of Independence. Who was interested in the true America? On the contrary, everyone was interested in the idea of a utopia brought to fulfillment. In the nineteenth century it fell to America to play the part that Russia would play in the twentieth."[1]

Reinhold Niebuhr is one of those who has most contributed to demythologizing the figure of America in the imagination and thought of Americans themselves. And not only – or at least not as much – in the volumes destined for such a goal,[2] but through his entire literary production: it is the very structure of principles in which his thought is expressed that will not give in to mystification of any type or in any field.

The illusory figure of an ideal America was generated and nourished within the whole context of modern thought: "Though there are minor dissonances the whole chorus of modern culture learned to sing the new song of hope in remarkable harmony. The redemption of mankind, by whatever means, was assured for the future. It was, in fact, assured by the future."[3]

In America, a worthy part of this choir was the social and cultural movement known as the Social Gospel, into which flowed the most prepared and vigilant elements of Protestantism, according to visions that fell into forms derived from Puritan idealistic ethical inspiration

* Translator's note: Originally published in *La Rivista di Filosofia Neoscolastica*, LX (1968), fasc. II-III, 167–90.

or the hope of the great democratic community that Jackson had drawn from Perfectionist Evangelism.[4] Niebuhr's first work still, ultimately, participates in the redemptive forecasts and programs of the Social Gospel.[5] But his discourse, as a whole, is already marked and shaken by the subterranean jolt of the experience he lived in Detroit, in the world dominated by Ford and the men excited by his programs, the experience, therefore, of the contrast between proclaimed ideals and social reality.[6] In maturing his impassioned observation and reflection on this contrast, he clearly identified the main instrument of modern errors in thought and approach: a certain philosophy of history. Maritain's observation is perhaps relevant: "Applying [even true principles] intelligently depends to a great extent on a genuine philosophy of history. If we are lacking this, we run a great risk of applying good principles wrongly – a misfortune, I would say, not only for us, but for our good principles as well."[7] There is, as it were, an axiomatic principle that, according to Niebuhr "has given diverse forms of modern culture the unity of a shared belief," and this principle has the greatest share of culpability for modern man's illusory understanding of time and, thus, for hindering such an understanding from rising to the level of a genuine philosophy of history: "Modern men of all shades of opinion agreed in the belief that *historical development is a redemptive process*."[8]

In the second phase of Niebuhr's production, a discourse on history takes form and is systematically developed, one aimed at demonstrating the absurdity and the deadly nature of that axiom. Niebuhr's main work[9] functions as a pivot for his research, since the first volume – *Human Nature* – systematically expresses the central concern of his first works, that is, a conception of man and, thus, of society; whereas the second volume – *Human Destiny* – draws forth its corollary and completion, a mode of conceiving history, and posits the initial structures of a "philosophy of history" defined and documented in later studies.[10] Niebuhr would go on to define his vision as a "theology of history"; yet, his epistemology and his heuristic seem to allow for using the formula "philosophy of history."

1 THE SELF, SUBJECT OF HISTORY

In order to document certain aspects of this vision – which is, without a doubt, the most significant moment of Niebuhr's intellectual activity – we must recall his representation of the essence of the self.

Because the self is the true actor in history, far from boiling down the historical process as content and meaning to webs of activities with which an elite would voluntaristically lead and shape the inert masses, or to a dialectic of impersonal factors of human "nature" understood in any way whatsoever, it is in the self that reality functions as history, that is, takes on a significant becoming.

There are two dimensions that, ultimately, constitute reality, and in the self they are affirmed in existential unity. First, what Niebuhr calls *nature* or *creature* with a word taken from the Bible, the true source of his thought, which is profoundly original in its genesis with respect to contemporary historiographic concerns. "Nature" is the reality of the universe as it is expressed in its gradations to the level of animal life: in fact, "he is a creature, subject to nature's necessities and limitations."[11] Nature is characterized by determination, so much so that the word "necessity"[12] may be used as its synonym. A description of this level of humanity must highlight "all his natural endowments, and determinations, his physical and social impulses, his sexual and racial differentiations, in short his character as a creature imbedded in the natural order."[13] The idea of "nature" substantially highlights man's "finiteness" and, more specifically, the dependency of his life. Nothing new comes from nature: thus, it "knows no history but only endless repetition within the limits of each given form."[14]

Another dimension of the self stands in natural – and paradoxical – unity with the first. It is the spirit, which is defined as the capacity for "indefinite transcendence."[15] In fact, the phenomenon "spirit" is characteristically found in the possibility of rising above any *given* level of reality in which the self is relativized and which constitutes the *situation* into which the self flows. Thus, it is possible to insist on affirming that the self has "special capacity of standing continually outside itself," or, with a dramatic expression, it is the "essential homelessness of the human spirit."[16] As a synonym of spirit, and a more evident and intense term to indicate its vitality, Neibuhr uses the word "freedom." This, clearly, connotes the fact that the self, immanent as it may be to a situation (as a given moment of self-actualization as relationship with reality), cannot be identified with it, is not within it in a definitive way.

From the anthropological standpoint, once could say that Niebuhr is most concerned with pointing out the organic relation of the human structure's dual factor:[17] the entire history of philosophy is proof of the ease with which man gives in to the temptation to divide himself and assume a unilateral stance by exhausting his self-conception in natural determinisms or mysticism. In any case, the coexistence of these two terms within reality constitutes a process that is incommensurate with the procedures and measures of natural reality, the *historical process*.

The capacity for freedom – this energy of limitless restlessness – breaks forth in "nature which knows no history but only endless repetition within the limits of each given form."[18] Thus is organized "a new order of reality, which, though grounded in a temporal flux, is not completely governed by natural necessity, since human agents have the power to change the natural course. This distinctive realm is most succinctly defined simply as 'history.'"[19]

2 HISTORICAL EPISTEMOLOGY

Memory

The first expression of freedom is knowledge, the self's possibility to "step outside" of the situation it is in. The first result of this is a way of looking that grasps and follows the emergence and the design of things. Freedom, as a mirror of reality, is *reason* or conscience. Yet, there is a sharper distinction to make. There is a rational activity that is a pure reflection of the world, which it translates into concepts or measures, which it disassembles in analysis and assembles into connections, which it sketches out in its laws: Niebuhr distinctly names it "conceptual knowledge," and its proper object is "the changeless patterns and structures which underlie the world of change,"[20] and so it constitutes the legislative aspect of the spirit: "law-giving rationality."[21] Yet, there is an activity of freedom, a "a force of 'reason,'"[22] that impacts reality in implicating freedom itself, and that grasps it in its categorical uniqueness and irreducibility as event, and together inscribes the event within the category of motion and continuity, in other words, of time. This is *memory*: "Since both present and past realities did not follow necessarily from previous events, the bewildering mixture of freedom and necessity in every historical concretion is rightly understood if the particular and unique acts which constitute the flow of events are remembered in their uniqueness."[23] The phenomenon of freedom cannot be reduced to conceptual or mathematical forms, and its units cannot be described in the same way that reason establishes scientific or logical coherency. Memory is, therefore, the human instrument suited to discovering the presence of freedom in the stuff of history; it, therefore, allows the human being "to be aware of its self-identity in this temporal flux."[24] Thus, memory is the fundamental factor that makes historical knowledge possible, the knowledge of that kingdom in which freedom manipulates nature by introducing into its continuity a qualitative newness that cannot be grasped by the schemas of a merely rational vision.

Memory, precisely because it is such a knowledge, also becomes an important "organic historical factor."[25] Niebuhr gives the example of a company that is formed to carry out a gravely important task: doubtless its present meaning is determined by memory and its configuration in the future is qualified by it (approaches, relationships, articulations, convergences, and solidarities acquire depth, and the factors at play are integrated in a vital way). "Organisms" are generated in the movement of history. Niebuhr also speaks of "collective memory." Although it is inconclusive to attribute personality to communities, just like persons, they nevertheless, are "historical entities that have reacted to unique historical events."[26] The awareness of such events is really the memory of the people, the decisive factor in the community's consistency, and just as for the person, for its self-identification through the tide of facts.

Historical knowledge and awareness of what exists are, ultimately, the same event, precisely because the essential and absolute originality of freedom represents the substance of the object for both of them, and it is by memory that those cognitive moments are constituted.

With definitive precision, one must say that historical knowledge is the "profound" dimension of awareness of what exists in that "present realities can be rightly interpreted only through the memory of past events."[27]

Hermeneutics

Freedom is structured on a higher level of historical knowledge than memory: it is the interpretive level. Man, who "transcends nature, time and history," is able to "develop rational structures of meaning for his individual and collective life."[28] But how objective, how "really real," these structures may be is impossible to demonstrate. The complexity of the factors involved, the inexhaustibility of freedom's trajectories, the interpreter's ideological posture make it an "insoluble problem."[29] Historical vision contains an unquestionable ambiguity and insecurity. On the other hand, an interpretive evaluation is inevitable; if, as radical epistemological positivism would claim, it were necessary to eliminate the act of evaluation in order to avoid distorted interpretations, there would be no history. "Time is a succession of events. Yet mere succession is not time. Time has reality only through a meaningful relationship of its successions"[30] – so that "historical events are established in terms of coherence by precisely the 'evaluations' which are so embarrassing philosophically."[31]

An ultimate relativism underlies the zone of possibility of historical knowledge in Niebuhr: "there can be no definitive refutations of any interpretations of historical events, though the forces of history may conspire to refute some extravagantly 'biased' interpretations, or those which are too contradictory to facts so obvious that they do not depend upon interpretations for validation."[32]

Faith, or Affirmation of the Ultimate Meaning

Such precariousness of knowledge in the very sphere of its activity does not weaken freedom, but instead, tends to exalt it towards its extreme possibility of knowledge, the affirmation of an ultimate, total meaning of history. The word "meaning" must be understood according to its entire density, as a formula pointing to the event in which life's potential is expressed totally, in which the norm or the ideal of impetus that moves human existence is actualized. There is a presupposition upon which any philosophical effort for ultimately comprehending history is based: the presupposition "in some depth of reality a pattern may be found in which that which seems 'contingent and unforeseen' takes its place as a 'necessary' development, as a servant of the hidden logic which underlies and informs all things."[33] The classical idea of cyclical motion and the modern one of progressive development, by isolating them, emphasize these conditions of history, but not its direction or its meaning; they misconstrue the proper character of human freedom by forcibly and prejudicially boiling it down to a determination, a measure, a ratio. Human freedom possesses absolute spontaneity and limitless energy; the "meaning" of its operation cannot be reduced to webs of explanations induced in some aspect of its operation itself or from principles within a moment of existence. So the quest for an ultimate criterion of truth in history cannot be carried out with methods of empirical or scientific observation[34] or in a way that is "an *a priori* notion," to cite Maritain, "founded either on purely philosophical insights or on dialectical exigencies."[35] A meaning that is totally immanent to history is qualified by the limits of time-space coordinates, and cannot be exhaustive.

On the other hand, a meaning, in order to be *of* history, must in some way be *within* man's historical experience. There is an existential level in which human freedom unleashes a knowledge that outclasses all of rational graduality. There is a type of experience of the self that is part of the web of history and yet intuitively carries within itself something that completely transcends it, constituting an exhaustive criterion, in proportion to the limitless dimensions of human freedom, of which it assumes all of the precariousness of historical incarnations by "fulfilling" them, that is, restoring to them all of their significance, affirming them within the totality, of which they appear to be limited and contingent incarnations. That level of knowledge is *faith*, that type of experience is *revelation*.

Every particular happening, precisely because of its particularity, is circumscribed in its interpretive capacity, and the zone of reality that it can illuminate is limited. Nevertheless, some happenings, identical to others in their objective consistency, in a de facto way allow us to glimpse the law of their dynamism, thus becoming the key to understanding all of the events that make up the matter of history. These particular happenings, which clarify everything, are designated with the term "myth" or "'symbol' to avoid the skeptical connotation of the word 'myth.'"[36] In *Beyond Tragedy*, a volume of expanded sermons published in 1938, Niebuhr compares the revelatory phenomenon of myth to the way in which an artist evokes the three-dimensional space of the figure he depicts through the two-dimensional space of the canvas. Thus, in symbol, the depth of the meaning – which in all its consistency exceeds the contingencies of temporal events – is evoked precisely through the contingent lines of the historical fact.

Paradoxically, the meaning of everything is not determined by "recurrences and forms to which all historical phenomena conform," according to rationalistic interpretations, nor by "the endless development of human power and wisdom," following modern evolutionism, but instead, emerges "in significant events of history,"[37] "which cannot be fully rationalized."[38] Indeed, the awakening of the perspective of intuition that affirms the eternal meaning, that is, the event of faith, within what is contingent, is a mystery. It constitutes a dynamism that escapes our control; man feels passive in front of it: revelation is a "shattering of the self by a power from beyond ourself."[39]

The word "mystery" must not, however, cause us to forget the normality of faith, the continuity of faith within the dynamism of human knowledge. Faith, in fact, is the supreme surpassing of human freedom, which is thus actualized in all its natural capacity of "self-transcendence." The word "mystery" attributed to faith and to the fact of revelation, instead, recalls that irreducible spontaneity, that surprising gratuitousness (in fact, theologians call it "grace") which mark the level of the origin of things: "There is a profound arbitrariness in every given fact, which rational theories of causation seek to obscure. Thus they regard a given form of animal life as rational because they can trace it historically to another form or relate it in terms of genus and species to other types of life. Yet none of these relationships, whether historical or schematic, can eliminate the profound arbitrariness of the givenness of things."[40] The event of faith, however, is nothing if not the emergence and development of something qualitatively already implicated in human awareness at the beginning of its existence, as a need of man's very structure, as the dynamism of his self-transcendence. In fact, "there is of course no absolute beginning for anything in history, including the beginning of 'revelation.'"[41] Thus, the embryo of faith is given by the "tangents towards the eternal,"[42] that is, at the same time as the sense of limit, in which inevitably each and every human endeavour is reduced, with its consequent incapacity to fulfill the meaning of its own existence and history, and by the boundless impulse to discover the meaning of everything.

In his conception of revelation, Niebuhr defines the phenomenon in terms that are, therefore, substantially subjective, and its consistence is eminently psychological: a phenomenon of awareness proper to the structure of the human self, the perception of a meaning along the trajectory of the intelligent quest. Revelation, in fact, consists in the perception of truth that, by clarifying the time-eternity relationship, defines the structure and meaning of the existence and history of human awareness. As cues that trigger this perception, *symbols* are historical facts or historical moments without any ontological alteration of the common fabric of all temporal events.

The only thing necessary is that their particular historical instance have a mechanical foothold, that it hint materially at the factors of that meaning, from which it is distanced by a qualitative leap. Thus, in speaking of the historical Jesus, for example, Niebuhr observes that "the actual incidents in the drama serve to add vividness to this final meaning."[43]

Verification

The inferential and systematizing tension of the *ratio* is not frustrated by the level of faith, but is assumed and engaged in a labour of verification. The entire opus of Niebuhr, it could be said, is in tension towards the vital necessity of registering this "validation" of existence and of history, so that religion would be a factor with social impact (he is often known as an "apologist" in contemporary philosophical and theological literature). There are two categories of verification that Niebuhr sets out in chapter X of *Faith and History*, and to which he inspires his readers in the subsequent volume of *The Self and the Dramas of History*: "Negatively the Gospel must and can be validated by exploring the limits of historic forms of wisdom and virtue. Positively it is validated when the truth of faith is correlated with all truths which may be known by scientific and philosophical disciplines and proves itself a resource for coordinating them into a deeper and wider system of coherence."[44]

From a methodological standpoint, the intuitions of faith function as a working hypothesis which, when compared with the data of existence and of history, are found to be "in accord with experienced facts."[45]

Since the interpretations of faith do not proceed from a scientific analysis of natural and historical processes, they are often qualified in a pejorative way as "dogmatic." And yet, any comparison that interprets historical reality carries presuppositions that are inevitable and have diverse origins and even more diverse verifications in experience, since even where the scientific method is rigorously followed, it is possible to be "blind to some obvious facts about human nature and history."[46] Thus, an "allegedly 'dogmatic' faith should be justified by the experiences of the human self more than the allegedly 'empirical' approaches to selfhood, which obscure their potent, though implicit, dogmas within their prescriptions for empirical observation."[47]

The process of faith, if it is thus validated by experience, could nevertheless, not be substituted by a rational investigation of it. It is, in fact, an ultimate interpretation of existence and of history, and this can only come about through "a commitment of the self rather than a conclusion of its mind."[48] The self's commitment to its own existence is manifested as an experience of contradiction and sorrow ("repentance" or "contrition"), and within this experience, in spite of it, an experience of the grace-filled permanence of the ideal presence, as an unconquerable aspiration ("justification") and immediately as the bursting forth of a new energy for striving, for "new life" ("sanctification"), in which the clarification of the meaning of things is a fundamental factor. Engagement with existence cannot avoid becoming engagement with history, full of an instinctive reaction when faced with all of the misapprehensions of one's own nature that are formed in the attempts to alter the coherencies and equilibriums demanded by the dimensions of humanity. This precondition that gives origin to faith – and that is the existential and historical engagement of the self – could also be designated as "the truth of the self." So only the self in its truth can discover the true meaning of the self and history. Reducing the truth of faith, or symbols, or myths, to facts that can be demonstrated through historical investigation, or to statements that are "validated by [their] coherence with a total system of rational coherence"[49] would mean emptying them of a truly ultimate, and therefore redemptive, meaning, one which would transform man, which would not constitute a continual objection to the limit of human situations and an active appeal to conversion. If myth is the content of faith, it is such an authenticity of the self that "saves the myth from caprice."[50]

It may be said that, analogously to Niebuhr's statements on the Church (as peripheral as they may be), the self's engagement and the vision of faith that springs from it are always inscribed within a paradigmatic place, where the interpretation of the meaning of things is objective in a provisory way so as to impede its corruption into pure fantasy or individual whim: this place is the community. The faith community, in a certain sense, has an epistemological value, albeit secondary and derivative. It, nevertheless, has no consistency prior to or outside of the faith experience of the individual; it may be said that a natural connotation of faith is the need for a convergence, for communion. "Dogma" expresses the convergence of experiences in a formulation that marks out their ultimate seriousness. It is only in such a climate of seriousness that "verification" can take place; it is, in fact, a procedure that cannot be disassociated from "repentance."

3 THE LAWS OF HISTORY

Within the constantly moving web of history, the heuristic force of faith in the experience of revelation is able to highlight some fundamental aspects that constitute an ultimate web of true laws, which shed a profound light of "intelligibility" on the entire flux of time. This is explained not in the sense that its events must necessarily be deciphered or its articulations be reconstructed, but in the sense that a luminous wellspring, as it were, at the origin of the flow of history permits us to discern the direction and some fundamental features of the tumultuous torrent of things. It is the articulation of myth that establishes the physiognomy of that wellspring.

The terminology used by Maritain, which identifies axiomatic laws and vectorial laws, can come to our aid as the most adequate one for categorizing this aspect of Niebuhr's thought.

Axiomatic Laws

(1) THE BIBLICAL MYTH OF CREATION, OR THE LAW OF GOD'S SOVEREIGNTY That *quid* by which reality has consistency and meaning is totally other, such that no moment of historical experience can consider it its own possession or program. It is also totally *immanent*, such that no situation of historical experience can constitute itself within something without it and avoid exhausting its own value within it. These are the two connotations of myth: "To speak of God as Creator of the world, is to regard the world in its totality as a revelation of His majesty and self-sufficient power … The supra-rational character of this doctrine is proved by the fact that, when pressed logically, it leads to the assertion that God creates *ex nihilo*, the idea at which all logical concepts of derivation must end – and begin."[51]

One primary feature derives from this double connotation of history's physiognomy: the flow of history has a profound *unity* that is not the sum of the individual cases, but as an existential universality that determines the meaning of each and every historical moment and factor.

Neither historical science nor the philosophy of history (without presupposing a creator God) can deal with such a problem without reducing it to abstractions and inappropriate generalizations or finding irreducibly impenetrable situations. Niebuhr gladly gives Hegel and Toynbee as examples.

A second feature springs from the fact that in history the good is universal: "The kingdom of truth is consequently not the kingdom of some other world … it is of this world. It is not some realm of eternal perfection which has nothing to do with historical existence.

It constantly impinges upon man's every decision and is involved in every action ... [It is] through man and in man."[52]

Since the good and the Divine are one, it also possible to confirm and clarify this definitive positivity that lies within the flow of history with another affirmation, which Niebuhr contextualizes well within the sphere of the "empiricist" philosophy and religion that dominated the world of Protestant thought at the turn of the nineteenth and twentieth centuries: "The experience of God is not so much a separate experience, as an overtone implied in all experience."[53]

A third factor lies in the fact that the process of this Kingdom of God, or the value of universal history, drawing its occurrence from absolute transcendence – and its actualization in the unforeseeable spontaneity of human freedom is its experiential indicator! – cannot tolerate any *foretelling* of its development in terms of meaning and moral value: "There is [in the New Testament] the awesome suggestion that history remains open to all possibilities of good and evil, including the destruction of the faith."[54] And Niebuhr, evidently, directly opposes Toynbee's "progress of religion."

(2) THE BIBLICAL MYTH OF THE CROSS, OR THE LAW OF THE NEGATIVITY OF HISTORY If God is the consistency and value of reality, human actions and historical instances have as their *proprium* negation, failure, in its etymological connotation as lie and delusion.

Indeed, the Divine exhaustively defines human capabilities. The infinite is meaning and perfection for man, so freedom's action in existence inevitably "mortifies," repudiates the ideal. The universality of this "law" is absolute. It is absolute for individuals, and thus, "there is no justification in the revelation for any good man."[55] It is absolute for any collective existence and for each and every human social manifestation, and it is a significant connotation of this law that it is all the more valid the more a human place is called to be a bearer of meaning: "The judgment [of the prophets] falls with particular severity upon Israel, precisely because it has been singled out for a special mission in history ... Israel's special mission gives it no special security in history."[56] And the law of human defeat burdens not only every human existence, individual or collective, but every theoretical expression of it: "There is therefore no pure ethical norm in history; nor any hope of history gradually purifying itself so that it will achieve this norm."[57] In Christian tradition, the symbol of the

Antichrist, as the supreme form of evil, which manifests itself at the extreme point of the line of history, refutes the mitigation or resolution of the universality of evil in time.

A new tragic aspect is inscribed within the sphere of this law. If the consistency and value of existence lie exactly in how much existence realizes the Divine – "freedom" – upon which it is structured, each and every affirmation of existence itself that does not live up to its "definitive" level ("definitive" in the etymological sense of the word) is self-destruction: "the true self dies."[58]

Existential activity is always, frustratingly, an encroaching judgment, as if the existing being's act unleashed from its constitutive core a wrath upon itself. But, the self invades the world and composes history. The universality of evil, thus, caries a pessimistic vision of history, felt as an immense deficit.

The ancient "nemesis" is recovered and transformed into the most evident category for interpreting history: "The most obvious meaning of history is that every nation, culture and civilization brings destruction upon itself"[59] in disproportion to its immanent paradigm: "The judgment of God is always partly the effect of the structure of reality upon the vitalities of history which defy that structure."[60] A sovereignty that controls the destiny of things is reaffirmed in this law, a destiny that is not defined deterministically, but as a tension within freedom, which in that sovereignty, nevertheless, finds its origin and consistency, but against which it "rebels" (another semanticism dear to Niebuhr) in the attempt to substitute it as the reason and consistency of its own existential moment. This new version of St Thomas' "conversio ad creaturas" illuminates history as an immense dramatic action, full of meaning, of tragic meaning; the Divine, as the fundamental structure of things, has the last word, but it breaks apart and destroys the self that clashes with it.

(3) THE BIBLICAL MYTH OF THE RESURRECTION OR THE LAW OF RENEWAL The relationship of dependence upon the Divine constitutes man. Thus, the ideal remains as an energetic immanence in every action, representing the active presence of value and the "possibilities of genuine newness of life."[61] Good and evil coexist as the two components of the identical moment of existence. The shadow of downfall "upon all historical achievements does not destroy the possibility of such achievements nor the obligation to realize truth and goodness in history."[62] The physiognomy of history

sustains neither skepticism nor defeatism. The nature of history is defined by the category of *renewal*.

Described in its genetic aspect, the category of renewal points to the fact that the permanence of the ideal and its stimulus within the freedom of the self constitute for the existing being the presence of its own meaning and, thus, the certainty of its advent. The self experiences its own total value already actualized "in principle" according to the formula that Niebuhr constantly uses. Thus, certain that existential deficiencies cannot prejudice one's own completion, which is safely beyond ambiguous history, the historical agent experiences itself as a continuous impulse to live up to the ideal, to "incorporate [the ideal] into the fabric of history." He is not afraid that "it can never be so embodied that it does not also stand in contradiction to history in judgment";[63] nor does he despair that the norm of existence may be an "impossible possibility."[64] It is important to stress that the entire event of renewal – that immanent energetic comparison with the ideal, that is, with what is beyond oneself – is often unconscious: almost the encounter with a "hidden Christ."[65] Therefore, despite the Lutheran inspiration documented in the preceding law, history appears characterized by "positive corruptions, as well as by partial realizations and approximations of the meaning of life."[66]

Yet, it is impossible to clearly identify the whole value of the law of renewal for Niebuhr if one does not pause to describe its theological dimension. The raw material of history, that is, the existential moment, subsists as a good-evil dialectical tension, and yet, the factors in action in such a dialectic are irreducible to any historical measure and, therefore, to any definitive judgment. Such a measure and such a judgment upon the historical gesture or upon a historical vector and, clearly, upon all of history belong to a moment that is outside of history.

Indeed, that measure and that judgment belong to a "final mystery of divine fulfillment beyond all provisional meanings."[67] In order to signify this, which is the extreme word on time and history, the symbol of the Resurrection pierces through from the existential version of its beginnings to the eschatological one.

In remembering that the last three articles of the Creed were derided by the Liberal mentality, Niebuhr writes, "There is no part of the Apostolic creed which … expresses the whole genius of the Christian faith more neatly than just this despised phrase: 'I believe in the resurrection of the body.'"[68] It is, in fact, the myth that resolves the problem of the coexistence of nature and spirit within the unity of man and the problem of the eternal value of the history of this coexistence. Niebuhr interprets as an alternative to this myth the symbol of the immortality of the soul that many would adopt because it is felt to be more rationally conceivable. However, the idea of the immortality of the soul would be the attempt to isolate one element that in itself would be capable of overcoming death: this would break apart man's unity, denying any meaning to the indefinite range of actions in which this unity exists in history; space and time as well as "nature" would be deprived of any value. If this were followed "to its logical conclusion nothing remains in eternity but an undifferentiated unity, free of all particularity and distinctions."[69]

In the symbol of the Resurrection, the "body" means everything that is contingent, all the elements of the natural situation that are united to spiritual self-awareness in order to determine the human individual, or the ideal values of freedom in order to create history's constructs. In the very symbol, "resurrection" means that all these elements, and all the situations they are reduced to, but which activate the transcendence of the spirit, have an eternal significance. The final confirmation eliminates nothing from the existing being, but conserves each and every aspect, by integrating it into the harmony of the whole.

As the final myth, the resurrection of the body clarifies the fact that history does not redeem itself through its own development. This is the most dangerous of utopias. On every level, history is something lacking and its fulfilment is at the end, that is, "beyond" its events. Yet, history reveals and incarnates an eternal meaning. History is not a useless struggle that eternity flattens or nullifies. Every existential act contains an approach to the ideal, whence it derives its characteristic value. Eternity will make it absolute not by absorbing it into an indistinct whole, but by assuming it and preserving it in its unmistakable individuality. Any human endeavour, either personal or social, contains a specific value which eternity, while completing it, will maintain, as it were, as marked and distinct.

The great axiomatic laws that emerge within the sum total of Niebuhr's thought constitute a dialectic in which the third law functions as the synthesis. Indeed, the connotations that lie within the myth of the resurrection of the flesh are the Parousia and the Last

Judgment. And the Parousia represents faith in the final victory of God over all the forces of evil that seem to undermine the meaning of existence and challenge the sovereignty of the Absolute with impunity. The Last Judgment confirms the inevitable ambiguity, the deluding partiality of existence and of history, and yet, it peremptorily establishes the distinction between good and evil within existence and within history – hence, moral struggle is shown to be full of meaning – which the resurrection of the flesh ultimately defines.

It is in this myth that revelation provides existence with the necessary basis of security and serenity for the strength and resistance to act, and it remains as the pledge of its desired fulfilment. This is the imperative of existence, of individual life or collective history, an effort, tirelessly renewed and indomitably overcoming of its own limits, to progressively realize the ideal in personal perfection and social justice.

Yet, in Niebuhr, the meaning of "progressive" is tied to the suggestion that lies within the idea of "renewal." At the level of value judgment, it does not represent a historical measure, nor is it the sign of an outcome that is a law within history. In this, there is only one thing that has a clarity that participates in the absolute: faith, the summit of freedom as the knowledge of the certain fulfilment of history beyond history, of the eternal meaning of time. Beneath this summit, the events of temporal flux are, as it were, drawn into a dark abyss – the resistance of human "imperfection" to meaning – yet, nevertheless, casting a light of value over them onto the transcendentally tangential backdrop of the freedom of existence: "Thus history as we know it is regarded as an 'interim' between the disclosure and fulfillment of its meaning."[70]

Vectorial Laws

Vectorial laws are those, according to Maritain, that regard "given segments [of human history] determined in extent and direction and in significance."[71] Among all of those that can be identified within the complex web of Niebuhr's notation, we would like to highlight the one whose presence delves deepest into the field of history.

Judeo-Christian Heilsgeschichte. Why do only certain historical events serve as cues for faith, and why does faith only arise in response to them? In that fact, what is typically documented is the sovereign transcendent power that governs, that is, leavens, history itself and causes it to rise towards the manifest actualization of its meaning. A series of specific facts, of precise historical contingencies, seems to constitute the privileged space of the phenomenon of revelation and, thus, the most precise location where "faith discerns the self-disclosure of God,"[72] in other words, where human freedom grasps God's actions that clarify the meaning of time and existence. These key events in the historical drama of all times are not independent from one another, but also in moving "by tortuous historical development"[73] compose an evolutionary trajectory, forming a history within history, a *Heilsgeschichte*. It is useful to recall that the events in question are not miracles that bring about "an impossible combination of the divine and the historical. The God who is both powerful and good by reason of being the source of all power, and not some particular power in history, cannot remain good if he becomes a particular power in human society."[74]

The true miracle, the true "act of God" in history is the existence of faith, which "recognizing the triumph of God's sovereignty in what seem to be the very ambiguous facts of history,"[75] that is, without a precise indication of their meaning, like all human occurrences. God's intervention in history is not so much a datum that causes faith to arise, as an enkindled faith that gives value to a datum. Naturally, the datum – once it is suffused with the light of faith, which breaks through the limits of its original meaning, making it "something more than a mere event"[76] – becomes, for the believer, an objective intervention of God, one of his "portentous acts."

The Judeo-Christian *Heilsgeschichte* represents a channel of faith that is exceptional for its concretely organic historical nature, for the depth of its significant observations, for the precision of its correspondence to the awareness of the situation that man lives, as well as for the way it exemplifies all of human history. This comes about in three chronologically successive and decisive phases.

(1) *The Hebrew prophetic movement* enlivens the struggle of the Hebrew people – a struggle common to all peoples – with mythic significance so as to enlarge "the frame of history to include all national stories, the rise and fall of empires, and ultimately both the origin and the end of man's existence on this earth."[77] Thus, God's promise to Abraham or the Covenant of Sinai are the primordial symbols through which the prophet, with the absolute and universal lordship of God, affirms the permanent value (the "mission") of history and the people. A further connotation qualifies this primordial

nucleus and gives the prophetic contribution of constituting a precise symbol of the supreme value of existence, a precise symbol, that is, of God's sovereignty: the idea of the Covenant also implies the idea of the infidelity of the people to the Pact with God.

God is, thus, shown not to be the expression of certain particular human forces or situations, the instrument of a people (albeit a chosen one), but so superior to everything that everything is inferior and in debt to him, the judge.

(2) *The life of Jesus* represents the second emergence of the *Heilsgeschichte*. This is a case of a historical figure, objectively of great moral value; yet, faith has grasped something beyond the limits that constitute that figure, "focal point of God's self-disclosure."[78] Herein lies the meaning of the Christian doctrine of the Incarnation: it does not state what *Jesus is*, ontologically,[79] but rather says something about who God is in relation to man and what the mystery of God brings to man's knowledge through the circumstances of Christ's life. The Word manifested itself in the flesh, even though it did not become flesh. In Niebuhr there is still the distinction of Liberal Theology between the Christ of faith and the Christ of history; yet, whereas for Liberals, the Christ of faith is a creation of believers that is applied to the Christ of history, in Niebuhr the Christ of faith is *discovered* by believers in the Christ of history, because he is present as an act of God.

There is a climactic point in God's self-disclosure in Christ: "The Cross is the symbolic point where this story most obviously ceases to be merely a story in history and becomes revelatory of a very unique divine 'glory.'"[80] It is the glory by which the Divine shows itself as the final and exhaustive norm of existence. The prophetic word is fulfilled in the myth of Christ: God takes upon himself the contradictions of history. He suffers his very own judgment on them, and he overcomes it by resolving it, "forgiving," fulfilling on his own level the unfilled aspect of human existence. The Christ of history was the first one to have the awareness of this meaning of his.

(3) The third link in the chain of revelation is *the first community of the faithful*.

In effect, the "revelation of Christ is not completed until the little Christian community surveys the whole Christian epic, which includes the life and teachings of Christ, but also and supremely the sacrificial death upon the Cross."[81]

The discovery of its meaning, by which the absolute triumph of God over evil is unveiled, is expressed in a conclusive faith experience, the resurrection of Christ. Death does not conquer him: in death he triumphs. It is death that truly reveals him to be "Son of God," "image of the Father." Faith in the Resurrection is, thus, the fullness of the faith in the Cross. The Cross as historical event was an evident fact. As "fact," the Resurrection is shrouded in the mysterious emergence of the experience of communion between the disciples and the resurrected Lord in Galilee. As it was handed down, the fact of the Resurrection "contained an alteration in the story through faith's apprehension of the significance of the story."[82] It was, therefore, not an evolutionary phenomenon, a persuasion that formed over time. Rather, it was a truly miraculous phenomenon, out of which the Church as "society of believers" sprang forth.

4 A CRITICAL NOTE

A philosophy of history is the corollary of a moral philosophy. Man's responsibility is the true central factor in Niebuhr's overall vision, and herein lies the cornerstone of his acute polemics with Barth, whom he scolds from the pages of the *Christian Century* in 1949: "this dreadful, godless, ridiculous opinion that man is the Atlas who is destined to bear the dome of heaven upon his shoulders."[83] Not the dome of heaven, but the web of history: heaven "judges" it, but history's capacity to build will come to fruition only through the dialectic of its personal responsibility. Of course, Niebuhr is quite far from the quasi-idolatry of free will proper to the pluralism of William James, whose admiring disciple he is (as is his entire cultural world).[84] If the drama of history is not ultimately an anarchic mass of human pronouncements, it is by "God's power, revealed in the structures of existence."[85] But divine power acts, and history is built with freedom and its dialectic.

The strong sense of values in Niebuhr is, culturally speaking, derived from Ritschl rather than from Puritanism; his interest exhausts itself in the *Werturteile*, to the point there is no longer space for *Seinsurteile*.

Yet this, too, together with the Jamesian stress on freedom, supports the concrete and committed sense of human time that Niebuhr has, one full of moral insistence and appeal to social urgency. Beyond any modification of his thought, even today, at seventy-six, Niebuhr would repeat what he wrote at thirty-five: "the final test of ideals must include their ability to qualify human action."[86]

History is, thus, shown to be full of leaps towards the good that are, on one the hand, prophecy and, on the other, verification. Thus, in his conception of history, Niebuhr clearly distances himself from the most noted contemporary Protestant historiographers, H. Butterfield, with his *Christianity and History*, and above all, K. Löwith, with his *Meaning of History*. Arguing with the Lutheranism that followed from the latter,[87] Niebuhr stated that Christian faith cannot be "reduced to a purely individual transcendence over a very inscrutable collective life."[88]

It has also been mentioned that the commitment of the self is the epistemological condition for grasping historic meanings, and in that sense Niebuhr seems to echo, albeit in another sphere of investigation, Marrou.

And yet, in the end, one cannot avoid the impression that Niebuhr's vigorous appeal to the responsibility of the self and to the constructive nature of history lacks an adequate basis. Niebuhr's way of looking at history seems to be that of a long *epochè* [suspension of judgment], because judgment of value, in order to be a sure measure, lies in what is beyond time. Now, in the dialectic of freedom, the aspect of agency in history, the certainty and nature of ultimate meaning, and therefore, the clarity and the practicability of its final value, make an operative synthesis possible, without which human factors would be "puppets of the *Weltgeist*."[89] If action cannot be based on a sure judgment, if relationships cannot be formed around evaluations that are certain, everything may spring from generous volunteerism, but it is no longer a case of a rational and, therefore, stable foundation for human behaviour, and it cannot be a sure function of social and historical constructivity. Paul Ramsey, one of the most noteworthy scholars of ethics in the United States, observes that, since for Niebuhr not even the principles upon which society is built are firm, "Such unlimited freedom means unlimited war ... there would then have been found no positive basis for community."[90]

In my view, the root of this slippage in Niebuhr's conception is found in some inadequate aspects of his epistemology. Within it, the focal point is constituted by the intuition of myth. Now, it is impossible to avoid observing what a precarious bridge this type of "existential experience" or "personal encounter" can be in terms of a possibility of a sure, stable, and communicative ultimate relationship with the real, God, and men. For man, only the idea casts light on things and gives them meaning: only the concept makes experience intelligible. Without this, any encounter or experience whatsoever would remain obscure, incommunicable, and inexpressible in itself, not so much because of personal intensity and realism, the realism of the intuition, but rather insofar as the subject itself is opaque. Niebuhr must tell himself and for others translate his experience into conceptual terms. Yet, these seem to become more or less pictorial and descriptive means, almost segments of a figure sketch, so as to affirm the presence of a fact and its overall features; they are summary indices, testimonies to reality, not an adequate and critical, albeit intentional, depiction of reality. Through what critical instrument is the objective value of the event assured? Existential intuitions are necessarily complex things, as is experience, and they express themselves more through paradoxes than through precise terms, more through ideas in tension than through defined ideas. In general the danger of such positions lies in a possible reduction of the necessary objectivity, precisely because of the will to adhere completely to the existential object. In fact, one is condemned to ambiguity to the degree that he claims to renounce the rational way of looking at things, which demands a certain detachment (or "abstraction") from existence, without which it cannot be specified as "obiectum," and therefore, the judgment upon it does not develop an adequately critical truth.

That ambiguity has consequences in Neibuhr's ontological conception, where there is a certain identification of the superior human element with the properly divine element. Consequently, theoretical perfection and moral perfection, in addition to being Socratically merged, are conceived as an infinite whole without degrees. And, since existence inevitably poses limits and imposes gradations, it must necessarily be seen as full of error and evil. But if the spirit-nature unity that will take place in existence is the condition that inexorably forces imperfection, how will the Divine eliminate this inevitability?

The only logical possibility would be the dissolution of that unity, that is, a dissolution of the historical self that this constituted by such a unity. The eschatological self would need to be another.

The serious *aporia* mentioned above, nevertheless, cannot take away from the wealth of wisdom with which Niebuhr conceives of man as agent of history: "We can participate in the fulfillment of the meaning [of things] only if we do not seek too proudly to appropriate the meaning as our secure possession or to effect the fulfillment by our own power."[91]

APPENDIX TWO

Reinhold Niebuhr and the Foundations of His Ethics*

Two facts belonging to the second half of the nineteenth century had a decisive influence on the consolidation of America's cultural orientation: (1) the colossal development of commerce and industry, which led to a rapid growth in wealth, and (2) scientific discoveries, in particular, the affirmation of evolutionary theory, which, when applied to human society, seemed to remove any possible limit on human achievement. The lay/secular culture of the young nation, thus, presents two fundamental features of a consequential optimism and pragmatism.

Out of the diversity of American Protestantism, a movement developed – the Social Gospel – that accepted the trends of secular culture in the new context, and sought to imbue them with a Christian spirit: "The Christian ideal is the same thing as pure Democracy." The Social Gospel managed to create a new social atmosphere, even if "this interest often was confined to declarations of programs and reports, without unleashing a truly renewing force which would be transformed into a great social reform brought about by the Church."[1]

It is in just such an atmosphere that there emerges the figure of a young Lutheran minister of Detroit's tiny Beth Evangelical Church: Reinhold Niebuhr. It is the era of Henry Ford's industrial initiative, which seemed to be the purest confirmation of the enthusiastic positions that saw the imminent destiny of humanity's perfection within inevitable social progress, and to which the Social Gospel offered an

* Translator's note: Previously published in *La scuola cattolica*, 1968, 49–507.

almost theological consecration. There is no doubt that Niebuhr is the most representative figure in the movement that would soon present a radical alternative to the Social Gospel itself, thus, changing the face of the most erudite thought of American Protestantism, known as the "new realism" or later "neo-orthodoxy," after Edwin Lewis in *The Faith We Declare* (1939) a term borrowed from European Barthian currents.

His diary of those years (1915–28), published in 1929 with the title of *Leaves from the Notebook of a Tamed Cynic*, documents the profound pastoral experience in which the key outlines of his thought were sketched. The acclaimed results of Ford's organization were achieved through the sacrifice of the whole mass of workers; the hiring conditions of those workers, favourable at the outset, turned out to be an exploitative manoeuvre – albeit an unwittingly hidden one. The young Niebuhr, thus, learned "the penetration of idealism by the corrupting element of self-interest; the inevitability of self-deception in the best intentions; the underlying cruelty and brutality in every class culture."[2] There emerged in him a pessimistic vision of human nature, which appeared to him as profoundly tragic and contradictory at all levels. Yet, most of all, it was pastoral activity, which caused him to note that "the ministry is particularly tempted to the self-deceptions which afflict the moral life of Christians … If it is dangerous to entertain great moral ideals without attempting to realize in life, it is even more perilous to proclaim them in abstract terms without bringing them into juxtaposition with the specific social and moral issues of the day."[3] During an interview, he recalled the moment when he abandoned Yale for Detroit, in other words, when he traded studies for ministry: "Epistemology bored me … and frankly the other side of me came out: I desired relevance rather than scholarship."[4] Thus, realism, concreteness, and currency characterize his intellectual expression, and ethical and social concerns would deeply mark his life in terms of both speculation and praxis.

Within his vast mass of scholarship, there are some works that serve as milestones in the evolution and definition of his ethical conception. His first work, *Does Civilization Need Religion?* (1927), "was still safely within the Social Gospel presuppositions,"[5] identifying social progress with man's redemption, and the automatic correspondence between commitment to an ideal and its worldly realization: "A merely realistic analysis of any given set of facts is …

as dangerous as it is helpful. The creative and redemptive force is a faith which defies the real in the name of the idea, and subdues it."[6] And yet, the disconnect between ideal and praxis is acutely, albeit discreetly, stressed; Christian ethical norms are always a bit "foolish"[7] in the face of real life; and the relation between the absolute and history is not one of simple harmony, but of tension and contrast.

The year following this first publication, Niebuhr left his Detroit parish to assume the Chair of Applied Christianity at Union Theological Seminary in New York, and the unique features of his ethical vision rapidly matured and took on a systematic nature. In 1932, he published *Moral Man and Immoral Society: A Study in Ethics and Politics*. This book gained him justifiable fame and transformed him into the leader of the opposition to the optimistic current of both the Protestantism of the Social Gospel and of John Dewey's confident secularism. Neither ascesis, in the name of the evangelical law of love, nor scientifically pursued education can assure a wise and perfect social structure, and therefore, simply translate into political ideal or a peaceful organization of society. In the area of social relationships, egotism unleashes all its uncontrollable virulence that only force, that is, power, can resist: "an uneasy balance of power would seem to become the highest goal to which society could aspire."[8] The kingdom of power is sundered from the kingdom of brotherhood and love: "It would therefore seem better to accept a frank dualism in morals than to attempt a harmony between the two methods which threatens the effectiveness of both."[9]

In 1935, *An Interpretation of Christian Ethics* radicalized the analysis of the moral possibilities of man as such: "The ethical demands made by Jesus are incapable of fulfillment in the present existence of man." "The full dimension of human life includes not only the impossible ideal, but realities of sin and evil which are more than simple imperfections and which prove that the ideal is something more than the product of a morbidly sensitive religious fantasy. Anything less than perfect love in human life is destructive of life. All human life stands under an impending doom because it does not live by the law of love."[10] An "impossible possibility" defines the status of man's ethical tension.

The stances taken in the works cited above gained a systematic foundation and a powerful, yet balanced development in the Gifford Lectures, given by Niebuhr in Edinburgh in 1939 and 1940, published in 1941 and 1943, and collected into a single volume titled *The Nature and Destiny of Man* (1949).

A given solution to ethico-social problems is obviously dictated by a given prior concept of man. In Niebuhr, the solution to these problems is constantly inspired by an overarching vision of human nature, its existence or "situation," its history. It is a vision that he deduces from an existential analysis whose fundamental factors he finds fully announced in the Bible. Indeed, for Niebuhr, all biblical teachings are exhausted in their explanation, and the reality of Christian Revelation itself is identified with the historical emergence of "myths" that are the natural vehicles for those factors.

There are two fundamental mythical formulations that spring from Christianity's wisdom about man: the Adam myth (man as "creature" and "*imago Dei*" with his "*iustitia originalis*" and his "original sin") and the Christ myth ("man-God," "who died on the Cross," and "Resurrected").

His criteria of analysis and his methods of biblical referencing position Niebuhr within the current of theological existentialism or of Dialectical Theology.

I THE "ADAM MYTH"

Niebuhr is quite absolute in his opposition to any conception of "natural law," either in its Stoic version, its medieval or Catholic version, or in its Enlightenment version. Yet, the noted scholar of ethics, Paul Ramsey, in his critical commentary on Niebuhr's system,[11] rightly insists that it is not an alternative or a subversion, but rather a revision of the traditional concept of natural law. If, as Maritain says,[12] the natural moral law is a set of things to do and to not do deduced "from the simple fact that man is man, nothing else being taken into account," it is true that for Niebuhr, as well, the basic ethical emphasis and formulation derives explicitly from "certain unchangeable aspects of human existence." In his main work, he speaks of the sense of obligation as "the claim which the essential nature of man makes upon him."[13] It must, therefore, be seen how Niebuhr defines the terms of this "essential nature," whose permanence he reaffirms in the face of all modern relativisms normally unable to recognize them "in their obsession with the changing aspects in the human situation."[14]

Two antithetical elements fundamentally subsist within man: "nature" and "spirit," in biblical language, "creature" and "*imago Dei*."

The idea of *creature* essentially highlights man's finiteness and, thus, the limited nature of any manifestation of humanity, the dependency of his life, and the determinedness of his forms. The term "nature" is what is normally used, in a technical sense, as a synonym for "creature"; together, though, it is also used generically to indicate the essence of the human self.[15]

But, within man's structure, Revelation finds an element that is incommensurable with any created entity, an element of divine proportions: the *imago Dei*. The divine proportions of this element come from a capacity that is irresistibly in act, of unceasingly surmounting any position in which the human being is realized. The impulse for this movement, which is inherent to man's structure, is indefinite, by nature limitless; it is, therefore, sharply distinct, and essentially transcendent in the face of the characteristic of man as creature. If the latter characteristic defined man as limit and as dependence and insufficiency, the *imago Dei* defines man as an unlimited capacity of boundless fulfilment: as capacity for God. That is what within man is defined as *spirit*: "[In biblical psychology] spirit is conceived of as primarily a capacity for and affinity with the divine."[16]

That is how Niebuhr indicates that characteristic phenomenon that is man's capacity to raise himself above any given level of reality, to surpass any given limit he has, a capacity of "self-transcendence." Often, this capacity of transcendence is explicitly called *freedom*, in that it denotes the fact that the human spirit is not bound or determined in a definite way by anything, nor can it be bound by any of its acts.

This transcendence of the spirit is enacted on two levels. In the first place, in going beyond – standing "outside of" – nature and its process: it is the human spirit as "capacity for making general concepts." This first level is called "conscience" or "reason." But, reason does not exhaust the reality of the spirit and of freedom. It does connote a certain overcoming of the natural process, but in ultimate analysis, it is still completely bound to the limits that are "given" within it, to the "deterministic causal chains."[17] Thus, "reason is … both a symbol of the freedom of man over nature and of his involvement in it."[18] But, within the spirit, there is a capacity for further activity that is not concluded in reason, not hindered by "rationality." Conscience itself and rational values become the object of a higher viewpoint, the *self-transcendence* of the spirit. Through it, man has a centre of knowledge that goes beyond his being as part of the natural world. And herein lies the true principle that emancipates the spirit from the necessities of the natural process and, thus, is found the principle of freedom. It is an impulse of continual and indefinite overcoming of the situation into which the self is placed: it, therefore, gives man "the possibility for those endless variations and elaborations of human capacities which characterize human existence."[19] It is, therefore, the principle of man's creativity and, above all, of man's creativity within the very space of his individuality, of his self-governance, his self-dominion.

As necessity and freedom, as finiteness and infinity, the two elements of the human composite are in opposition. Yet, in active life, they subsist in absolute unity, in "organic relation." More than a composite of elements, one could speak of man as a tension between two opposite poles. The tension that makes up human unity is expressed and realized as *will*. The will is more precisely the function of freedom as it manipulates the givenness of the self. Through the will, therefore, the self's individuality is characterized concretely, it is shaped in a determined way, rising thus, to the level of personality. Hence, Niebuhr declares, "[man's] essence is free self-determination."[20]

Existentially, the relationship between the two essential elements that are so antithetical brings about a characteristic and inevitable state of mind, anguish, with a double connotation, in the same way as its structural tension is bipolar: (a) Freedom, or the capacity for transcendence, opens up further horizons and urgent perfections to man. Within man, therefore, there is an irrepressible agitation towards ever more perfect ideals. In this connotation, anxiety is a source of creativity: "Anxiety for perfection." (b) Yet, natural finiteness and contingency force freedom to constantly be realized in terms that are inevitably reduced and precarious. This continual and irremovable frustration – as partial as it may be – of the ideal creative impulse poses to the human spirit the question of whether its achievements have value. And, since this impulse constitutes a properly human characteristic, the problem pervades the very meaning of existence, of whether it is destined to failure. Within the human conscience, there perennially exists a fear about one's own situation: "anxiety of freedom."[21]

The situation of the self as anxiety seeks a resolution. Theoretically, the sinless solution would be found if freedom were to no longer be affected by the self to which it belongs and, therefore, by the anxiety connected to it; if freedom were thus capable of translating into act its capacity for the infinite to such a complete degree so as to bring itself "beyond" any possible determination by the self, to exclusively focus on the "ultimate," "eternal" reality of those possible determinations – in other words, on God's will. The human self should interpret the ambiguity and uncertainty of its finite situation from the standpoint of God's hidden design. What is needed is an actualization of the self that represents a "leap" from the limit in which the self subsists to that which is not limit. The sole possibility for the finite self to actualize itself in all the purity of its capacity for infinity consists in this qualitative leap. The "centre" of the life of the self is outside of the self and its world.

In short, what is necessary are the "theological" virtues of faith and hope, which in man make up that "original justice" of the biblical myth that marks the ideal dynamism of what is essential to the self. Faith and hope generate harmony in love as relationship to others, and in respect towards the "natural law" as relationship to situations.[22]

In point of fact, the theoretical possibility of "original justice" is inevitably frustrated. It is evident that the solution cannot be generated by the action into which the self is launched, since the problem springs from the very structural condition of the self. And yet, the self feels bent on an autarchic attempt to overcome this situation. The self seeks equilibrium within the sphere of its own present contingent possibilities. Thus, evil – sin – inevitably springs forth.

This attempt at self-transcendence can take place in two ways. (1) [It can do this] by giving undue value to its own capacity for transcendence or freedom, in an attempt to give an ideal or absolute value to one's own finite knowledge (the sin of ideology); or to render one's own contingent position secure by overcoming, through his own strength, the limits established by nature, using one's energies independently from these limits (the sin of the wish for power). This aspect of the attempt [at self-transcendence] is the sin of pride or "self-love." (2) [It can do this] by denying one's own capacity for self-transcendence or freedom, and seeking to immerse oneself completely in a particular aspect of natural reality: the sin of "sensuality."

The inevitability of sin should absolutely be understood as something that belongs to the essential nature of man. It could be said that sin is "natural" for man, "in the sense that it is universal but not in the sense that it is necessary." Yet, it is universal: "there is no level of moral goodness upon which the sense of guilt can be eliminated."[23] What does this inevitability consist of? It is something present in situation of the self prior to any other act. In every actual sin, there is an evil that is prior to the action, which is its determining matrix. Every human action has at its origin an "inclination to evil" that always determines it. It is precisely in this "prior" wherein lies "that aspect of which is designated as 'original.'"[24] Each human action is evil, based on this evil that is found at its very origin. Niebuhr cites the famous paradox of Kierkegaard in which "sin posits itself."

This original evil is in the will – which is the place where freedom existentializes itself (thus, evil is not part of human essence) – it is a native "defect" by which the will cannot succeed in adequately translating that capacity for the infinite or freedom that, nevertheless, constitutes it. In short, one could say that this defect lies in the fact that the will is *the self's* will, and not *God's* will. Precisely as the executive, existential aspect of freedom, the will realizes freedom in its dialectical relationship with the finite nature of the contingent and limited element of the self; it does not realize freedom in its purity, but freedom in tension. As essence, therefore, the will is freedom. In terms of actualization, it is the denial of freedom. Since the will is the self that determines itself in existence, it could be said that the existence of the self is contradiction, rupture of the essential order and harmony: "[Man's] sin is the wrong use of his freedom and its consequent destruction."[25]

The original defect of the will, by which it does not know the "leap," which we have mentioned as the sole solution, and seeks to resolve its restless situation in an autarchic way, plunging ever deeper into it, from an ethical standpoint is defined as a lack of "perfect trust in divine security." Thus, the more profound evil from which actual evil springs, given the state of anxiety, is *disbelief*: "The anxiety of freedom leads to sin only if the prior sin of unbelief is assumed. This is the meaning of Kierkegaard's assertion that sin posits itself."[26] This is the *original sin* that lies at the root of *actual sin*, that is, each and every human action.

Sin's inevitability paradoxically subsists along with its personal imputability. It is, in fact, a defect of the will, and the will is the organ that expresses freedom: freedom is the antithesis of necessity. So, despite the "original" character of evil in the will, it should not be attributed to a necessity of human nature, but it is, rather, something extraneous to its essence, which comes about within its voluntaristic determinism. Man is, therefore, responsible for it. This judgment is completely motivated by man's psychological experience. Seen from the outside, "sin may seem to be the necessary consequence of previous temptations";[27]

and yet, the interior experience of sin dismantles this deterministic explanation. Inner experience always registers the presence of a certain degree of "conscious dishonesty." This *sense of guilt* and the phenomenon of *repentance* highlight the presence of this connivance. Adam and Eve, after sinning, were "ashamed."

And yet, the fullest experience of human freedom lies in the sense of guilt. Action "reduces" freedom of spirit to limits; but once an action is complete, that is, as soon the will has determined the self, the mind re-emerges from the confines of action, goes beyond it, and turns to dominate it with its gaze. It is precisely in this moment that the self recognizes that the ideal object of the spirit has been voluntarily sacrificed to the contingent necessity of natural, limited life. Thus, the maximum affirmation of the freedom of the self in action – that is, of the self that posits itself in existence – is at the terminus of action and is manifested as the acknowledgment of one's own insufficiency, of a *voluntarily* realized insufficiency, an acknowledgment of *existing as sin*. This means the definitive affirmation of the inevitability of evil in each and every action: "The ultimate proof of the freedom of the human spirit is its own recognition that its will is not free to choose between good and evil." Or "Man is most free in the discovery that he is not free."[28]

2 THE "CHRIST MYTH"

From a psychological standpoint, man's ethical dynamism would, at this point, be impeded, blocked; the permanent impetus of "original justice" would be "corrupted" and disappear, if faith, the vigilance of freedom over the transcendent, did not discover in the symbol of Christ on the Cross the definitive form of the ethical ideal that urges the human spirit on. In the Cross, God reveals to man the terms of his relationship with him, and in this revelation man grasps the supreme rule that undergirds life and to which life must conform in order for existence to avoid collapsing into chaos. God reveals himself as wise ruler and final goal in that he is the norm for man. Thus, Niebuhr affirms: "The same Christ who is accepted by faith as the revelation of the character of God is also regarded as the revelation of the true character of man."[29] Christ is God-man. The figure of Christ mediates the phenomenon of the encounter with God such that the elements of the human-Divine relationship do not remain suspended in that vague flux of uncertainty into which the each and every human being's native religious sentiment drifts, but rather become clearly defined. The spirit feels itself to be placed in the "right" position, from which the impulse towards the ideal acquires dynamism and efficiency. Existence, thus, can count on resources that come from beyond its own energy, which is naturally centred on the self. It is a "beyond" that opens up and communicates itself, gives itself: it is *grace*.

The word "grace" has different connotations, but the analogy between them is clear, and everything boils down to the affirmation of that redemption of existence man aspires to.

One could speak above all of a "*common*" *grace*, which precedes grace proper. It may be defined as that bit of perception and realization of the ideal fixed within every human act by the very fact that it exists. Man can never wholly deny the element of freedom that he possesses. Since the norm of that freedom is love, an absolute and total refusal of it would eliminate the very possibility of existence.[30]

But grace, strictly speaking, is light and strength that man experiences as intervening in his situation in a clear way from "outside" it. Everything within man that surpasses cognition and act, in that they are ruled by the particular and restricted interests of the self, must be attributed to this grace. Oftentimes, this energetic encounter with what is beyond the self is unconscious: "frequently it is the 'hidden Christ' and a grace which is not fully known which initiates the miracle [of the self that goes beyond its center]."[31] But, historically, what is properly called grace manifests itself and is unleashed in its constitutive dialectic by means of the encounter with the Cross of Christ.

The dialectic of the Cross begins as light, or as the *grace of wisdom*. The ethical imperative of freedom, in its *iustitia originalis*, is love. Love demands that action not be centred on the self, but on the other. If the law of love implies this selflessness, in reality, what we see is the fact "that the highest form of human goodness embodies a heedlessness of self which endangers the self in its physical security."[32] Christian wisdom urges one to have no fear of any implication. Christ reveals God to be interested in man; God's love for man is an infinite love. Existentially, that boundless love – love in its authenticity – is manifested as giving one's life for others, hence, the symbol of the Cross. Man's perfection "is not so much a sum total of various virtues or an absence of transgression of various laws; it is the perfection of sacrificial love."[33] Man's ethical ideal is only the *agape of the Cross*, the sacrifice of oneself in order to be consumed in the other as the motive for one's action.

Yet, existence, with fundamental problems of preservation of life and life in common, seems necessarily to impose a law of calculation, of compromise, of prudence; it would seem to place limits on the indefinite impulse of freedom in love. Reason would, in fact, find that the adequate norm for historical existence is not disinterested love (*sacrificial love*, or agape), but love founded on a predictable reciprocity, love as studied harmony in contact, as equilibrium in social life, *mutual love*.[34] Yet, neither is mutual love in its apparent consistency an exhaustive practical rule, nor is sacrificial love an abstract utopia without a real impact on historical existence. This very calculated approach, this very equilibrium of compromise could not occur if the self used them as its exclusive motor for action. Each and every act of the self demands, at the outset, the presence of an impulse that transcends the particular interests of the self: an ideal impulse, which action would impede and betray, yet which lies at its very root. Without it, existence would be missing its leaven, it would dry up: "If mutual love is not constantly replenished by impulses of grace in which there are no calculation of mutual advantages, mutual relations degenerate first to the cool calculation of such advantages and finally to resentment over the inevitable lack of complete reciprocity in all actual relations."[35] Each initiative must have a margin within which the self is risked, is forgotten: it "loses itself."

It is evident that all this does not take away the fact that the presence of the ideal in existential acts is always to the detriment of the self, that it is always "Cross." Yet, the existential situation is always the fruit of the collision of different interests: the proportion in which the pure ideal is accepted within the situation is the exact proportion in which the self does put into question its own interests, and the interests of others overwhelm it. By its very nature, agape cannot avoid being realized at the expense of the historical life of the self.[36] It is precisely for this reason that one can say that any form of life, of historical activity, by the very fact that it exists and acts and affirms itself, as an exception, in varying degrees, to the ethical ideal of life itself and, therefore, of history.[37] For man, the wisdom of the Cross is the supreme possibility towards which he is pushed, but it is impossible to realize. It is the "impossible possibility" of human existence. So, "there are no righteous," nor does there exist a "pure ethical norm in history."[38] From this standpoint, man's ethical ideal, which only faith can define, is *judgment* and *condemnation*: Christ is also the judge of the last day.

Thus, when, through the figure of Christ, the self comes face-to-face with God – God as the law of its being, as unavoidable affirmation of the ideal – it feels, as it were, a jolt within, wherein lie the sense of its own lack and the feeling of its own incapacity of overcoming it. In that moment, the self is forced to deny its own self-sufficiency and to recognize that its salvation can only come from "an accession of power from beyond the self." Egocentrism is "broken," "contrite." It is the phenomenon of *conversion*. We must point out that this is the dialectical counterpoint to the "original fall" that, theoretically, accompanies every action, just as every action is accompanied by a sense of guilt. Indeed, it is not a *metanoia* that changes the attitude of existence in a lasting way as much as its activity; "the shattering of the self is a perennial process,"[39] just as that inclination to evil that provokes a deficit in every human action is a permanent characteristic of existence.

The symbol of the Cross does not contain only the connotation of the pure affirmation of the ethical ideal. The summit of its content – the vicarious atonement – lies in the affirmation that the ultimate value of God for man is that of forgiveness. God as justice is, on the one hand, wisdom that is affirmed in the structure of the cosmos as its law; on the other hand, he is power that acts upon those who rebel against that law. But God's merciful agape towards those who challenge his will as constitutive of the structure of things reveals in him a power of freedom over its own law without abrogating it; it reveals a power of self-transcendence without self-betrayal.[40] And whereas divine power that reveals itself as justice conquers but does not remove the disorder of evil, merciful love represents the extreme expression of the power and sovereignty of God in the world, posited as the principle of a final completion of the human. Forgiveness is the power of God over man, the power that God has to overcome his very own justice and to continually eliminate with his infinite capital the inevitable deficit of every human action, the power to tirelessly fill the void that is at the heart of every existential instant. This is the capital and cardinal grace, by which the human being feels complete, not desperately lacking, and yet, his completion does not come from himself. Rather, another completes him.

The perception of the Cross as "God who forgives" is the grace of justification. This must not be determined based upon preconceived theological ideas, but upon the individual's existential experience. The self, in the instant in which it feels "contrite," converted by facing the divine ideal, and it recognizes it as its completion by feeling within the nostalgia for it, experiences an influx of serenity, peace, and equilibrium. This is the proof that the ideal is reconciled with it, becomes its "possession," and "covers" what is lacking. In fact, in re-emerging from the "swamp" in which the unity of the self in action has overturned and misunderstood the ideal, and recovering its recognition, man becomes "just," because he possesses the ideal in a certain true way, that is, intentionally. The healthy sense that springs forth within the soul in that renewed perception of the ideal is exactly the rebuke that the unfulfilled realization of it in action is not the definitive situation, but a contingency that God overcomes, "forgiving it." In the final analysis, justification is resolved for man in the experience of the intentional contact with the law of his life as surpassing and completing action, as redemption of its unfulfilment. Since God himself is the law of life, God himself completes man's existence, he "takes" his defect "unto himself" and redeems it: "God takes the sinfulness of man into Himself."[41]

A further clarification of the meaning of that intentional contact with God is necessary. It is not just any knowledge of Christ and his significance. It is a contrite knowledge of the past that is full of aspiration for the ideal. The contrition that the comparison with the ideal produces could close in on itself in desperation. The formal element of justifying faith is the nostalgia and the enlivened desire for perfection: "the newness of life in principle is ... a gift, which must subsequently be realized progressively in volition and aspiration."[42] In a certain way, justice, which is Christ, enters into man and man possesses it. He possesses it not in fact, but in principle, in as much as in that determined experience of faith the contrite self repudiates the principle of egocentrism and its animated by the principle of devotion to the ideal: God, revealed in Christ. In other words, by faith man possesses justice "as sentiment" and not "as act." Actualization would corrupt this sentiment, this attitude of interior aspiration, and the dialectical process that governs the historical existence of the human spirit will continue on. It is, therefore, a new life that remains at the root of the self without managing to translate itself into a complete reality, just as the spirit's infinite transcendence remains at the root of the self without managing to be completely realized. Justice, for existing man, is never something wholly in his possession. It is always something on loan from what lies beyond existence, and it is granted as tension and desire, not as act. Christ is never fully "Christus in nobis"; only "Christus pro nobis" is true for man. He is man's ideal only in the sense that he is "ideal for" man, and, if grasped through faith, is attributed, "imputed" to man by God: "Christ in us is not a possession but a hope"; "divine mercy 'imputes' the perfection of Christ and accepts the self's intentions for achievements."[43]

The Cross, in as much as it is the revelation of God's mercy on man, is completed in the symbol of the *Resurrection*. The announcement that eternity assumes responsibility for the failings of time and eliminates them, by fulfilling them "at the end," has an impact on time and contingency. From the "justified" position, the impulse towards the ideal takes on dynamism and efficacy. Existence becomes capable of new and greater approaches to its ideal, that is, capable of greater *perfection*. This is the aspect that most properly belongs to redemption, the experience of a new life that succeeds judgment and mercy. The self experiences a real "accretion of power" because "the justification by faith is a release of the soul into action."[44]

It is through this burst of energy that history becomes "a realm of endless possibilities of renewal and rebirth."[45] The new life lies in the whole self's renewed engagement with reality: the recovery of the unity of the self and the unity of the self with reality, the recovery of the possibility of action and the intensity of action. This is grace as the *power of God in* man: "it represents an accession of resources, which man does not have of himself, enabling him to become what he truly ought to be."[46] It is the grace of *sanctification*.

It is important to point out that as long as man is immersed in the natural process, the taint of attachment to self will be unavoidable both as a standpoint on the problem of truth and as a calculus in the life of relationships. Furthermore, the same grace that provides existence with a way of overcoming its own actual disproportion to the ideal law posits a new motive of disproportion, because it increases the self's sensibility to the ideal, and it, therefore, opens it up to new and vast urgencies for application. Sanctity and sin, thus, always coexist as two points of the same existential point; grace as power within man is undergirded by grace as mercy towards man. Sanctification is always actualized in dialectical tension with justification. Each and every moment of existence carries within itself this "paradox of grace, that is a having and not having."[47] No achievement of thought would every have an absolute value and no human action could ever conform so perfectly to the ideal as to not contradict it in some way.

The amount of agape that can be incorporated into the dynamic structures of human relationships is the value of *justice*. Emil Brunner objects that Niebuhr does not possess "a clear concept of justice."[48] But, as Harland correctly points out, for Niebuhr, justice does not have a different formal principle other than that of agape: "Justice is not a definable entity in itself. Justice is a relational term in Niebuhr, it is the relative embodiment of *agape* in the structures of society."[49] So, love demands justice, precisely because it seeks its existence in the world, otherwise it would be reduced to inconsequential sentimentality. In that sense, the norms and laws of justice help provide love with a content.

Conversely, it must also be stated that justice without love would be a crude "calculation of competing interests."[50] The wisdom of justice would boil down to a "balance of power."[51] Yet, it must be said that agape denies justice insofar as it cannot be balanced between the concrete factors of the relationship. Thus, its directives codify the limits of the ideal of fraternity, the ideal of agape: directives that are essentially contingent, the fruit of an evolving situation and, therefore, always open to being transcended by a more inclusive, more universal point of view, one that is more agape.

It is to this concept of justice that Niebuhr anchors his strict aversion to any concept of "natural law." The indefinite mobility of human situations and the essentially undetermined nature of freedom make a normative definition of human expressions and human relationships *impossible*.[52] The confidence of Catholic moralists derives from their misunderstanding of the immanence of the dimension of freedom in every contingency, which is made absolutely unique by the qualifying power of freedom itself. The concept of an "original fall" acquires an abstract meaning, by which man's reason would remain intact in its capacity; a universal value and sanctity is attributed to particular points of view and conditioned perspectives. Thus, Thomism is reduced to a "religious sanctification of the feudal social system."[53]

The codification of the directives of human behaviour into natural laws precludes the comprehension of the emergence of the new, of the true concrete human situation: "There is no possibility of giving any rational definition of a just relation between man and man or nation and nation short of a complete love in which each life affirms the interests of the other."[54]

In defining justice independently from love, justice loses its redemptive power as incarnate relation to love, and love loses its relation to life as a whole. An abstract moralism, thus, hovers over a skeptical practice of life (since history sweeps away the premature and unilateral definition of things): "The final dyke against relativism is to be found, not in these alleged [natural] fixities, but in the law of love itself."[55]

This last statement provides the point of departure for a brief concluding observation, given the expository aim of this work. Niebuhr's conception, as noble and lively and provocative as it is, does not seem to so easily be a "dyke" against uncertainty and relativism as is claimed. The authentic Protestantism of Niebuhr recognizes psychological experience as the privileged "place" for verifying values, that is, of the inherent sense of the essential fabric of the human fact. On this terrain lies their foundation, the criteria for their recognition, and also the factors for their safeguarding and their permanence. A rational reading of reality is inevitably codified into formulae and, therefore, firm and fixed relationships which, by their nature, are nothing more than contingencies that are continually pressed in on by human energy, the unstoppable vehicle of change and newness.[56] Against such a precarious rational reading, Niebuhr proposes a prophetic attitude; such is his appeal to the ideal of absolute love, and the judgment from it which is incumbent on every action. Derived from it is an energetic encouragement to the moral man, as Niebuhr feels and describes him, to be serious and engaged. Yet, there is, as it were, a disproportion between the energy of the appeal to an existential engagement and the adequacy of the norm that is produced, since an ethical norm ought to be characterized by the existential concreteness of its indications. Thus, Brunner notes (and not incorrectly): "Brilliant as Reinhold Niebuhr is in his analysis of existing social conditions or of historical movements and cultural trends, this critical analysis seldom gives rise to definite, concrete ethical postulates for social action."[57] His ethical discourse is impressive, but he easily leaves one ill equipped to face the urgency of relationships, ultimately risking falling into that abstraction that Niebuhr wanted to avoid with all his heart. More recent commentators frequently accentuate this unease, reminding themselves of Niebuhr's first works, in which his thought had not yet achieved fullness and equilibrium.[58] But, in his thought, certain fundamental implications of his vision can never be radically avoided: "[The ethic of Jesus] has nothing to say about the relativities of politics and economics, nor of the necessary balances of power which exist and must exist even in the most intimate social relationships."[59] Yet, an ethics that has no possibility of articulation and mediation to this point cannot avoid an ultimate skepticism.

This is made even more likely by another consequence of Niebuhr's Protestant epistemology. For Niebuhr, as for Luther, the value judgment on the perfection of the self should be provided by the experience of an actual complete harmony. Biological substrata, psychological antecedents, and situational determinations all condition an act and, therefore, its moral value. Thus, the presence of *motus primo primi*, the unprovoked eruption of desires, the irremovable dynamism of impulses, all of this makes the order of the self impossible and the value judgment on the moments of its existence negative. For this reason, the value of an act of the will is not determined by something totally immanent to the will itself, and precisely by the direction that it assumes; the value of the will is given by the limits into which the indeterminacy of freedom is compelled to fit, out of the necessity of existence. With such a definition of the moral agent, it does not seem possible to easily save (to recover and educate), the seriousness and the engagement of the self with reality in its ultimate significance, in its ethical worth.

Yet, as we have already noted, Niebuhr has been a powerful voice of appeal to such a seriousness and engagement. It is evident that a prophet might not necessarily be a lucid and systematic moralist.[60]

APPENDIX THREE

The Recovery of Religious Values in American Personalism and the Philosophy of Edgar Sheffield Brightman*

I

The inspiration for American Personalism is fidelity to the most fundamental values of religious tradition, God and "the freedom and dignity of the soul."[1] The imposing nature of the fact of the human individual, original and irreducible, would suggest the point of departure for a certain epistemology and would establish the basis for a certain metaphysics; but it is that fidelity to religious values that determines its reactions and facilitates its intuitions.

Thus, George Holmes Howison (1834–1916), whose name is linked to the first expression of a personalistic philosophy – a member of the Kant Club of St Louis, the blossoming of a passionate and systematic study of Kant and Hegel in America[2] – rebels against the pantheistic implication of Hegel's absolute wherein every individuality, divine and human, is denied (he would transfer to Hegel's absolute the irony that Hegel aimed at Schelling when he spoke of the "night in which all cows are black"). And he immediately contradicts the early expressions of Royce, whose *deeper* or *larger self*, or whose *whole world of ideas* dissolved every authentic individual specificity into modalities of the Absolute. For Howison, reality is, instead, constituted at the base of persons who are irreducible and indestructible, like spiritual atoms. These spiritual unities are essentially in communication among themselves (and, thus, the cognitive process begins). Thus, the universe is like an immense social order, a

* Translator's note: Previously published in *Filosofia e vita*, 8, 1967, 71–85.

great community, whose unity is continually generated in the immanent tension of every person towards the one sole Ideal, the Personal God. "City of God," "Eternal Republic," are the terms Howison uses to indicate the reality as he conceives it, to which he applies the traditional concept of "prime mover," because, he asserts, it is the totality, made up of human personalities and of God "living Bond of their union," who constitutes "the genuine *Unmoved One that moves all Things*."[3] Such a conception specified an attitude that not only attacked any idealistic interpretation which tended to dissolve the datum of the person into an abstract totality, or the concreteness of reality itself into "mentalistic reductions," but which was openly at war with the epistemology and anthropology that evolutionism fed into. The scientist, Howison clearly holds, can only reach the phenomenon, the psychic and physiological aspects of man. He cannot touch his essence, which is spirit, and he must not seek to transform his findings into metaphysical claims.

At the very outset of the history of Personalism, we see the recovery, albeit according to an original idealistic inspiration, of certain aspects of traditional metaphysics, which Wilbur M. Urban, one of the most influential philosophers of the American academic world, called "the natural metaphysics of the human mind,"[4] and with which a religious vision of reality could find a rational foundation.

Concurrently with Howison's initiative in California, at the opposite geographic extreme, the teaching of another personalist current was being developed by another important thinker, formed in old Boston, the most significant location for the history of American thought; an imposing movement, from which, due to its very religious nature, a great many Protestant clergyman drew a schema of explanation and rational organization. "The intellect has its inalienable rights in religion," the founder of this new movement would write, one whose thinking would provide a liberalizing ferment within traditional theology, to the point that the conservative wing of the Methodist Church would condemn him as a heretic (without, however, harming his position as professor): "He became the Socrates of the Methodist church."[5] Thus, the figure of Borden Parker Bowne (1847–1910) shows that passion for religious values that marked the very positing of the subject of American Personalism.

What dominates in his philosophy is the reality of the individual self, according to the essence of philosophical inquiry, the starting point and the content that concretize and solidify the systematic consideration of reality. Thus, Bowne abandons from the beginning the attitude (which is also that of Kant and of Lotze, his master and friend)[6] that obscures within the concern over categories, the consideration of the substantiality of the self that is the subject actor of the categories themselves. All of reality is a plurality of persons, each one an autonomous source of movement and relationships, a law unto himself (reminiscences of Leibnitz's monadism, especially through its echoes in Lotze's forms, are logically easy – and inevitable in a certain sense – in pluralistic Personalism). Material reality itself is nothing if not the phenomenic appearance of personal activity: "The material world is realized idea – idea which has somehow had force put into it."[7]

The experience of the self connotes, even more so, the fact that the totality of its "external" reference constitutes a "universe," an ordered unity, full of intentionality. The eminent intelligibility of the universe, even more evident than in the operation of the individual, therefore, implies a universal regulating mind, and the inexhaustibility of the meaning of the relationships that make up the universe postulates the infinity of that mind. Thus, God is the being-foundation of which finite reality is the manifestation that on the level of persons is consistent, is "creation." God could be called the intelligence and the will of the universe as a whole, the world and its activity (although it is clear in Bowne, in any case, that God in his essence transcends the process of reality as *totum*). In particular, God determines among the multiplicity of persons an interaction from which inevitably springs the harmony of the overall intention. So, our human existence, the dynamics of social life, the course of history are essentially "moral"; values have undying consistency or validity; and undying optimism is a fundamental consequence.

In the optimism of his cosmic and historical vision, Bowne, on the one hand, was more in line with the impetus of the Methodist spirit, and on the other, he conformed perfectly to the dominant interpretation of Christianity of his time, made into the code of social evolution and the Redemption identified with progress. Such an interpretation was expressed in the New Theology and in the movement known as the Social Gospel, which characterized the most lively and cultured front of American Protestantism in the second half of the nineteenth century and early in the twentieth century. Yet, that optimism was also a subversive factor in the conception of God and of man's consequent relationship with him, which characterizes the entire Calvinist Puritan tradition and especially the classical theology of Jonathan Edwards: "The God of theology for a long time hardly attained to any real active goodness, such as the thought of ethical love implies. This God, too, was rather metaphysically conceived, and his holiness consisted mainly in making rules for men and in punishing their transgression. He was conceived largely after the fashion of the medieval despot, and the conception of any obligation on his part to his creatures would have been looked upon almost as blasphemy ... We see that the law of love applies to power as well as to weakness."[8] It is also true, however, that the echo of Edwards' "sultanic" – as it was called – idea of God can still be heard in Bowne's metaphysics in a radical moment, in which, in order to save the reality of the interaction between finite persons, a necessary factor in the cosmos, Bowne reduces this interaction completely to divine activity, which "passes through individualities," ultimately the independence and, therefore, the self-determination of the human self.

The criterion that Bowne sets into motion in moments of decisive value appears without a doubt to be related to those "needs of the soul" that Lotze invokes at the beginning of his Mikrokosmos in order to motivate the resistance to a totally mechanistic vision of reality and to integrate the naturalistic level of the perception of the real into a theistic spiritualism. Thus, Bowne makes explicit a principle of verification: "Whatever the mind demands for the satisfaction of its subjective interests and tendencies may be assumed as real in default of positive disproof."[9] But, Bowne's critical awareness is clearly documented: "When we have lived and described the personal life we have done all that is possible in sane and sober speculation. If we try to do more we only fall a prey to abstractions. This self-conscious existence is the truly ultimate fact."[10] In particular, if the system of references and indications of which the self's experience is woven were to be denied in its epistemological value, the mind should declare itself to be unreliable, and therefore deny itself: "As philosophy can never be allowed to commit suicide, it is bound to take those views which are consistent with its own existence. Hence philosophy, when it understands its own conditions, must always be theistic."[11] For this reason, Blau spoke of the presence in Bowne's epistemology of a "a realistic vein of common sense," a judgment that recalls the title of Bowne's most famous work, *Personalism: Common Sense and Philosophy* (1908).

II

Out of Bowne's activity, there originated a long-lasting and influential school, whose most noted member was Edgar Sheffield Brightman, born in 1884 at Holbrook, Massachusetts. E.S. Brightman and W.E. Hocking may be considered the last two great American philosophers to have sought to preserve a foundation in "traditional" religion (albeit with all the possible Liberal connotations), deriving inspiration, although in a different way, from a "traditional" philosophy prior to the great revolution of existentialism of Niebuhr and Tillich. A metaphysical foundation for religious thought that would be able to flourish even within the already universally accepted reduction of the "true" to the "experimentally verifiable": this is the understanding that animates Brightman's work. He, thus, sharpens his logical tool, his "concrete and comprehensively critical reason," wherein religious values appear to be the ultimate coherence in the totality of experience. Hence, the philosophy of religion represents the highest vantage point in the adventure of thought, the summit of that metaphysics which is "the mind's effort to view experience as a living whole,"[12] that "living whole" of Goethe's verses which Hegel's citation consecrated for general consideration.

Brightman is not simply a follower. Although he cannot be defined as "the greatest representative" ("il maggior representante") of Personalism, as Luigi Stefanini does,[13] within its history he is certainly the one who developed the whole web of traditional components of the system into a more complete and systematically critical structure. Those components are, thus, revived into a robust synthesis attentive to the evolving cultural situation and in some respects truly original.

For Brightman, it is no longer, as it is for Howison and Bowne, mainly a polemical effort to create an alternative to the idealistic abstractions and naturalistic reductions into which the supreme values, the self and God, dissolve. Brightman starts in a positive way from within the intelligence of his moment, and he attempts to integrate Personalist ontology into the dominant "empiricist" framework, to merge the tradition of idealist[14] forms with the encroaching novelty of pragmatism: "After James' death, his plea that religion break its alliance with Rationalism and follow the method of Empiricism was heeded beyond his expectations ... The new 'Empiricism' affected deeply the philosophy of religion of the twenties and thirties ... In several seminaries, theology came to be regarded as, in its basis, an 'empirical science.'"[15]

Brightman entered into this climate of thought wholeheartedly. Yet, whereas James had proclaimed that in conceiving religion it was necessary to "abandon metaphysics and deduction for criticism and induction,"[16] Brightman wished to propose a synthesis and not an alternative.

At the beginning of his *The Philosophy of Religion*, he states, "The keynote of this book is experience" (p. vii), and it is also the key to his whole system. Beyond experience one cannot go and outside of experience there is nothing: "it is the present consciousness which is the sole possible starting point, and the sole possible source of evidence for any statements about the absent."[17] Experience is the epistemological starting point, and at the same time the exhaustive sphere of "reason," that is, of "concrete" thinking.

Concreteness, which Brightman defines as the feature most proper to rational activity, has a purely Hegelian flavour, and it coincides with tension towards totality, that is, to the connection between the parts with the integral unity of the system (cf. "the truth is the whole" of *Phenomenology of Spirit*). Thus, philosophy is "thinking which seeks to discover connected truth about all available experience."[18] Consistency (the principle of non-contradiction) is not enough for reason; its supreme criterion is "coherent" thinking: "(*a*) that all the facts of experience be considered and (*b*) that propositions about these facts be related in an orderly and significant way."[19]

Personalism posits itself as an empirical method. The appeal to reason as coherency not only does not contradict that presumption, but it confirms it as the sole attitude that is adequately empirical: "To demand coherence is to demand full attention to all the facts of experience, to neglect none, in short, to 'save the appearances,' as Simplicius said in his commentary on Aristotle's *De coelo*."[20]

The experience that is the starting point for everything is what Brightman calls the *situation-experienced* or, with a more poetic formula in *Person and Reality*, his final work, edited by Bertocci, *the shining present*. It is the actual datum of awareness, the immediacy of experience. Brightman still uses the expression *empirical situation*, and above all *datum self*: "The word *self* is used for any and every consciousness, however simple or complex it may be. A self is any conscious situation experienced as a whole."[21]

The traditional concept of the soul as a spiritual and substantial reality aims to explain this connotation of the unity of experience. Yet, it is a definition that is not sufficiently empirical and, thus, abstract. The fact of awareness, albeit within the fact of change and variety, can be experienced in a belonging that is unitary and unmistakable, complex and indivisible; we can, therefore, speak exclusively of the self as a synthesizing reality (a *synthesizer*).

But, the experience of ourselves imposes the evidence of a type of awareness, of unity, of permanence, and of dynamism that are much clearer than in the concept of pure ego, a power of self-identification that integrates into the empirical moment the past and tentatively the future, forecasting it and aspiring to it; with it the ego is structured within the categories of "esse" (of substance) and of "evolvingness" (of time). It is the emergence of the fact of the person, and *person* is "reflective and critical self-consciousness," capable of devotion "to any ideal enterprise."[22] The personality is, thus, the capacity that a certain *self* has of developing in a conscious way and of realizing itself critically on higher levels according to an experienced inner directive: "A self is given; a personality is achieved."[23] The experience of fulfilment, which constitutes the personal self, defines value. The world of personal experience coincides with the world of values, in that each and every experience is activity, and each activity is a function of a fulfilment, of a perfection: "values are satisfactions."[24] Hence, the person, just as it is one who experiences, is also a "valuer," a generator of values.

Rational or coherent reflection on experience forces other developments to take place. Indeed, an experience "always means more than it is."[25] According to the hierarchy of awareness that forms it, in order for it to be itself, something "beyond" itself is implied, something "other" than itself, something not present – because the only presence is the experience of self – but which is "believed in," as a postulate or a presupposition, and thus Brightman denominates it "situation-believed-in"; and it is believed in so that the experience of self may be lived in terms of a necessary fulfilment, a fullness, a total enlightenment. Hence, Brightman also calls it "illuminating absent." One could say that the experiencing subject postulates the object, as a factor within reality, as what solicits and qualifies experience, that is, as the "cause" of experience itself.[26]

The person as experience – or "experient" – is, so to speak, a whole web of active directions, of dynamic indices, which strive to form a picture of reality in which it may be settled in place, with precise relationships.

This is the theoretical tension, the "impetus towards the system," as W.E. Hocking said, that is the life of the personal self. In function of its own experience, as datum and as implication, the human ego expresses with rationality its own awareness of reality by means of a theory, it defines reality within a system. Theory or system are essentially attempts, true working hypotheses, which reference to continually mobile experience "will verify," that is, will mobilize towards the goal of ever more perfect coherence. An absolute definition is not possible, but the degree of probability will depend upon the courage and the coherence with which the "metaphysician must embark on his own voyage of exploration."[27]

The impetus towards the system is not abstract or purely intellectual. It is "full" of respect, of sympathy, of desire. The experient is teleogically striving: "All experience is temporal, always moving ahead into a future as if it were reaching for purposes yet to be attained."[28]

The concept of *ideal* represents the ultimate and ungraspable terminus of that tension; it is the perfect, integral – infinite! – formulation of the picture, that is, of the whole person: "fundamentally ... a conception of the kind of person that one approves and ought to become."[29] The ideal is not a presence within experience; it is postulated ("illuminating absent") in the experience of values ("shining present"), as connoted in the active direction inherent to them. But, this priority from the epistemological standpoint of the experiential datum establishes a dialectical interaction between value and ideal, because the ideal is perceived by consciousness as "judgment" on itself, on lived experience. Within that role, the ideal is norm, that is, "a rational concept of what ought to be."[30]

Experience, thus, mobilizes itself at new levels, and this inner tension towards a teleological future constitutes the fact of the *will*: "'Will' means the fact of choice and the fact of purposeful effort."[31] In implying selection and choice within the sphere of its own datum, experience as will is a fact of *freedom*, a *conflictive* fact in which the whole personality strives towards "the 'war aims' of the universe. That goal is to be found in the realm of true value,"[32] in other words, of ideals in the kingdom of the spirit. Spirit is the aspect at the summit of experience as awareness of the good and as energy towards it, a capacity of self-transcendence of the human self: "To know, to feel, to will, to grow in conscious scope and power – this is spiritual."[33]

This is exactly the religious level of experience, in that "religion has always been the worship of, and striving toward, what has been believed to be the source and guarantee of highest values,"[34] and therefore, "the goal of religion is the development of worthy consciousness,"[35] where "worthy" has the same meaning as "noble" as used in *The Spiritual Life*. Brightman agrees with Harald Höffding when he asserts, "That which expresses the innermost tendency of all religions is the axiom of the conservation of values"[36] – only noting that the essential dynamism of the experience of values would suggest substituting "conservation" with "continuity."

J.A. Leighton rightly stated that the "only world view in which values and meanings can have a permanently real status is one in which minds, personalities, and their values are supreme."[37] The idea of God arises with the same dynamism with which all of the experiences of human consciousness tend to complete themselves; it points to the extreme level of the "illuminating absent"; the quest for God is "a search for the purpose of life and for an unfailing source of eternal value."[38] As the wellspring of the real, God is not adequately knowable; indeed, a complete rational comprehension of the relations that make up reality is not possible. And yet, human speculations "may serve to direct life from chaos and contradiction toward integration and coherence."[39]

Brightman is perfectly aware of such limits, and he has statements that echo the scholastic *via negationis* and *via sublimationis*: "The Eternal Divine Spirit must have properties which no human being ever experienced, and must be devoid of many of the limitations which human persons experience."[40]

In the theoretical effort, in any case, the explanation must be homogeneous and coherent with the data of our conscious personal experience. Otherwise abstractions would be hypostasized or there would be a risk of depriving the divine of its highest notes, flattening it into a brute mechanism (a mention of the essential factors of a theory on God would be helpful, precisely because of the epistemology proper to it, also for further clarifying the essential features of a theory of the person). In terms of experience, God is known as the wellspring or meaning of values, their source and redeemer. If we keep in mind that a person is "a conscious self able to develop ideal values,"[41] it is possible to understand how to affirm that God is person: "the unbegun and unending energy of the universe is conscious rational will."[42]

But, the person is reality in contrast because of his original condition of structural limit, of the constitutive "datum," and because of freedom, which often chooses poorly. The experience of values is thus complicated by the problem of evil. Now, it is true that "the problem of evil admits no final, no completely enlightening solution."[43] There is still the need to formulate the most coherent hypothesis in light of the person's experience, and it seems to be that of a finite God: "No possible experience could reveal unlimited and absolute power."[44]

God is a perfect vision of the ideal and a perfect energy of actualization (perfect will), and this is the essence of the concept of him. Yet, this dual divine perfection is marked by a "datum" (the "given") that is structurally immanent to him, which allows any point of the divine will limited possibilities of ideal acts; finite possibilities, in infinite evolution and progression. This is essential to the coherence of the concept of God with experience. Thus, the divine goodness necessary for defining God as the creator of values is safeguarded; it is saved in that his will acts out perfectly the possibilities that a "given" allows it. God's lordship is also safeguarded, in that his will always bends the "given" towards the ideal direction. Still, consequently, in God there is truly memory, of the aims to achieve, of ideals to obey: "The Spirit is eternal; but as friends and interpreters of the Spirit we must choose between a view of Eternal Spirit as immovable and unalterable and a view of Eternal Spirit as developing life."[45]

The concept of perfection finally becomes coherent with experience: "[God's] perfection and the perfection of his world consist in their perfectibility."[46] The infinitely evolving experience of the divine will, in other words, the divine experience of values, is nature, that "area that can be approached through the senses."[47] There is no essential metaphysical difference between God and nature; the latter is totally immanent to the former "as part of the immensity of his eternal being."[48]

Brightman recognizes that "belief in a personal God (theism) does not entail of itself any particular view of matter," but immediately adds that some "(including the writer) are idealists and regard matter as being an order of organization of the experience of God."[49] In other words, matter is a form of activity, of experience, divine experience. In a more definitive way, we could say that in nature divine perfectibility, that of the given is actualized, and time and space are the constitutive elements of that limit, like the lines that form an angle opening on infinity, which moment by moment limit the expressive potential of the origin.

Since all of nature is part of the divine person, "nothing is real save purposing beings, namely, persons."[50] Beyond God, "outside" of God, therefore, are human personalities; the experience of imperfection cannot coincide with what is perfect. Brightman numbers himself among those who "agree with pantheists in holding that God is immanent in nature," but who "deny that spiritually imperfect human persons could without contradiction be regarded as parts of a spiritually perfect divine person."[51] But, how does this ontological distinction occur?

The answer must call back into effect the concept of creation: "The concept of creation is difficult but unavoidable."[52] This is applied also to nature, because evolution is an ongoing creation of newness, yet nevertheless, since it remains an aspect within God, that concept is more properly applied to the fact by which the natural situation flourishes in something that transcends itself, and has "self-awareness," has personhood. Therefore, it is another source of the production of values, together with God. Thus, nature, in which God expresses his ideals and posits the norms of human consciousness, becomes the field of interaction between God and man, in which every solipsism is overcome structurally by necessary metaphysical collaboration; and collaboration with the one sole Cosmic Spirit automatically establishes also solidarity among human spirits. Progress and history become a collective building of the world of values, together with God, in an infinite becoming: "To interpret the human spirit as being the sign of the presence of a Divine and Superhuman Spirit in the cosmos is to be committed to the faith that there is a common purpose for all spirits, a common problem with a possible co-operative solution."[53]

The intensity with which he defines experience and the solid coherence with which he creates the unity of his theory about it are the most immediately impressive aspects of Brightman's thinking.

His definition of person in terms of consciousness recalls the comment that Whitehead made to Descartes' "Cogito, ergo sum,"[54] but it is even more "powerful, noble, rich, courageous, free," to quote what he says about "spirit." This intensity always provides evidence and surety in its juxtaposition: "If a person believes that the only approach to truth is the approach of the laboratory, he will never be able to find a spiritual God. God is a property of the universe as a whole, and not of its observable parts,"[55] and determines its clear distinction from attempts made in the Protestant academic world to base religion on an empirical method that is too "reduced" to the scientific or naturalistic level; here, I am alluding to the highly influential school of D.C. Macintosh of Yale and H.N. Wieman of Chicago.

Brightman's most profound proposition lies in the coherency with which he defines the unity of life in terms of religiousness. That religiousness is not some a priori or autonomous experience à la Fries or Otto, or even his old master Knudson. Rather, it is the ultimate value of every experience, the full coherency to be sought in every situation: "Religious experience is *any experience of any person taken in its relation to his God.*"[56]

Religion, in Brightman, is the realistic valuing of each and every experience; hence, its energy and at the same time redemptive comprehension, which carries forward Bowne's anti-Edwards inspiration – "[God is not defined] by might, nor by power, but by [his] spirit,"[57] and which echoes the ultimate positivity that Lotze's *Gültigkeit* assigned to things.

Yet, the consequentialness with which experience is utilized as an epistemological principle, if it is logically unassailable, doubtless leads to such conclusions that it could also suggest a revision of the principle itself, not to mention the confusion that the theory of the self brings to the boundaries between subhuman and person, as Brightman coherently recognizes:[58] if it is impossible to leave the experient, how can one posit overcoming the solipsism? As Experient par excellence, can God create? Bowne considered the affirmation of an "extra-mental" universe to be "unreflecting" because it "arises from confounding extra-human with extra-mental."[59] This, in a certain sense preserves the objectivity of rational statements on nature as truly "other" than man, even if it is within the "mind" of God. But, what objectivity does possession of things have, and its marriage with the human energy, for progress? In such conditions, to speak of cause and effect and to recall these concepts in order to explain relationships within reality raises the doubt that perhaps one is speaking into the void, a purely nominalistic use of those words, in order to cover the metaphysical void that lies between creatures with a common sense empirical appeal.

Yet, the greatest unease arises in the face of the concept of the "Given" of perfectibility, of God's changeability. What Collins observes[60] is true: "Hegel accustomed a whole generation to accept the presence of development in the absolute … [Thus,] a finitizing, changing aspect in the absolute spirit came to be regarded as the surety of divine life and actuality." And it is also true that James has accustomed us to the resolution of the ideal of perfection within the empirical and relative finiteness of his "meliorism." But, it is also true that our intelligence, as groping as it may be, experiences discomfort when faced with such a conclusion: "We must acknowledge a duality of nature at the very eternal heart of things, in which the active is indeed in control, but maintains its control with struggle and pain."[61]

Thus, there is not one *ultimate*; the concept of resistance, in any case, connotes a contradiction. The *ultimate* is not the ideal, but struggle, that is, contradiction, once again. Neither mind nor desire are experienced in correspondence, in "coherence" with this theory.

Yet, this is purposely an attempt, a hypothesis. In following it, there is found not a shadow of skepticism, or a relativistic temptation to disengagement: Brightman communicates the healthy energy of one who has truly "embarked on a voyage of exploration."

At exactly fifty years since the death of its first leader, George Holmes Howison, American Personalism could not be better represented.

Notes

INTRODUCTION

1 J.B. Baillie, "Introduction" in G.W.F. Hegel, *The Phenomenology of Mind* (New York: Harper and Row, Torch Book Series, 1967).

2 Giussani's book was originally published under the title *Teologia protestante americana. Profilo storico* (Milano: Marietti, 2003)

3 The author is grateful for the excellent article written by John Zucchi, titled, "Luigi Giussani, the Church, and Youth in the 1950s," in *Logos*, vol. 10, no. 4 (2007), 131–50.

4 This English edition will follow the shorter title.

5 Zucchi, "Luigi Giussani," 132.

6 What makes these three works a trilogy is the fairly loose yet clear connections made between each work, the subsequent two building on *The Religious Sense*. See Giussani, *The Religious Sense* (Montreal: McGill-Queen's University Press, 1997); *At the Origin of the Christian Claim* (Montreal: McGill-Queen's University Press, 1998); *Why the Church?* (Montreal: McGill-Queen's University Press, 2001).

7 It is clear from the slate of speakers and presenters who have been given opportunity to speak at the Meeting that a significant part of Giussani's *charism* has been his ability to transcend certain religious differences and enable a greater degree of dialogue purely on the basis of human religious nature.

8 Archie J. Spencer, "*The Religious Sense*: A Review," *McMaster Journal of Theology and Ministry*, vol. 2 (1999). Available at http://www.mcmaster.ca/mjtm/2-r4.htm.

9 A subsequent essay by Eliza Buzzi on the influence of Edwards' thought on Giussani confirms this intuition. See her essay, "Jonathan Edwards on

Religious Experience," *Questio*, vol. 4 (2004), pp. 345–86. See also her introduction in her edited volume, *A Generative Thought: An Introduction to the Works of Luigi Giussani* (Montreal: McGill-Queen's University Press, 2003), ix–xii.

10 "*The Religious Sense*: A Review," 1.
11 Giussani, *The Religious Sense*, 6ff.
12 Ibid, 7.
13 Ibid., 10.
14 Ibid., 12.
15 Ibid., 14.
16 Ibid.
17 Ibid.
18 Ibid, 32.
19 Ibid, 34.
20 Thomas Aquinas, *Summa Theologiae*. 1, q 1.2.
21 Luigi Giussani, *At the Origin of the Christian Claim*, Introduction, 9.
22 Ibid., 21.
23 Ibid.
24 Ibid., 30.
25 Ibid., 79.
26 Ibid.
27 Ibid., 83.
28 Ibid.
29 Giussani, *Why the Church?*, 7.
30 Ibid., 65ff.
31 Henri De Lubac, *Catholicism: Christ and the Common Destiny of Man*, translated by L.C. Sheppard and E. Englund (San Francisco: Ignatius Press, 1988), 76; quoted in *Why the Church?*, 72.
32 Ibid., 111.
33 Ibid., 114.
34 Ibid., 119.
35 Ibid., 189.
36 Ibid., 204.
37 Ibid., 205.
38 Ibid.
39 Ibid.
40 Ibid., 209.
41 Ibid.
42 Eduard Schillibeeckx, *Christ the Sacrament* (New York: SCM, 1975).

43 Gary Dorrien, *The Making of American Liberal Theology*, vols I–III, (Louisville: Westminster John Knox Press, 2001).

44 Ibid., 3–4. As Dorrien's introduction clearly indicates, he is more interested in noting the development within the American religious consciousness as a specific method within the *Religionswissenschaft* mode than is Giussani, whose phenomenological approach is less driven by a philosophical agenda than a genuine interest in the intersection between human experience and divine claims upon the human.

45 Dorrien, *The Making of American Liberal Theology*, vol. I, 3–4.

46 Ibid., 4–5.

47 See ibid., 435.

48 Dorrien calls this "the founding idea of a new theological establishment." *The Making of American Liberal Theology*, vol. I, introduction, 1.

49 See Zucchi, "Luigi Giussani," 149nn14–15.

50 Reinhold Niebuhr, *Nature and Destiny of Man*, 2 vols (New York: Scribner, 1949).

51 See his superb critique of modernity in his section on "The Loss of the Self in Idealism," ibid., 74–92.

52 Ibid, 93

53 Ibid.

54 Ibid.

55 Ibid., 221.

56 Guissani, *The Religious Sense*, esp. chapter 3.

57 As per Paul Tillich, *Systematic Theology*, vol. I (Chicago: University of Chicago Press, 1951), 8.

58 See, Paul Tillich, *Theology of Culture*, ed. by R.C. Kimbal (New York: Scribner's, 1962).

CHAPTER ONE

1 Cited in W.W. Sweet, *The Story of Religion in America*, New York 1950, 30.

2 A. Keller, *Amerikanisches Christentum Heute*, Zurich 1943, 115.

3 Cf. D. Horton, *Congregationalism: A Study in Church Polity*, London 1952, 52–61, or – earlier still – P. Miller, *Orthodoxy in Massachusetts, 1630–1650: A Genetic Study*, Cambridge (Mass.) 1933, chapters III and IV.

4 H. Jacob, *A Declaration and Plainer Opening of Certain Points*, 1611, cited in H.S. Smith, R.T. Handy, and L.A. Loetscher, *American Christianity: An*

Interpretation with Representative Documents, vol. I, *1607–1820*, New York 1960, 84. This work, at the end of every period examined, includes an anthology of significant texts: it is from these texts that I have drawn my documentation for certain authors.

5 Sweet, *The Story of Religion in America*, 55.

6 A. de Tocqueville, *De la démocratie en Amérique* (1835), translation *Democracy in America* by Arthur Goldhammer, Library of America, 2004, 37.

7 "Our Thomas Hooker does not fear comparison with ... Richard Hooker," the classical author and English theologian of the "middle way" – so asserts W.L. Sperry, *Religion in America*, New York 1946, 135.

8 P. Miller, *The New England Mind: From Colony to Province*, vol. I, Cambridge (Mass.) 1962, 65.

9 M.C. Tyler, *A History of American Literature*, New York 1890, vol. I, 216, cited in L. Ziff, *The Career of John Cotton: Puritanism and American Experience*, Princeton 1962, vii.

10 "The most influential of all New England statements," Ziff, ibid., 191.

11 Miller, *The New England Mind: From Colony to Province*, vol. I, in chapter II documents the use of this criterion through the so-called Jeremiad sermon, in which God's judgment on his people was inferred precisely from natural or social events.

12 Chapter IV, sec. 3. See the edition of H.W. Foote, *The Cambridge Platform of 1648: Tercentenary Commemoration at Cambridge, Massachusetts, October 27, 1948*, Boston 1949.

13 "John Davenport's Creed," in J. Cotton, *The Covenant of God's Free Grace*, London 1645, appendix, cited in Smith et al., *American Christianity*, vol. I, 113.

14 Foote, *Cambridge Platform*, chapter XV, sec. 1; chapter XVI, sec. 1.

15 Ibid., chapter X, sec. 2; chapter VI, sec. 1.

16 J. Cotton, *The Keyes of the Kingdom of Heaven*, Boston 1843, 7ff, cited in Ziff, *The Career of John Cotton*, 194.

17 In C. Mather, *Magnalia Christi Americana*, published by T. Robbins, Hartford 1855, vol. I, 437, cited in Miller, *Orthodoxy in Massachusetts*, 186.

18 See S.E. Morison, *Builders of the Bay Colony*, Boston 1930, 85.

19 Sweet, *The Story of Religions in America*, 59.

20 J. Cotton, *An Exposition upon the Thirteenth Chapter of Revelation*, London 1655, 238, cited in Ziff, *The Career of John Cotton*, 175.

21 In T. Hutchinson, *The History of the Colony of Massachusetts Bay*, Boston 1764, vol. I, 497, cited in Miller, *Orthodoxy in Massachusetts*, 229. For the theocratic ideal of Cotton, see esp. *Discourse about Civil*

Governement in a New Plantation Whose Design Is Religion, Cambridge 1633, which is certainly his in content, even if it was materially written up by John Davenport, a minister of the New Haven Colony.

22 Foote, *Cambridge Platform*, chapter XVII, sec. 5.

23 J. Cotton, *The Keyes of the Kingdom of Heaven*, 95, cited in Ziff, *The Career of John Cotton*, 195.

24 Foote, *Cambridge Platform*, chapter XVII, sec. 6 and 9.

25 Cotton, *The Keyes of the Kingdom of Heaven*, 95, cited in Ziff, *The Career of John Cotton*, 196.

26 Miller, *The New England Mind: The Seventeenth Century*, 2nd ed., Cambridge, Mass. 1963, 48.

27 In his introduction to the Italian translation of the cited work of P. Miller, *The New England Mind: The Seventeenth Century* (*Lo spirito della Nuova Inghilterra: Il Seicento)* translated by P. Forghieri, Bologna 1962, xvi.

28 J. Cotton, *A Treatise of the Covenant of Grace*, London 1659, 199 ff, cited in Ziff, *The Career of John Cotton*, 110ff.

29 T. Hooker, *The Application of Redemption*, London 1659, 376, cited in Miller, *The New England Mind: The Seventeenth Century*, 50.

30 Cited in ibid., 51.

31 J. Cotton, *A Modest and Cleare Answer to Mr. Balls Discourse of Set Formes of Prayer*, London 1642, 43, cited in Ziff, *The Career of John Cotton*, 186.

32 Cf. J. Davenport, *An Answer of the Elders of the Severall Churches in New England unto Nine Positions Sent over to Them*, London 1643; R. Mather, *Church-Governement and Church-Covenant Discussed*, London 1643.

33 J. Cotton, *The New Covenant*, London 1654, 14f., cited in Ziff, *The Career of John Cotton*, 109f.

34 Cf. J. Cotton, *Sixteene Questions of Serious and Necessary Consequences Propounded unto Mr. John Cotton together with His Answers*, London 1644, cited in Ziff, *The Career of John Cotton*, 119. Even reliance on the true church is dangerous: "while you enjoy them, trust not in them, nor thinke not to stand upon this, that you are blessed in regard of them; but looke at them all as losse, and drosse, and dung, that you may win Christ," J. Cotton, *Christ the Fountaine of Life*, London 1651, cited in Ziff, *The Career of John Cotton*, 110.

35 Cited in Miller, *The New England Mind: The Seventeenth Century*, 389.

36 P. Bulkeley, *The Gospel-Covenant,* London, 1651, IV, cited in Ziff, *The Career of John Cotton*, 113.

37 Regarding Roger Williams, it is useful to recall his famous debate with Cotton: *The Bloudy Tenent, of Persecution, for Cause of Conscience, discussed, in a conference between truth and Peace*, London, 1644.
38 In F.H. Foster, *A Genetic History of the New England Theology*, Chicago 1907, 28, cited in W.A. Visser 't Hooft, *The Background of the Social Gospel in America*, St. Louis 1963, 77.
39 T.J. Wertenbaker, *The Puritan Oligarchy*, New York 1947, 137.
40 J. Cotton, *Christ the Founder of Life*, 145, cited in Ziff, *The Career of John Cotton*, 80.
41 Cited in Smith et al., *American Christianity*, vol. I, 201.
42 Ibid., 197.
43 Miller, *The New England Mind: From Colony to Province*, 189.
44 Ibid., 417.
45 S. Stoddart, *The Doctrine of Instituted Churches*, London 1700, 6, cited in Smith et al., *American Christianity*, vol. I, 220.
46 Ibid., 20, cited in Smith et al., *American Christianity*, vol. I, 220.
47 *"Articles," A Confession of Faith Owned and Consented to by the Elders and Messengers of the Churches in the Colony of Connecticut*, New London 1760, vol. II, chapter VI, cited in Smith et al., *American Christianity*, vol. I, 226 ff.

CHAPTER TWO

1 In W.E. Roush, "Arminian Theology," in V. Ferm (ed.), *An Encyclopedia of Religion*, New York 1945, 38.
2 Later integrated into one single work, *Elementa Philosophica*, Philadelpha 1752.
3 Miller, *The New England Mind: From Colony to Province*, 462.
4 In Miller, *The New England Mind: The Seventeenth Century*, 377.
5 Ibid., 388.
6 In Miller, *The New England Mind: From Colony to Province*, 462.
7 W.G. McLoughlin Jr., *Modern Revivalism: Charles Grandison Finney to Billy Graham*, New York 1959, 7.
8 E.H. Davidson, *Jonathan Edwards: The Narrative of a Puritan Mind*, Boston 1966, 6.
9 P. Miller, *Jonathan Edwards*, New York 1949, 177.
10 J.E. Smith's 1959 critical edition of *Religious Affections* published by Yale University Press is almost 380 pages long.
11 J. Edwards, *Religious Affections*, ed. J.E. Smith, New Haven 1959, 89.
12 Ibid., 95.

13 Ibid., 205
14 Ibid., 209.
15 Davidson, *Jonathan Edwards*, 17.
16 J. Edwards, *A Divine and Supernatural Light*, in C.H. Faust and T.H. Johnson, *Jonathan Edwards: Representative Selections*, New York 1935, 106.
17 See ibid., 103.
18 Faust and Johnson, *Jonathan Edwards*, xiv.
19 S.E. Dwight, *The Life of President Edwards*, in *The Works of President Edwards*, 10 vols. New York 1829, vol. I, 533, cited in J. Edwards, *Freedom of the Will*, ed. P. Ramsey, New Haven 1957, Editor's Introduction, 7.
20 Edwards, *Freedom of the Will*, 181, 185.
21 Ibid., 144.
22 Ibid., 220.
23 Ibid., 453ff. The letter was written 25 July 1757 and published first in Scotland and thus as an appendix to the third edition of *Freedom of the Will* (1768), with the title *Remarks on the Essays on the Principles of Morality and Natural Religion, in A Letter to a Minister of the Church of Scotland*. The *Essays* were published by Henry Home, Lord Kames, Edinburgh 1751.
24 Edwards, *Freedom of the Will*, 157ff.
25 Ibid., 428.
26 Cited in Miller, *Jonathan Edwards*, 49.
27 bid., 285.
28 J. Edwards, *The Great Christian Doctrine of Original Sin Defended*, in *The Works of President Edwards*, ed. S. Austin, Worcester 1808, vol. VI, part IV, 423.
29 J. Edwards, *Dissertation Concerning the End for Which God Created the World*, in *The Works of President Edwards*, vol. VI, part IV, 59ff.
30 Cited in Davidson, *Jonathan Edwards*, 98.
31 Ibid., 99.
32 Ibid., 102.
33 Ibid., 88.
34 J. Edwards, *The Nature of True Virtue*, with a foreword by W.K. Frankena, Ann Arbor 1960, v.
35 Ibid., 1.
36 Ibid., 98.
37 Ibid.
38 Ibid., 2ff.

39 Ibid., 3.
40 Ibid., 100.
41 Ibid., 26.
42 Miller, *Jonathan Edwards*, 288.
43 Cited in ibid., 307.
44 Cited in ibid., 165.
45 Ibid., 175ff.
46 Quoted in ibid., 175.
47 Ibid., 176.
48 C. Chauncy, *Twelve Sermons*, Boston 1765, 23, quoted in Smith et al., *American Christianity*, vol. I, 381.
49 J. Mayhew, *Sermons*, Boston 1775, 268, cited in Smith et al., *American Christianity*, vol. I, 378.
50 J. Mayhew, *Two Sermons on the Nature, Extent and Perfection of the Divine Goodness*, Boston 1763, 24, cited in Smith et al., *American Christianity*, vol. I, 379.
51 H.C. Mather, *Manuductio ad Ministerium*, The Facsimile Society, New York 1938, 50, in Smith et al., *American Christianity*, vol. I, 376.
52 In Miller, *The New England Mind: The Seventeenth Century*, 160.
53 S. Willard, cited in ibid., 205.
54 W.H. Channing, *Memoir of William Ellery Channing: With extracts from his correspondence and manuscripts*, Boston 1848, vol. II, 403ff., in H.W. Schneider, *A History of American Philosophy*, New York 1963, 65.
55 Ibid., vol. III, 38, in ibid., 66n14.
56 Cited by J.S. Bixler, "Liberal Theology," in Ferm, *Encyclopedia of Religion*, 443.
57 W.H. Channing, "Unitarian Christianity," in *Discourses, Reviews, and Miscellanies*, Boston 1830, 290–326, passim, in Smith et al., *American Christianity*, vol. I, 495ff.
58 Ibid., 498ff.
59 Ibid., 500ff.
60 Ibid., 501.
61 Miller, *Jonathan Edwards*, 270.
62 P. Miller and T.H. Johnson, *The Puritans*, New York 1938, 21.
63 Cited in W.M. Horton, "Samuel Hopkins," in Ferm, *Encyclopedia of Religion*, 346.
64 S. Hopkins, *The System of Doctrines Contained in Divine Revelation Explained and Defended*, 2nd ed., Boston 1811, vol. I, 465-8, 474–7, cited in Smith et al., *American Christianity*, vol. I, 541ff.
65 Ibid., 542–3.

66 Also among the most important denominations, Congregationalists and Presbyterians, there emerged an initially operational solidarity in the foundation of churches (as was laid out in the Plan of Union of 1801) and, therefore, an administrative and disciplinary solidarity as well (Accommodation Plan of 1808).
67 G.P. Fisher, *Life of Benjamin Lilliman*, 2 vols, New York, 1866, vol. I, 83, cited in Smith et al., *American Christianity*, vol. I, 521.
68 C. Beecher, ed., *Autobiography, Correspondence, etc. of Lyman Beecher, D.D.*, 2 vols, New York 1864–65, vol. I, 552, cited in ibid., vol. II, 24.
69 Cited in W.M. Horton, "Nathaniel Taylor", in Ferm, *Encyclopedia of Religion*, 762.
70 N.W. Taylor, *Concio ad Clerum, A Sermon Delivered in the Chapel of Yale College, September 10, 1828*, New Haven 1828, in Smith et al., *American Christianity*, vol. II, 31, 29.
71 A. Mahan, *Scripture Doctrine of Christian Perfection…*, 4th ed., Boston 1840, cited in Smith et al., *American Christianity*, vol. II, 43ff.
72 Ibid., 47.
73 W.M. Horton, "Charles Grandison Finney," in Ferm, *Encyclopedia of Religion*, 280.
74 C.G. Finney, *Lectures on Revivals of Religion*, ed. W.G. McLaughlin Jr., Cambridge, Mass. 1960, 9.
75 C.G. Finney, *Sermons on Various Subjects*, New York 1835, 14, cited in ibid., Introduction, xxiv ff.
76 Finney, *Lectures on Revivals of Religion*, 21.
77 A. Dod, "Finney's Sermons," *Biblical Repertory and Theological Review* 7 (July 1835), 524, cited in Finney, *Lectures on Revivals of Religion*, Introduction, xxx.
78 Finney, *Lectures on Revivals of Religion*, 13.
79 Ibid., 207.
80 Ibid., 379.
81 See ibid., Introduction, xlii.
82 Ibid., xliii.
83 Ibid., 404.
84 C.G. Finney, *Lectures on Systematic Theology*, ed. G. Redford of Worchester, London 1851, 540.
85 Finney, *Lectures on Revivals of Religion*, 306.
86 See Finney, *Lectures on Systematic Theology*, lect. XX–XXI: "Human Government."
87 A.N. Whitehead, *Essays in Science and Philosophy*, New York 1947, 153.

88 H. Nichols (ed.), *The Mercersburg Theology*, New York 1966, Introduction, 7.
89 Y. Brilioth, *Three Lectures on Evangelicalism and the Oxford Movement*, London 1934, 57, cited in ibid., 11.
90 J.W. Nevin, "The Theology of the New Liturgy," *Mercersburg Review*, XIV (1867), 28–44, cited in ibid., 15ff.
91 J.W. Nevin, "Our Union with Christ," *Weekly Messenger*, 14 Jan. 1846, cited in ibid., 200.
92 J.W. Nevin, "The Mystical Union," *Weekly Messenger*, 8 Oct. 1845, cited in ibid., 197.
93 P. Schaff, *The Principle of Protestantism*, Chambersburg, Pa. 1845, in ibid., 125.
94 Ibid., Introduction, 9.

CHAPTER THREE

1 H.W. Schneider, *A History of American Philosophy*, New York 1946, 261.
2 T. Manferdini, *Studi sul pensiero Americano*, Bologna 1960, 125.
3 O. Brownson, "Two Articles from the Princeton Review," *Boston Quarterly Review*, III (1840), 275, cited in Smith et al., *American Christianity*, vol. II, 125.
4 R.W. Emerson, *The Complete Essays and Other Writings of Ralph Waldo Emerson*, ed. B. Atkinson, New York 1940, 37.
5 Ibid., 124.
6 Ibid., 267, 262.
7 T. Parker, *The World of Matter and the Spirit of Man*, ed. G.W. Cooke, Boston 1907, 305, cited in Smith et al., *American Christianity*, vol. II, 123.
8 Emerson, *The Complete Essays*, 156.
9 G. Ripley, *Discourse on the Philosophy of Religion*, Boston 1836, 442, cited in Smith et al., *American Christianity*, vol. II, 127.
10 E.W. Emerson and W. Emerson Forbes (eds.), *The Journals of Ralph Waldo Emerson*, 10 vols., Boston 1909–1914, vol. III, 474, cited in ibid., 129.
11 L. Marcuse, *La philosophie américaine*, trans. Fr. D. Bohler, Paris 1967, 92. [Translated from the Italian.].
12 A. Keller, *Amerikanisches Christentum-Heute*, Zurich 1943, 118 [translated from the Italian].
13 J.L. Blau, *Men and Movements in American Philosophy*, New York 1952, 130.
14 Cf. C.H. Hopkins, *The Rise of the Social Gospel in American Protestantism, 1865–1915*, 6th ed., New Haven 1961, 123.

15 H. Bushnell, "A Discourse on Dogma and Spirit; or the True Reviving of Religion: Delivered Before the Porter Rhetorical Society, at Andover, September 1848," in *God in Christ*, Hartford 1849, in H.S. Smith (ed.) *Horace Bushnell*, New York 1965, 45.
16 *Twentieth Anniversary: A Commemorative Discourse, Delivered in the North Church of Hartford, May 22, 1853*, Hartford 1853, 19ff., cited in ibid., 43.
17 "The Kingdom of God as a Grain of Mustard Seed," *New Englander*, 11 (1844), 610, cited in ibid., 375.
18 H. Bushnell, *Christ in Theology*, Hartford 1851, 333, cited in ibid., 44.
19 H. Bushnell, *God in Christ*, Hartford 1849, cited in ibid., 58ff.
20 Ibid., 129
21 Ibid., 139, 151, 130.
22 Ibid., 131.
23 "Concio ad Clerum: A Discourse on the Divinity of Christ; Delivered at the Annual Commencement of Yale College," 15 Aug. 1848, *God in Christ*, cited in ibid., 169, 174ff.
24 Ibid., 175.
25 H. Bushnell, *The Vicarious Sacrifice, Grounded in Principles of Universal Obligation*, New York 1866, ibid., 280.
26 Ibid., 312.
27 Cf. H. Bushnell, *Forgiveness and Law, Grounded in Principles Interpreted by Human Analogies*, New York 1874, chapter I: "Forgiveness and Propitiation, Without Expiation."
28 P. Tillich, *Systematic Theology*, Chicago 1951, I 3.
29 L.F. Stearns, "The Present Direction of Theological Thought in the Congregational Churches of the United States," in *Present Day Theology*, New York 1893, cited in H.P. van Dusen, *The Vindication of Liberal Theology: A Tract for the Times*, New York 1963, 46ff.
30 H.E. Fosdick, *The Living of These Days*, New York 1956, vii.
31 K. Cauthen, *The Impact of American Religious Liberalism*, New York 1962, chapter 2.
32 W. De Witt Hyde, *Outlines of Social Theology*, New York 1895, Preface, cited in A.S. Nash, *Protestant Thought in the Twentieth Century: Whence and Whither?*, New York 1951, 108.
33 W.A. Brown, *Christ, the Vitalizing Principle of Christian Theology*, New York 1898, 20, cited in van Dusen, *The Vindication of Liberal Theology*, 40.
34 G.A. Gordon, *The Christ of Today*, Boston 1895, 184, cited in Smith et al., *American Christianity*, vol. II, 258.

35 J.H. Randall, Jr., *The Making of the Modern Mind*, Boston 1926, 419.
36 J.C. Bennett, "After Liberalism, What?," *Christian Century*, 3 Nov. 1933, 1403.
37 Cauthen, *The Impact of American Religious Liberalism*, 219.
38 W.N. Clarke, *An Outline of Christian Theology*, New York 1898, 298, cited in Smith et al., *American Christianity*, vol. II, 264.
39 Cauthen, *The Impact of American Religious Liberalism*, 56.
40 G.B. Smith, *Current Christian Thinking*, Chicago 1928, 83.
41 W.A. Brown, *Christian Theology in Outline*, New York 1906, 353, cited in Cauthen, *The Impact of American Religious Liberalism*, 262n5.
42 G. Hammar, *Christian Realism in Contemporary American Theology*, Uppsala 1940, 138.
43 W.A. Brown, *The Essence of Christianity*, New York 1902, 303, cited in Cauthen, *The Impact of American Religious Liberalism*, 44.
44 W.A. Brown, *The Church in America*, New York 1922, ix, cited in ibid., 59.
45 J.W. Buckham, *Progressive Religious Thought in America*, Boston 1919, 273, cited in Smith et al., *American Christianity*, vol. II, 279.
46 H.E. Fosdick, *The Living of These Days*, New York 1956, 230ff.
47 Cauthen, *The Impact of American Religious Liberalism*, 66.
48 H.E. Fosdick, *The Power to See It Through*, New York 1935, 35, cited. in ibid., 73.
49 J.W. Buckham, *Progressive Religious Thought in America*, Boston 1919, 316ff., cited in Smith et al., *American Christianity*, vol. II, 301.
50 A.C. McGiffert, "The Kingdom of God" in *Christianity as History and Faith*, A.C. McGiffert, Jr (ed.), New York 1934, cited in Smith et al., *American Christianity*, vol. II, 287.
51 E.W. Lyman, *Theology and Human Problems*, Boston 1910, 193, cited in Cauthen, *The Impact of American Religious Liberalism*, 140.
52 E.W. Lyman, *The Meaning and Truth of Religion*, New York 1933, 343, cited in ibid., 137.
53 S. Mathews, *The Faith of Modernism*, New York 1924, 23, in Smith et al., *American Christianity*, vol. II, 238.
54 S. Mathews, *Atonement and the Social Progress*, New York 1930, 205, cited in Cauthen, *The Impact of American Religious Liberalism*, 166.
55 S. Mathews, *The Spiritual Interpretation of History*, Cambridge, MA 1916, 210, 219, viii, cited in ibid., 62.
56 S. Mathews, *The Gospel and Modern Man*, New York 1910, 48, 45, cited in ibid., 154.
57 S. Mathews, *The Growth of the Idea of God*, New York 1931, 232, cited in ibid., 157.

58 E.S. Ames, *The Psychology of Religious Experience*, New York 1910, 26, cited in Smith et al., *American Christianity*, vol. II, 429.
59 F. Mayer, *A History of American Thought*, Dubuque 1951, 236.
60 W.H. Werkmeister, *A History of Philosophical Ideas in America*, New York 1949, 103.
61 B.P. Bowne, *Metaphysics*, Boston 1898, 294.
62 B.P. Bowne, *Metaphysics: A Study in First Principles*, Boston 1882, 56.
63 B.P. Bowne, *Personalism, Common Sense and Philosophy*, Boston 1908, 297.
64 Ibid., 325.
65 H.C. King, *The Ethics of Jesus*, 19, cited in J. MacQuarrie, *Twentieth-Century Religious Thought: The Frontiers of Philosophy and Theology, 1900–1960*, New York 1963, 90.
66 Cauthen, *The Impact of American Religious Liberalism*, 110.
67 A.C. Knudson, *The Doctrine of God*, Nashville 1930, 297.
68 Ibid., 241.
69 Ibid., 366.
70 A.C. Knudson, *The Doctrine of Redemption*, Nashville 1933, 466.
71 Cf. Hopkins, *The Rise of the Social Gospel*, 196ff.
72 Cf. H.F. May, *Protestant Churches and Industrial America*, New York 1963, 163–81.
73 S.E. Mead, *The Lively Experiment: The Shaping of Christianity in America*, New York 1963, 142.
74 Hopkins, *The Rise of the Social Gospel*, 316.
75 Cf. H.R. Niebuhr, *The Kingdom of God in America*, New York 1959, 45–126.
76 Cf. Visser 't Hooft, *The Background of the Social Gospel in America*, 123ff.
77 Hopkins, *The Rise of the Social Gospel*, 91.
78 G.G. Atkins, *Religion in Our Times*, New York 1932, 46.
79 W. Gladden, *Working People and their Employers*, Boston 1876, in R.T. Handy (ed.), *The Social Gospel in America, 1870–1920*, New York 1966, 38.
80 Ibid., 45.
81 Ibid., 48.
82 Ibid., 28.
83 W. Gladden, *How Much is the Bible Worth? A Book for the People*, Boston 1891, cited in ibid. 85ff.
84 W. Gladden, *How Much is Left of the Old Doctrines? A Book for the People*, Boston 1899, cited in ibid., 26.

85 W. Gladden, *Present Day Theology*, Columbus 1913, cited in ibid., 159ff.
86 W. Gladden, *Ruling Ideas of the Present Age*, Boston 1895, cited in ibid., 27.
87 W. Gladden, *The Church and the Kingdom*, New York 1894, cited in ibid., 103–5.
88 R. Niebuhr, *An Interpretation of Christian Ethics*, London 1948, 7.
89 Cited in Hopkins, *The Rise of the Social Gospel*, 217.
90 Handy, *The Social Gospel in America*, 263.
91 R.D. Cross, in the introduction to W. Rauschenbusch, *Christianity and the Social Crisis*, ed. R.D. Cross, New York 1964, viii.
92 Ibid., 54, 56.
93 Ibid., 59–61.
94 Ibid., 65ff.
95 Ibid., 73.
96 Ibid., 91.
97 Ibid., 418, 421.
98 Ibid., 420ff.
99 W. Rauschenbusch, *A Theology for the Social Gospel*, New York 1945, 158.
100 Ibid.
101 Ibid., 1.
102 Ibid., 46, 49.
103 Cf. H.S. Smith, *Changing Conceptions of Original Sin*, New York 1955, 198ff.
104 Rauschenbusch, *A Theology for the Social Gospel*, 78.
105 Ibid., 79–81.
106 Ibid., 90.
107 Ibid., 81.
108 Ibid., 98ff.
109 Ibid., 101ff.
110 Ibid., 102ff., 142.
111 Ibid., 131, 133.
112 Ibid., 136ff.
113 Ibid., 142ff.
114 Ibid., 139, 141.
115 Ibid., 95.
116 Ibid., 141.
117 In the *Rochester Democrat and Chronicle*, 25 July 1913, cited by M.L. Stackhouse in the "Editor's Introduction," to W. Rauschenbusch, *The*

Righteousness of the Kingdom, ed. M.L. Stackhouse, New York, 1968, 16ff.
118 Ibid., 87.
119 W. Rauschenbusch, *Christianizing the Social Order*, New York 1912, 49, 93.
120 Ibid., 124.
121 Ibid., 458.
122 J.C. Machen, *Christianity and Liberalism*, Grand Rapids 1943, 2, 20.
123 C.W. Reese, *The Meaning of Humanism*. Boston 1945, 50.
124 J. Dewey, *A Common Faith*, New Haven 1934, 50.
125 A.E. Haydon, *The Quest of the Ages*, New York 1929, cited in W.M. Horton, "Systematic Theology," in Nash, *Protestant Thought in the Twentieth Century*, 113.
126 C.F. Potter, *Humanizing Religion*, New York 1933, 1, 9.
127 C.F. Potter, *Humanism a New Religion*, New York 1930, 97.

CHAPTER FOUR

1 R. Niebuhr, *Faith and History*, New York 1949, 6.
2 In H.E. Fey (ed.), *How My Mind Has Changed: Thirteen Distinguished Religious Thinkers Assess the Impact of the Last Decade on Their Lives and Thought*, Cleveland 1961, 11.
3 W.M. Horton, in Nash, *Protestant Thought in the Twentieth Century*, 115.
4 Sperry, *Religion in America*, 153.
5 D.C. Macintosh, *Theology as an Empirical Science*, New York 1919, ix.
6 Ibid., 29.
7 D.C. Macintosh, *The Reasonableness of Christianity*, New York 1925, 220.
8 Ibid., 46, 49.
9 Ibid., 82, 84.
10 Ibid., 241.
11 H.N. Wieman, *Man's Ultimate Commitment*, Carbondale, IL 1958, 12.
12 H.N. Wieman and W.M.Horton, *The Growth of Religion*, Chicago 1938, 292.
13 H.N. Wieman, *The Source of Human Good*, Chicago 1947, 7.
14 Cited in W.M. Horton, in Nash, *Protestant Thought in the Twentieth Century*, 116.
15 E.S. Brightman, *A Philosophy of Religion*, 10th ed., New York 1954, vii.
16 E.S. Brightman, *An Introduction to Philosophy*, New York 1951 (rev. ed.), 12.

17 Brightman, *A Philosophy of Religion*, 192ff.
18 E.S. Brightman, *The Finding of God*, New York 1931, 23.
19 E.S. Brightman, *The Spiritual Life*, New York 1942, 44.
20 Brightman, *A Philosophy of Religion*, 226.
21 Brightman, *An Introduction to Philosophy*, 257.
22 Brightman, *The Finding of God*, 115.
23 E.S. Brightman, *The Problem of God*, New York 1930 (henceforth PG), 129, 134ff.
24 M.F. Thelen, *Man as Sinner in Contemporary American Realistic Theology*, New York 1946, 131.
25 Cited in Keller, *Amerikanisches Christentum-Heute*, 183.
26 W.M. Horton, *Christian Theology: An Ecumenical Approach*, New York 1958 (rev. ed.), 33.
27 Cf. H.R. Niebuhr, *The Social Sources of Denominationalism*, Cleveland 1964, vii.
28 H.R. Niebuhr, *The Kingdom of God in America*, New York, 1959, ix.
29 Ibid., ix ff.
30 Ibid., 17.
31 H.R. Niebuhr, *The Meaning of Revelation*, New York 1964, vii.
32 H.R. Niebuhr, *Christ and Culture*, New York 1956, 255ff.
33 R. Niebuhr, *Faith and History*, 1, 6ff.
34 A. Schlesinger Jr., "Reinhold Niebuhr's Role in American Political Thought and Life," in C.W. Kegley and R.W. Bretall (eds.), *Reinhold Niebuhr: His Religious, Social and Political Thought*, New York 1956, 131.
35 R. Niebuhr, *Does Civilization Need Religion?*, New York 1927, 45.
36 Cf. ibid., 44.
37 A.C. Outler, "Ahead Again," *Christian Century*, 1 June 1955, 654.
38 R. Niebuhr, *Moral Man and Immoral Society: A Study in Ethics and Politics*, New York 1932, 232.
39 Ibid., 270ff.
40 R. Niebuhr, *Reflections on the End of an Era*, New York 1934, 230.
41 Ibid., 59.
42 Ibid., 93ff.
43 Ibid., 275.
44 R. Niebuhr, *An Interpretation of Christian Ethics*, London 1948, 67, 70ff.
45 In 1951 Scribner's, New York, published a one-volume edition of the work.
46 In the excellent edition by Il Mulino, with an introduction by Sergio Cotta, this is the first work of Niebuhr's to be translated into Italian: *Fede e Storia: Studio comparator della concezione cristiana e della concezione moderna della storia*. Tr. F. Giampiccoli, Bologna 1966.

47 R. Niebuhr, *The Self and the Dramas of History*, New York 1955, 97.
48 R. Niebuhr, *Beyond Tragedy: Essays on the Christian Interpretation of History*, London 1947, 4.
49 R. Niebuhr, *Faith and History*, 105.
50 R. Niebuhr, *The Nature and Destiny of Man: A Christian Interpretation*, New York 1951, vol. II, 100.
51 R. Niebuhr, *Faith and History*, 141.
52 R. Niebuhr, *The Nature and Destiny of Man*, vol. II, 53.
53 Ibid., 56.
54 R. Niebuhr, *Faith and History*, 141, 144, 151.
55 R. Niebuhr, *The Nature and Destiny of Man*, vol. I, 270.
56 Ibid., 152.
57 Ibid., vol. II, 74.
58 Ibid., vol. I, 252, 16.
59 Ibid., 255.
60 R. Niebuhr, *Faith and History*, 144.
61 R. Niebuhr, *Christianity and Power Politics*, New York 1940, 112.
62 R. Niebuhr, *The Nature and Destiny of Man*, vol. II, 81.
63 Ibid., vol. I, 140ff.
64 Ibid., vol. II, 43, and vol. I, 142.
65 Ibid., vol. II, 67.
66 Ibid., 188.
67 R. Niebuhr, *Faith and History*, 213.
68 Ibid., 28.
69 A. Schlesinger Jr., in Kegley and Bretall, *Reinhold Niebuhr*, 149.
70 R. Niebuhr, *The Children of Light and the Children of Darkness: A Vindication of Democracy and Critique of Its Traditional Defenders*, New York 1960, 110ff.
71 R. Niebuhr, *Discerning the Signs of the Times. Sermons for Today and Tomorrow*, 1946, 12.
72 R. Niebuhr, *The Irony of American History*, New York 1952, 155.
73 R. Niebuhr, *Man's Nature and His Communities*, New York 1965, 16.
74 Ibid., 15, 125.
75 Doxa Editions in Rome published an Italian translation until 1929 edited by A. Banfi with the title: *Lo spirito borghese e il Kairos*.
76 *In Religionshphilosophie der Kultur*, Berlin 1919, 28–52.
77 W.M. Horton, in Nash, *Protestant Thought in the Twentieth Century*, 121.
78 G. Weigel, S.J., "Contemporaneous Protestantism and Paul Tillich," *Theological Studies*, XI (1950), 185.

79 Keller, *Amerikanisches Christentum-Heute*, 187 [Translated from the Italian].
80 Ibid., 188ff.
81 Cf. *The Interpretation of History*, New York 1936, part 1: "On the Boundary: An Autobiographical Sketch."
82 Ibid., 40.
83 Ibid., 38ff.
84 In 1967 the University of Chicago Press published a one-volume edition of the whole work.
85 P. Tillich, *Systematic Theology*, vol. I, Chicago 1951, 8.
86 Cf. ibid., 6.
87 Ibid., 8.
88 Ibid., 62.
89 Ibid., 12, 14.
90 Ibid., 23ff.
91 Ibid., 24.
92 Ibid., 25.
93 P. Tillich, *Systematic Theology*, vol. III, Chicago 1964 (2nd ed.), 283.
94 Ibid., 297ff.
95 P. Tillich, *The Courage to Be*, New Haven 1952, 176.
96 Ibid., 155.
97 P. Tillich, *Love, Power and Justice. Ontological Analyses and Ethical Applications*, New York 1954, 36ff.
98 Ibid., 25
99 Ibid., 99.
100 P. Tillich, *Dynamics of Faith*, New York 1957, i.
101 Ibid., 18, 20.
102 Ibid., 126ff.
103 P. Tillich, *Theology of Culture*, ed. R.C. Kimball, 3rd ed., New York 1962, v.
104 Ibid., 41.
105 Ibid., 42.

CHAPTER FIVE

1 Sperry, *Religion in America*, 156.
2 D.D. Williams, *What Present-Day Theologians Are Thinking*, New York 1967, 106.
3 J.B. Cobb, *A Christian Natural Theology*, Philadelphia 1965, 149.
4 Williams, *What Present-Day Theologians Are Thinking*, 159.
5 J. Macquarrie, *Principles of Christian Theology*, New York 1966, ix.

6 W. Hordern, *Speaking of God: The Nature and Purpose of Theological Language*, New York 1964, 190ff., 197.
7 Cf. W.K. Frankena, *Ethics*, New Jersey 1963, 42–4.
8 P. Ramsey, *Deeds and Rules in Christian Ethics*, Edinburgh 1967, 3.
9 P. Ramsey, *Basic Christian Ethics*, New York 1950, 100.
10 Cf. P. Ramsey, *Nine Modern Moralists*, Englewood Cliffs NJ 1962, 122–31, 212–23, where he refers sympathetically to the positions of J. Maritain.
11 Ramsey, *Deeds and Rules*, 2.
12 P. Lehmann, *Ethics in a Christian Context*, New York 1963, 77, 101, 366.
13 J. Fletcher, *Situation Ethics: The New Morality*, Philadelphia 1966, 158.
14 Ibid., 29, 65.
15 J. Fletcher, "Six Propositions: The New Look in Christian Ethics," *Harvard Divinity Bulletin*, Oct. 1959, 18, cited in H.H. Barnette, *The New Theology and Morality*, Philadelphia 1967, 41.
16 G. Vahanian, "'La fine dell' 'epoca religiosa': Il problema nel suo significato teologico" (The End of the 'Religious Era': The Issue in Its Theological Significance) *Concilium* (Italian ed.), II (1966), 4, 131. [Translated from the Italian].
17 D. Bonhoeffer, *Letters and Papers from Prison*, ed. E. Bethge, trans. R.H. Fuller, New York 1953, 195, cited in T.W. Ogletree, *The "Death of God" Controversy*, London 1966, 14.
18 T.J.J. Altizer, *Mircea Eliade and the Dialectic of the Sacred*, Philadelphia 1963, 13.
19 W. Hamilton, "The Shape of Radical Theology," *Christian Century*, 6 Oct. 1965, 1220.
20 W. Hamilton, *The New Essence of Christianity*, New York 1960, 30.
21 His contributions can be found in Italian in *Dio è morto?* (Documenti nuovi, n1) Milan 1967, 175–90, under the title "Cosa è la morte di Dio?" [What Is the Death of God] and in *Dibattito sull'ateismo* [The Debate on Atheism], Brescia 1967.
22 P.M. van Buren, *The Secular Meaning of the Gospel: Based on an Analysis of Its Language*, New York 1966, 103.
23 Translated into Italian as *La morte di Dio: La cultura della nostra epoca post-cristiana*, Roma 1966.
24 Translated into Italian as *La città secolare*, trans. A. Sorsaja, Firenze, 1968, and *Il Cristiano come ribelle*, intro. and trans. S. Maggiolini, Brescia 1968. Another recent work of Cox's is *On Not Leaving It to the Snake* (1967).
25 H. Cox, *The Secular City: Secularization and Urbanization in Theological Perspective*, New York 1966 (rev. ed.), 18.

26 Ibid., 125.
27 Cf., e.g., the citation of the Freedom Schools, in ibid., 127.
28 See ibid., 26–32, chapter I: "The Sinai Covenant as the Deconsecration of Values."
29 Ibid., 27ff.
30 f. W. Hamilton, "The New Optimism – from Prufrock to Ringo," in T.J.J. Altizer and W. Hamilton, *Radical Theology and the Death of God*, Indianapolis 1966, 159.
31 Ibid., 169
32 T.J.J. Altizer, *The Gospel of Christian Atheism*, Philadelpha 1966, 132ff.
33 Ogletree, *The "Death of God" Controversy*, 86.

APPENDIX ONE

1 Marcuse, *La philosophie américaine*, 14.
2 R. Niebuhr, *The Irony of American History*, New York 1952; *Pious and Secular America*, New York 1958; R. Niebuhr and A. Heimert, *A Nation So Conceived*, New York 1963.
3 R. Niebuhr, *Faith and History*, New York 1949, 6. Henceforth referred to as *FH*.
4 Niebuhr and Heimert, *A Nation so Conceived*, 28 and in general the entire chapter.
5 "The creative and redemptive force is a faith which defies the real in the name of the idea, and subdues it," Niebuhr exclaims with characteristic Liberal optimism in *Does Civilization Need Religion?*, New York 1927, 45.
6 Cf. his journal from those years: *Leaves from a Notebook of a Tamed Cynic*, New York 1929.
7 J. Maritain, *On the Philosophy of History*, trans. Joseph W. Evans, New York, 1957, 17.
8 *FH*, 1ff; emphasis added.
9 *The Nature and Destiny of Man: A Christian Interpretation*, New York 1941–43. The first volume will be referred to as *HN*, the second as *HD*.
10 *FH*; *The Self and the Dramas of History*, New York 1955; *The Structure of Nations and Empires*, New York 1959.
11 *HD*, 1.
12 Cf., e.g., *HN*, 123; *FH*, 56.
13 *HN*, 270.
14 Ibid., 26.
15 *HD*, 74.

16 *HN*, 13ff.
17 Cf. ibid., 11.
18 Ibid., 26: cf. also 40, and *FH*, 172.
19 *FH*, 18.
20 Ibid., 16.
21 *HN*, 114.
22 *The Self and the Dramas of History*, 4. This work will be abbreviated as *SDH*.
23 *FH*, 18ff.
24 *SDH*, 4.
25 Ibid., 205.
26 Ibid., 39.
27 *FH*, 18. "Therefore history is never simply something 'back there,' it is the depth dimension of our present," is Niebhur's thought in a nutshell. G. Harland, *The Thought of Rienhold Niebuhr*, New York 1960, 91.
28 *FH*, 57.
29 *SDH*, 54.
30 R. Niebuhr, *Beyond Tragedy*, London 1947, 5; hereinafter *BT*.
31 *SHD*, 57.
32 Ibid.
33 Ibid., 50.
34 "No induction from empirical facts can yield a conclusion about ultimate meaning because every process of induction presupposes some canon and criterion of meaning." *BT*, 14.
35 J. Maritain, *On the Philosophy of History*, 11.
36 *SDH*, 97.
37 *FH*, 105.
38 *BT*, 7.
39 *HD*, 100.
40 *BT*, 8.
41 *HD*, 26n13.
42 Ibid., 76.
43 *FH*, 143.
44 Ibid., 152.
45 *SDH*, 242.
46 Ibid., 127.
47 Ibid., 71ff. Cf. also *FH*, 118: "History in its totality and unity is given a meaning by some kind of religious faith in the sense that the concept of meaning is derived from ultimate presuppositions about the character of time and eternity, which are not the fruit of detailed analyses of historical events."

48 *SDH*, 242.
49 *FH*, 170.
50 *SDH*, 97.
51 *HN*, 132, 135
52 *BT*, 227.
53 *HN*, 127. Cf., e.g, the definition of religious experience given by the most significant representative of "personalism" at Boston University: "Religious experience is any experience of any person taken in its relation to [the Ultimate Value]." E.S. Brightman, *Philosophy of Religion,* 10th ed., New York 1954, 415.
54 *FH*, 112.
55 Ibid., 144.
56 *HD*, 25. Cf. also the preceding work: *Christianity and Power Politics*, New York 1940, 112ff: "the claim of ultimate and absolute validity is always involved in religion." For Niebuhr, idolatry is always involved in religion qua religion. In coherence with this approach, Niebuhr could make this fundamental accusation against the Amsterdam Assembly of the World Council of Churches: "The assembly was distressing as well as heartening because it is so apparent that most churches actually do assume that they have the only right order, theology, or way of life." Quote from the *Union Seminary Quarterly Review*, Nov. 1948, cited in E.W. Zeeden, "Über die innere Entwicklungs-Geschichte des Protestantismus seit der Reformation," *Theologie und Glaube*, XL (1941), 229.
57 *HD*, 81.
58 *FH*, 174.
59 *HN*, 140.
60 Ibid., 142.
61 *HD*, 107.
62 Ibid., 213.
63 *FH*, 213.
64 *HD*, 76.
65 Ibid., 123.
66 Ibid., 213. Cf. the beautiful ending of chapter XIV of *BT*, 286.
67 *FH*, 215.
68 *BT*, 290.
69 *HD*, 296.
70 Ibid., 288.
71 Maritain, *On the Philosophy of History*, 77.
72 *HN*, 136.
73 *FH*, 25.

74 *HD*, 22.
75 *FH*, 148.
76 Ibid., 141.
77 Ibid., 25.
78 Ibid., 144.
79 The orthodox interpretation of the two natures of Christ is for Niebuhr rationally absurd and is made "within the limitations of Greek terms." *HD*, 60.
80 *FH*, 169.
81 *HD*, 53.
82 *FH*, 147.
83 Cited in J. Bingham, *Courage to Change: An Introduction to the Life and Thought of Reinhold Niebuhr*, New York 1961, 338.
84 Cf. R. Niebuhr, *Christian Realism and Political Powers*, London 1954, chapter XL.
85 *FH*, 27.
86 *Does Civilization Need Religion?*, 189.
87 "The possibility of a philosophy of history rests on secularized eschatology"; "the eschatological history of salvation also cannot impart a new and progressive meaning to the history of the world." These are some of the statements that K. Löwith makes in his debate with Niebuhr: *History and Christianity*, in Kegley and Bretall, *Reinhold Niebuhr*, 282ff.
88 "Reply," in ibid., 440.
89 Maritain, *On the Philosophy of History*, 25.
90 Ramsey, *Nine Modern Moralists*, 129.
91 *HD*, 298.

APPENDIX TWO

1 Keller, *Amerikanisches Christentum-Heute*.
2 D.R. Davies, *Reinhold Niebuhr: Prophet from America*, New York 1948, 16.
3 R. Niebuhr, *Leaves from a Notebook of a Tamed Cynic*, 15ff.
4 Cited in Bingham, *Courage to Change*, 83.
5 Schlesinger Jr., "Reinhold Niebuhr's Role in American Political Thought and Life," 45.
6 R. Niebuhr, *Does Civilization Need Religion?*, New York 1927, 45.
7 Cf. ibid., 45.
8 R. Niebuhr, *Moral Man and Immoral Society*, New York 1953, 232.
9 Ibid., 270ff.

10 R. Niebuhr, *An Interpretation of Christian Ethics*, London 1948, 67, 70ff.
11 Cf. Ramsey, *Nine Modern Moralists*, 111–47.
12 J. Maritain, *The Rights of Man and Natural Law*, tr. Geoffrey Bles, London 1945, 36.
13 R. Niebuhr, *The Nature and Destiny of Man: A Christian Interpretation*, New York 1949, I 272 (henceforth *NDM*).
14 *FH*.
15 *NDM*, vol. I, 270.
16 Ibid., 152.
17 Ibid., 4, 259.
18 Ibid., vol. II, 14.
19 Ibid., I 55.
20 Ibid., 16.
21 See ibid., 185.
22 "[Natural law] defines the proper performance of [man's] functions, the normal harmony of his impulses and the normal social relations between himself and his fellows within the limitations of the natural order." Ibid., 270.
23 Ibid., 242, 257.
24 Ibid., 245.
25 Ibid., 16.
26 Ibid., 183, 252.
27 Ibid., 255.
28 Ibid., 258, 260.
29 Ibid., 146.
30 "In normal life consistent self-destruction through self-seeking, which could be defined as total depravity, is prevented by the various forces of 'common grace' which serve to draw the self out of itself." *FH*, 174ff.
31 *NDM*, vol. II, 123.
32 *FH*, 197.
33 *NMW*, vol. II, 68.
34 Cf. Niebuhr's debate with Liberal theologians, e.g., D. Day Williams, "Niebuhr and Liberalism," in Kegley and Bretall, *Reinhold Niebuhr* 210ff, and Niebuhr's "Reply," 442.
35 *FH*, 185.
36 "A love which seeketh not its own is not able to maintain itself in historical society. Not only may it fall victim to excessive forms of the self-assertion of others; but even the most perfectly balanced system of justice in history is a balance of competing wills and interests, and must therefore worst anyone who does not participate in the balance." *NDM*, vol. II, 72.

37 Cf. *FH*, 143, 197.
38 *NDM*, vol. II, 76, 44, 81.
39 Ibid., 109nn4 and 5.
40 "The revelation of the Atonement is precisely a 'final' word because it discloses a transcendent divine mercy which represents the 'freedom' of God in quintessential terms: namely God's freedom over His own law." Ibid., 67.
41 Ibid., vol. I, 142.
42 Ibid., vol. II, 103.
43 Ibid., 125, 114.
44 Ibid., 114, 188.
45 *FH*, 28.
46 *NDM*, vol. II, 99.
47 Ibid., 226.
48 E. Brunner, *Some Remarks on Reinhold Niebuhr's Work as a Christian Thinker*, in Kegley and Bretall, *Reinhold Niebuhr*, 30.
49 G. Harland, *The Thought of Reinhold Niebuhr*, New York 1960, 23.
50 *NDM*, vol. II, 248.
51 "Without a judgment upon even the best judicial process from a higher level of judgment, the best becomes the worst." Ibid., vol. I, 258.
52 Cf. *FH*, 183.
53 *NDM*, vol. I, 221.
54 R. Niebuhr, "Christian Faith and Natural Law," *Theology*, Feb. 1940, 89, cited in Harland, *The Thought of Reinhold Niebuhr*, 33.
55 R. Niebuhr, *Christian Realism and Political Problems*, London 1954, 173.
56 "The question is whether its general principles are not too inflexible on the one hand and their definitions too historically conditioned on the other hand ... what I was trying to deal with was the problem of the historical elaboration of man's essential nature on the one hand, and the historical bias which crept into the definition of that essential nature on the other hand." R. Niebuhr, "Reply," in Kegley and Bretall, *Reinhold Niebuhr*, 435.
57 Brunner, *Some Remarks on Reinhold Niebuhr's Work*, 30.
58 Cf., e.g., F. Herzog, *Understanding God: The Key Issue in Present-Day Protestant Thought*, New York 1966, 112.
59 R. Niebuhr, *An Interpretation of Christian Ethics*, 61.
60 Niebuhr notes autobiographically, 'I have never been very competent in the nice points of pure theology; and I must confess that I have not been sufficiently interested heretofore to acquire the competence." "Intellectual Autobiography," in Kegley and Bretall, *Reinhold Niebuhr*, 3.

APPENDIX THREE

1 F. Mayer, in *A History of American Thought: An Introduction*, Dubuque 1951, 244, points to F.C.S. Schiller (1864–1937) as an exponent of a non-theistic personalism. Schiller came from Oxford to the University of Southern California, where his teaching had great influence. His best-known work is *Riddles of the Sphynx* (1891). Brightman, however, who speaks of him as a "brilliant and prolific writer" and who attributes to him the introduction of the term "humanism," qualifies him as a "pragmatic humanist," in *A Philosophy of Religion*, 10th ed., New York 1954, 62, 336, as does W.H. Werkmeister, in *A History of Philosophical Ideas in America*, New York 1949, 580.

2 Cf. H.W. Schneider, *Storia della filosofia Americana*, ed. A. Pasquinelli, Bologna 1963 (the work was published in New York in 1947), 211–16 and 473–82. See also, W.H. Werkmeister, *A History of Philosophical Ideas in America*, 73–9.

3 *The Limits of Evolution and Other Essays*, New York 1901, xiv and xv, cited in J.L. Blau, *Men and Movements in American Philosophy*, New York 1952, 192.

4 G.P. Adams and W.P. Montague (eds.), *Contemporary American Philosophy*, London 1930, 373, cited in Blau, *Men and Movements*, 304.

5 Mayer, *A History of American Thought*, 236.

6 After graduating in Philosophy at New York in 1871, Bowne spent a crucial period in Germany studying with Erdmann, Ulrici, and above all, Lotze, to whom he dedicated his *Metaphysics, A Study in First Principles*.

7 Blau, *Men and Movements*, 201.

8 *Personalism: Common Sense and Philosophy*, Boston 1908, 297, cited in Mayer, *A History of American Thought*, 243.

9 *Studies in Theism*, New York, 1880, 18, cited in A.C. Knudson, *The Validity of Religious Experience*, New York 1937, 116.

10 *Personalism*, 265, cited in Mayer, *A History of American Thought*, 241.

11 *Metaphysics*, 169, cited in Blau, *Men and Movements*, 204.

12 *Person and Reality, An Introduction to Metaphysics*, ed. P.A. Bertocci, New York 1958, 18 (henceforth *PrR*).

13 "Personalismo," in *Enciclopedia Filosofica*, Venezia-Roma 1957, col. 1316.

14 For Brightman, personalism would be "the most coherent and concrete form of idealism," in *An Introduction to Philosophy*, rev. ed., New York 1951, viii (henceforth *IP*).

15 G.F. Thomas, *The Philosophy of Religion*, in A.S. Nash, *Protestant Thought in the Twentieth Century*, New York 1951, 80ff.

16 W. James, *The Varieties of Religious Experience*, New York 1902, 445.
17 *IP*, 12.
18 Ibid., 5.
19 Ibid., 69.
20 *A Philosophy of Religion*, 10th ed., New York 1954, 192ff (henceforth *PR*).
21 Ibid., 350.
22 *The Spiritual Life*, Nashville 1942, 61 (henceforth *SL*).
23 *PR*, 362.
24 *Nature and Values*, New York 1945, 83 (henceforth *NV*).
25 *Persons and Values*, Boston 1952, 15 (henceforth *PV*).
26 Cf. *PR*, 359.
27 *PrR*, 88.
28 *PR*, 384.
29 *IP*, 145.
30 Ibid., 142.
31 Ibid., 299.
32 *NV*, 68.
33 *SL*, 20.
34 *PrR*, 302.
35 *PR*, 349.
36 H. Höffding, *The Philosophy of Religion*, London 1906, 215, cited in *PR*, 16.
37 J.A. Leighton, "The Principle of Individuality and Value," in C. Barret (ed.), *Contemporary Idealism in America*, New York 1932, 160, cited in R.E. Gibson, *God, Man and Time*, Philadelphia 1966, 64.
38 *The Finding of God*, New York 1931, 23 (henceforth *FG*).
39 *PR*, 202.
40 *SL*, 164.
41 Ibid., 44.
42 *PR*, 226.
43 *IP*, 257.
44 *FG*, 115.
45 *SL*, 149.
46 *The Problem of God*, New York 1930, 130 (henceforth *PG*).
47 *NV*, 40.
48 Ibid., 126.
49 *PR*, 226.
50 *IP*, 262.
51 *PR*, 158.

52 Ibid., 367.

53 *SL*, 139.

54 A.N. Whitehead, *Modes of Thought*, New York 1938, 228.

55 *Is God a Person?*, New York 1932, 30, cited in A.J. Reck, *Recent American Philosophy*, New York 1964, 314.

56 *PR*, 415.

57 *FG*, 189. Cf. B.P. Bowne, *Personalism*, Boston 1908, 297, cited in Mayer, *A History of American Thought*, 243.

58 *PR*, 350, where he leaves the problem of the immortality of animals unresolved.

59 Bowne, *Personalism*, 109, in Mayer, *A History of American Thought*, 110.

60 J. Collins, *God in Modern Philosophy*, Chicago 1959, 286.

61 *PG*, 134ff.

Index